"The authors have done an excellent job of organizing this volume and have covered a huge array of trust-related topics. Given the current immense attention, concern, and perhaps even fear of upcoming political elections and Wall Street abuses, the attention to politicians and business leaders who have failed us in the past will be viewed as highly relevant to most people's interest. The figures and related statistics provide powerful tools to establish the importance of building trust in those leadership positions."

—**Linda K. Stroh**, Graduate School of Business, Loyola University Chicago

"In today's popular press, one encounters examples of the so-called trust deficit on a daily basis. And yet little is ever offered as a solution for rebuilding those relationships—reestablishing the trust that is the bedrock of all human relationships. For years, Drs. Aneil K. Mishra and Karen E. Mishra have been among the few thought leaders working on that important topic, and I have found their thinking and advice an essential ingredient of my culture-change work at several firms in different industries. In *Becoming a Trustworthy Leader: Psychology and Practice*, the Mishras elegantly lay out a road map for leaders to build (or restore) trust, drawing upon their expertise, primary research, and the thinking of others in this field. It is essential reading for thoughtful leaders in the public and private sectors, students of organizational behavior, and those involved in the political arena."

—**Steven Fitzgerald**, human resources, learning, talent management, workforce research, M&A, and shared services, Avaya

"Aneil K. Mishra and Karen E. Mishra have come up with another winner. Trust in today's global economy is more valuable than gold and is the very foundation of the Western capitalist economic system. Through the magic and transparency of the marketplace, producers and consumers trust that value will be provided at a fair price. Unfortunately, due to the misalignment of incentives in healthcare—its fatal flaw—such trust is lacking, as market forces are largely absent in determining value or price—thus, little or no trust. Despite this fundamental flaw, Aneil K. Mishra and Karen E. Mishra explore how trust can be established among the various stakeholders, providers, patients, and payers. They provide a cogent and credible template for trust in healthcare based on reliability, openness, competence, and compassion, providing compelling case study support of leaders in the field who successfully established trust and success. BRAVO, my friends, for a job well done!"

—**Thomas A. Schwann**, chief, cardiothoracic surgery at the University of Toledo, Ohio

"We may be living in trust's darkest days, but all hope is not lost. Drs. Aneil K. Mishra and Karen E. Mishra pick up where their last book left off, in redefining trust and relationships in the workplace. Backed by decades of research and a passion for the subject, they deconstruct the trust-building process into actionable compartmentalized techniques for today's leader. With trust in the workplace and society at its lowest recorded levels, a crisis of confidence is sweeping the nation. Drs. Aneil K. Mishra and Karen E. Mishra take readers through an introspective process, challenging and examining their assumptions while defining and sharpening the tools necessary to restore confidence in their organizations. In a time riddled with corporate fraud and governmental ineptitude, it's easy to lose confidence in our leaders and institutions. Drs. Aneil K. Mishra and Karen E. Mishra aggressively challenge the spirit of complacency enrapturing our institutions by devising methods to help restore trust in our society and ourselves. Readers are given a ground-up tutorial on how to become trustworthy leaders as they are challenged to reexamine their intellectual biases and assumptions."

—**Joel Levy**, senior municipal credit analyst, TIAA-CREF

"While managers grasp for control and reap mediocrity, leaders nurture trust and realize excellence. In an age of ever-increasing complexity, this book presents the key to progress. It is a must-read."

—**Professor Robert E. Quinn**, University of Michigan Ross School of Business

Becoming a Trustworthy Leader

Trust in leaders and in a variety of institutions is at an all-time low. Yet more than ever, we need strong leadership to address our present problems and our many long-standing economic and societal challenges. Based on our more than two decades of research, we discuss examples of leaders who have built trust with employees, teams, and other key stakeholders to foster innovation and lasting positive change in their organizations. We show how anyone can become a trustworthy leader by developing the ROCC of Trust through reliability, openness, competence, and compassion.

Dr. Aneil K. Mishra is managing partner of Total Trust Coaching & Consulting in Raleigh-Durham, North Carolina. He is the coauthor of *Trust Is Everything: Become the Leader Others Will Follow*. Aneil has been a business school professor at Penn State University, Wake Forest University, and Duke University. Aneil mentors leaders and teams, helping them to build trust in order to improve organizational performance. Aneil is a graduate of Princeton University and earned his PhD from the University of Michigan Ross School of Business.

Dr. Karen E. Mishra is a business school professor in Raleigh-Durham, North Carolina. She has been a business school professor at Michigan State University, Wake Forest University, and Penn State University. She conducts research on how leaders build trust and engagement through internal communication. She is the coauthor of *Trust Is Everything: Become the Leader Others Will Follow*. She is also an executive coach, helping leaders build trust with their teams. She earned her MBA at the University of Michigan Ross School of Business and her PhD at the University of North Carolina at Chapel Hill.

LEADERSHIP: RESEARCH AND PRACTICE SERIES

A James MacGregor Burns Academy of Leadership Collaboration

SERIES EDITORS

Georgia Sorenson, PhD, Research Professor in Leadership Studies, University of Maryland and Founder of the James MacGregor Academy of Leadership and the International Leadership Association.

Ronald E. Riggio, PhD, is the Henry R. Kravis Professor of Leadership and Organizational Psychology and former Director of the Kravis Leadership Institute at Claremont McKenna College.

Scott T. Allison and George R. Goethals
Heroic Leadership: An Influence Taxonomy of 100 Exceptional Individuals

Michelle C. Bligh and Ronald E. Riggio (Eds.)
Exploring Distance in Leader–Follower Relationships: When Near is Far and Far is Near

Michael A. Genovese and Janie Steckenrider (Eds.)
Women as Political Leaders: Studies in Gender and Governing

Jon P. Howell
Snapshots of Great Leadership

Aneil K. Mishra and Karen E. Mishra
Becoming a Trustworthy Leader: Psychology and Practice

Becoming a Trustworthy Leader

Psychology and Practice

ANEIL K. MISHRA AND KAREN E. MISHRA

Routledge
Taylor & Francis Group

NEW YORK AND LONDON

First published 2013
by Routledge
711 Third Avenue, New York, NY 10017

Simultaneously published in the UK
by Routledge
27 Church Road, Hove, East Sussex BN3 2FA

Routledge is an imprint of the Taylor & Francis Group, an informa business

© 2013 Taylor & Francis

The right of Aneil K. Mishra and Karen E. Mishra to be identified as authors of this work has been asserted by them in accordance with sections 77 and 78 of the Copyright, Designs and Patents Act 1988.

Library of Congress Cataloging in Publication Data
Mishra, Aneil.
   Becoming a trustworthy leader : psychology and practice / authored by Aneil K. Mishra & Karen E. Mishra.
      p. cm.
   ISBN 978-0-415-88281-1 (hardback : alk. paper) —
ISBN 978-0-415-88282-8 (pbk. : alk. paper)   1. Leadership.
2. Trust.   I. Mishra, Karen E.   II. Title. HD57.7.M575
2012658.4'092—dc232012030023

ISBN: 978-0-415-88281-1 (hbk)
ISBN: 978-0-415-88282-8 (pbk)
ISBN: 978-0-203-08041-2 (ebk)

Typeset in Palatino
by Apex CoVantage, LLC

SFI Certified Sourcing
     www.sfiprogram.org
     SFI-00453

Printed and bound in the United States of America
by Edwards Brothers, Inc.

CONTENTS

SERIES EDITORS' FOREWORD

We are very pleased to have this book, *Becoming a Trustworthy Leader*, as a part of our book series. The series is titled "Leadership: Research and Practice," and true to that title, this book is a practical guide, but one that is built upon a foundation of decades of research on leadership and trust. Authors Aneil K. Mishra and Karen E. Mishra have done an excellent job of taking a complex topic and making it accessible with their ROCC of Trust model and vivid examples of trust in leaders from organizations they have worked with across multiple sectors and professions.

In recent years, leadership scholars have realized that trust is a critical core element in the leader–follower dynamic, and it is finally receiving the attention it deserves. This could not happen at a better time because, as our authors point out, trust in institutions and in leadership is at an all-time low. The goal of this book is to draw on trust research and, from the authors' extensive experience in corporations and government, to offer practical insights for today's leaders on how to build trust in work teams, organizations, and across organizational (and national) boundaries.

As the authors suggest, without trust a leader will not be successful in the most challenging tasks of leadership, such as leading organizational change; motivating others to be innovative, entrepreneurial, and to take risks; and building a lasting commitment to an organization's mission. Their four-factor model—derived from 20 years of research with thousands of employees, managers, and top managers—includes a "how to" set of tips for leaders to build personal trust through being reliable, open, competent, and compassionate.

What happens when a leader violates trust or inherits a culture of trust infractions? In a chapter on the difficult issue of rebuilding broken trust in the workplace, the authors present examples from their research and consulting work where leaders face a disintegration of trust. Their research and that of other scholars indicates that the most common sources of broken trust in organizations are poor communication, unwillingness to acknowledge mistakes, performance issues, inconsistency between words and behaviors, and disrespectful behavior.

In sum, this book provides not only a thorough understanding of the role of trust in leading organizations but also a useful framework and helpful tips that can be used to become more knowledgeable and effective, regardless of one's leadership role. All in all, we consider this an essential piece of any practicing leader's or leadership educator's bookshelf.

Georgia Sorenson, PhD
Visiting Professor of Leadership Studies
Carey School of Law, University of Maryland

Ronald E. Riggio, PhD
Henry R. Kravis Professor of Leadership and
Organizational Psychology
Kravis Leadership Institute
Claremont McKenna College

AUTHOR BIOGRAPHIES

Aneil K. Mishra is managing partner of Total Trust Coaching & Consulting in Raleigh-Durham, North Carolina. He is an internationally recognized and widely published thought leader, educator, and consultant in the areas of trust, leadership, change management, organizational culture, and organizational downsizing. He develops and teaches executive programs in leadership and organizational change with a number of leading companies in fast-changing industries in the United States, Turkey, and South America. Aneil has published his research in a number of leading scholarly and practitioner journals, including the *Academy of Management Review*, *Administrative Science Quarterly*, *Sloan Management Review*, *Organization Science*, *Human Resource Management*, *Journal of Organizational Behavior*, *Medical Care Research and Review*, and *The Milbank Quarterly*, and he is a founding associate editor of the *Journal of Trust Research*. He is the coauthor of *Trust is Everything: Become the Leader Others Will Follow*. Aneil is a graduate of Princeton University and earned his PhD from the University of Michigan Ross School of Business.

Karen E. Mishra is a business school professor in Raleigh-Durham, North Carolina. She has been a business school professor at Michigan State University, Wake Forest University, and Penn State University. She conducts research on how leaders build trust and engagement through internal communication. She is also an executive coach, helping leaders build trust with their teams.

She is the coauthor of *Trust Is Everything: Become the Leader Others Will Follow*. Her research on trust, downsizing, crisis communication, and corporate social responsibility has been published in the *Sloan Management Review*, *Public Relations Review*, *Journal of Relationship Marketing*, *Human Resource Management*, and the *Journal of Historical Research in Marketing*. She is on the editorial board of the *Journal of Trust Research* and has taught negotiation at Vienna University. She earned her MBA at the University of Michigan Ross School of Business and her PhD at the University of North Carolina at Chapel Hill.

Trust Is Needed Now More Than Ever

☐ Trust Is Gone, but It's Been Gone for Decades

It's time to discover a new way for individuals to lead organizations and societies. Trust in our institutions, including government and business, is at an all-time low. To strengthen society and its major foundations, we need to build and rebuild trust. This will not be easy, but based on our own extensive field research, we have identified leaders from a wide variety of industries and circumstances who have done this. These leaders point the way toward creating and recreating the trust that is necessary to help meet the many seemingly insurmountable challenges in our political, economic, and cultural realms. More than 30 years ago, when we first began interviewing leaders about leading change, we learned about the importance of trust, and what occurs when distrust rather than trust is the norm. These leaders back then were in the midst of a crisis in the automotive industry in which U.S. firms were facing significant cost and quality pressures from their Japanese competitors. Those organizations that had established trust with key stakeholders responded quite differently than those that had not established such trust. As one supplier executive told us back in 1990,

> I trust those people with that division of General Motors. We have an open relationship, a give-and-take relationship. Last year we made significant productivity improvements in [making] some of their parts. But we also had some cost increases on some other parts that were out of our control: increases in the costs of paint and other materials, costs associated with preventing damage to parts during

handling. We were able to give them price reductions where we achieved productivity improvements. In turn, they gave us our legitimate price increases without any argument.

Now with other divisions of GM, it's an adversarial relationship, animosity on both sides, and issues never get resolved. With those other divisions of GM, we're not as likely to give them price reductions, and they're not as likely to give us our legitimate price increases.

The failure of leaders in that industry to deal with that crisis in ways that addressed the fundamental issues that precipitated the crisis not only led to subsequent crises, but also contributed to more than 25,000 automotive suppliers failing, and the associated loss of hundreds of thousands of jobs among the automotive manufacturers and their suppliers.[1]

Today, trust in business is at an all-time low. The Edelman Global Trust Barometer has been tracking trust levels in society since 1999, assessing both the United States and other countries. In 2011, Edelman found Americans' trust in business at one of its lowest levels ever, 46%, down from 54% the year before, and barely improved from 2009, when it was 38%.[2] In 2012, Americans' trust in business had improved only a further four percentage points, to 50%.[3] Trust in business in the United States is lower than it is in a number of other major countries, including Australia, Brazil, China, Canada, India, Indonesia, Italy, Malaysia, Mexico, and Singapore.[4] It is higher in the United States, however, than in France, Germany, Russia, South Korea, Spain, and the UK. Not surprisingly, this same survey showed that the financial sector was the least trusted business sector.[5]

Business is not alone in being distrusted or experiencing significant declines in trust, and indeed we can claim that there is a true crisis when it comes to a lack of trust in government in the United States and in many other countries. In a 2011 survey, the Gallup Poll of Trust in Government found that 81% of those polled have little or no trust in the U.S. federal government to do what is right.[6] By January 2012, only 10% of Americans approve of the job that Congress is doing, which is a record low, and represents a decrease of 50% or 10 percentage points from only a year earlier.[7] A CNN/ORC International poll in 2011 revealed similar findings, with only 15% of Americans trusting the U.S. federal government to do what is right. This is a full 10 percentage points lower than 2010, again an all-time low.[8] Gallup has found that trust in state government, as well as the executive and legislative branches of the federal government, have continued to decline over the past 15 years, and trust for the legislative branch is now at its lowest level ever.[9,10]

Globally, moreover, distrust in government is at an all-time high. Indeed, the Edelman Barometer for trust in government suffered its "steepest decline in Barometer history," with citizens in a majority of countries surveyed "not trusting their governments to do what is right."[11] Between 2011 and 2012, declines in trust in government in several counties were particularly noteworthy. "In Europe, trust in government dropped by more than 10 points in France, Spain, and Italy. In Latin America, Brazil experienced a 53-point plunge. In Asia, South Korea and China suffered declines of 17 and 13 points, respectively. In Japan, trust in government dropped by 26 points, driven by the catastrophic earthquake that struck the country in early spring (of 2011)."[12]

Not only do we distrust our institutions, but we also distrust our leaders and each other as individuals. A survey by the Center for Work-Life Policy, an American consultancy, found that between June 2007 and December 2008, the percentage of employees who professed loyalty to their employers plunged to 39% from a high of 95%, and the number voicing trust in their employers fell from 79% to 22%.[13] In 2011, the National Leadership Index reported that more than three quarters of Americans agreed with the statement that "we have a crisis of leadership in this country," and a similar fraction agreed that "unless we get better leaders in this country, the United States will decline as a nation."[14] Declines in trust have persisted since the 2008–2009 recession. In 2012, Edelman found that across the globe, only 38% of respondents believed information about companies as communicated by their CEOs to be credible, a 12-percentage-point drop, which was the largest in the history of the Trust Barometer.[15] Trust in our peers has also declined. Individuals' trust in the credibility of the information they receive from "a person like themselves" has declined from 47% to 43% from 2010 to 2011.[16] Sheldon Yellen, the CEO of $1.5-billion Belfor Holdings, told us,

> Trust is a hot issue right now. The world has changed since 2008. People are obviously hurting. I believe that the resentment toward CEOs out there is out of anger. People are complaining about corporate structures in America and the obvious abuse by certain CEOs. But the media focuses on the bad. I guess it's more popular to show that than the good guys. I think that if you see something wrong, you've got to get involved. You can make a change. You can make a difference. However, there are also good CEOs and good corporate structures that people can believe in—and they should! People have to find something to believe in as much as they've already found something to complain about.[17]

Clearly, we are suffering from a serious trust deficit. Yet now, more than ever, we need strong leadership to address our present problems and our many long-standing economic and societal challenges. In fact, GOP presidential hopeful Jon Huntsman used the term "trust deficit" to describe one of the most pressing problems facing our country right now.[18] Eric Kutner, a homeland security specialist and founder of Emergency Response Design Group, noted,

> We have what I call a culture of mediocrity right now in this country for many reasons. We don't raise the bar anymore. Instead we keep lowering the lowest common denominator. It's because we have lack of trust with a lot of leaders. Many people who are in leadership roles don't have the necessary credibility to be there in the first place. Leadership is not based upon titles. Leaders are people who get followed.

☐ Why Has Trust Declined?

Trust has declined for many reasons. First, we have become more suspicious over time, in part by being disconnected, "protecting ourselves from the harsh, unpredictable realities of the outside realities" as we "cocoon" in our homes, which researchers such as Robert Putnam, in his book *Bowling Alone*,[19] and Faith Popcorn observe.[20] In the United States, we have also witnessed massive institutional failures in the financial system, public education, governmental disaster responses, and the political system. Organizations have also failed us through their horrific malfeasance and misfeasance, including the Lockheed bribery scandals in the 1970s, the Red Cross HIV-testing failures in the 1980s, Long-Term Capital Management in the 1990s, and Enron and Tyco International in the early 2000s. Relentless organizational downsizing also continues to undermine people's trust in business organizations.[21] More recently, average Americans have suffered through the financial mortgage fraud and failures of Countrywide Financial, Freddie Mac, and Fannie Mae, *News of the World*'s phone hacking, and Hewlett-Packard's spying on board members and journalists.[22] In Japan, the meltdown of the Fukushima nuclear reactor after the tsunami of March 2011, the lack of preparation for potential disasters such as this, the lack of oversight of the nuclear industry by the Japanese government, and the lack of scrutiny by the Japanese press all contributed to the Japanese no longer trusting their government, or the nuclear energy industry it was supposed to regulate.[23] Indeed, as *The Economist* recently argued,

> If the Japanese nuclear establishment—industry and regulators alike—wants to earn trust, it must be seen to be learning every lesson it

can. It must admit how little it previously deserved trust and explain clearly how it will do better in future. Even then, such trust will not always be given.[24]

Perhaps most egregiously, business, political, and religious leaders have repeatedly violated our trust, acting individually or in concert with others. Simply listing prominent leaders who have resigned from office for violating trust could fill an entire chapter, but even in the last few years such failed leaders include politicians such as Governors Rod Blagojevich and Elliot Spitzer, Senator John Ensign, and Representative Anthony Wiener. Business leaders include Hewlett-Packard's Mark Hurd, UBS's Oswald Grbel,[25] and Galleon Group Founder Raj Rajaratnam. Even our religious and spiritual leaders fail us;[26] indeed, the Catholic bishop of Augsburg, Walter Mixa,[27] and Southern Baptist minister and leader George Alan Rekers[28] have left office in disgrace because they violated trust.

There are many possible reasons why trust has eroded. Julie Mitchell, a leadership coach to Fortune 500 organizations, summarized the roots of today's trust vacuum,

Trust has eroded in our society for many reasons, including glorification of bad, untrustworthy behavior, selfishness, quick fixes, and competition instead of collaboration, for starters. Trustworthy people and institutions don't get much attention and it's easy to believe no one can be trusted. We have deep, serious problems that have been largely ignored by our leaders. Time and again, empty promises are made while nothing changes. The U.S. culture is unhealthy at both individual and collective levels; this is reflected in our institutions. We are literally too tired, fat, sick, medicated, stressed, overworked, and impatient to deal with overwhelming challenges. Institutions are made of people who may be well intentioned but are too often severely limited in their ability to behave in ways that build trust. Too many leaders are blind to anything outside their privileged personal experiences; they lack self-awareness, and/or feel stuck or powerless in broken, dysfunctional systems.

Professor Gretchen Spreitzer (professor, University of Michigan Ross School of Business), suggested another cause,

Trust has eroded because leaders have acted in their self-interest in ways that have let others down. They take huge bonuses when others are being asked to sacrifice. They take a short-term perspective when a long-term one will deliver the most sustainable outcomes.

Despite the low trust levels across so many institutions and types of leaders, we argue in the pages to follow that trust can be built, rebuilt, and sustained if leaders have the courage, humility, and authenticity to take the initiative. Such leaders are not just those in positions of power, but really anyone who is willing to make the effort. Our focus, accordingly, is on trust between individuals or groups, especially between leaders and their followers.

☐ Overview of Our Book

Defining Trust and Its Vital Importance

Trust is important because it allows individuals and collectives to manage interdependence more easily by reducing the need for contracts and formal agreements.[29] Trust reduces uncertainty and helps us manage complexity.[30,31] Furthermore, it permits highly flexible work arrangements that promote risk-taking and innovation. Indeed, when trust has been established, entirely new ways of behaving are possible.[32] As Jack Beach of IBM told us,

> The most important benefits of trust are employee productivity, creativity, innovation, and engagement. Trust enables increased performance and employee satisfaction. It is also a measure of a leader's effectiveness. Leaders create organizational climates in which people trust leaders, leaders trust their people, people trust each other, and people trust themselves to be able to use their judgments, make choices, and act within corporate intent. Without that you can only boss and micromanage; you cannot lead.

Based on almost two decades of research involving thousands of employees, managers and top managers, we can define interpersonal trust as one party's willingness to be vulnerable to another party based on the belief that the latter party is Reliable, Open, Competent, and Compassionate.[33] We call these four dimensions of trustworthiness the **ROCC of Trust** (see Figure 1.1). Each of the trustworthiness dimensions contributes additively to a person's trustworthiness.[34] Our definition of trust is consistent with several decades of other research on trust and trustworthiness that incorporates the key elements of vulnerability,[35,36,37] risk and risk-taking,[38,39] rational choice,[40] and positive expectations about a core set of dimensions regarding others' intentions or behavior.[41,42] Because vulnerability constitutes the core of most definitions of trust, and because we are often quite vulnerable when we are ill, this book profiles several

FIGURE 1.1   The ROCC of Trust

physician leaders who have achieved path-breaking healing by building trust with their patients and staff.

The ROCC of Trust

The ROCC of Trust is based on the extent to which one person believes that another is reliable, open (honest), competent, and compassionate. These four dimensions of a person's trustworthiness contribute to the willingness of others to be vulnerable to that person. People trust others to be **reliable** when they can be counted on to do what they say they will do, keep their promises, and exhibit consistency between their words and actions.[43] To be trusted in terms of **openness** (honesty) means—at a minimum—that the person won't lie to us. At its fullest expression, openness means complete disclosure.[44,45,46] Openness takes time to develop, because it is only over time that we can learn another's true intentions and agendas, and because being open itself involves a willingness to be vulnerable.[47] Trust in terms of **competence**—at a minimum—means that we are able to perform and meet task or job expectations. At a maximum, competence means consistently exceeding expectations.[48] **Compassion**, at a minimum, means not taking advantage of another person, and at its highest level, compassion involves demonstrating genuine interest in the needs of another and unselfishly working to fulfill those needs.[49]

We trust others while recognizing the possibility that they might take advantage of us. Effective leaders not only accept this possibility, but through the quality of courage, are able to overcome barriers that may limit others from being trusting. Indeed, the most successful leaders with whom we've worked not only quickly identify those who are trustworthy in terms of the ROCC, but they also demonstrate the ROCC of Trust first, setting an example, and inspiring their followers to do the same. In our research, consulting, and coaching, we have found that leaders who demonstrate the ROCC of Trust to their followers and other stakeholders, and who are able to work with others who are also trustworthy, are able to create lasting positive change in their organizations.[50] Oftentimes, this positive change leads to outcomes such as improving quality and productivity more than tenfold, preserving or creating thousands of jobs, or remaking entire industries through innovative business strategies and generating hundreds of millions of dollars in annual revenue in the process. Trust can even have an important effect on a country's economic performance. At a national level, trust has been found to influence populations' perspectives of other countries and their purchasing decisions.[51] Indeed, "one standard-deviation increase in trust increases exports to a country by 10 percentage points."[52] This book focuses on how leaders can enhance trust within and across organizations—even across national borders. It is based on our own primary research and unrestricted access to leaders who we believe embody the qualities within the ROCC of Trust.

Trust as a Basis for Effective Leadership

Previous research has shown that leaders are critical to the process of building trust in organizations, and that trust in leadership is significantly related to a number of attitudes, behaviors, and performance outcomes among employees.[53,54] Leaders who are trusted by their followers, particularly in terms of competence, effect change more easily and more quickly in their organizations.[55] In our research about different kinds of leaders, we found that when the leader took the initiative to demonstrate his or her trustworthiness, others within the organization (and often beyond it) came to trust the leader, and through that trust, acted in positive ways that led to lasting change and performance improvements. These positive results then helped affirm the leaders' trustworthiness and trust-building efforts. Figure 1.2 describes a "virtuous trust cycle."

We found that this "virtuous trust cycle" often depended on three critical leadership characteristics: courage, authenticity, and humility. Leaders' courage made it easier for them to be vulnerable to others, for example by sharing sensitive information, or by empowering rank-and-file employees. Leaders' authenticity encouraged others, in turn, to be vulnerable

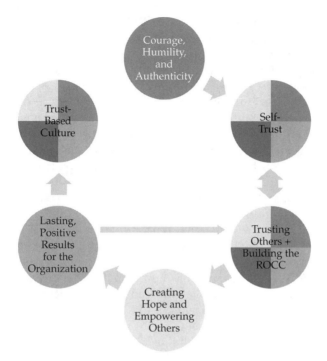

FIGURE 1.2   The Virtuous Trust Cycle

to them. If leaders' behavior was consistent with their rhetoric—if they "talked the talk and walked the walk"—it reassured followers and others that the leaders' motives, values, or goals did not need to be second-guessed. Finally, the leaders' humility engendered their followers and others to be vulnerable to each other. When leaders admitted that they didn't have all the answers and that they depended on their followers as much as the followers depended on them, humble leaders fostered a sense of shared fate. Far too often, this humility is missing in organizations,[56] especially those facing adverse circumstances. In contrast to organizations that compete for resources, especially when threatened or in crisis, we found that organizations led by humble and trustworthy leaders used collaborative approaches to allocating resources.

Consistent with a large body of research that has shown that leadership effectiveness does not depend on one "best" way or one particular combination of attributes or abilities,[57,58,59] we will demonstrate throughout this book how each of the leaders we've studied built the ROCC of Trust in his or her unique way. Whether influenced by upbringing, work experience, or another set of factors, each leader with whom we've worked typically started building the ROCC of Trust using a different piece or pieces of the ROCC. For example, Ted Castle of Rhino Foods found it essential to demonstrate openness by sharing his firm's financial and operations data transparently with all of his employees. In doing so, he created a sense of responsibility and urgency that allowed his ice cream novelty and baking company to successfully weather many economic changes over the years and grow into a $30-million-a-year business. Bob Lintz, former General Manager of the General Motors Parma, Ohio, plant, turned a money-losing stamping plant in the 1980s into a world-class and financially successful billion-dollar operation by initially demonstrating competence and compassion. He did this by spending millions of dollars on employee retraining and including the UAW in bringing in new business to the plant. As a result of these and other efforts, the Parma plant improved quality and productivity significantly. Melanie Bergeron, Chair of Two Men and a Truck International, demonstrated reliability by requiring all franchisees to pay their contractually obligated royalties, and do so on time, even though Home Office incurred hundreds of thousands of dollars in legal fees and months of effort to enforce the contracts. Nonetheless, to be effective change agents, these and all of the leaders we profile in this book have demonstrated all four components of the ROCC of Trust over time. We will show how they did this using their own approaches, which fit both their individual talents and the circumstances their organizations faced.

Are Leaders Born or Made?

This question remains ubiquitous and enduring among our students and clients. People who search the Internet to find an answer to this question frequently end up at our blog, www.totaltrust.wordpress.com, where we have wrestled repeatedly with this question. Based on the research we present in this book and from our own personal experience, leaders can be born *or* made. Some of us are born with a sense of leadership. In part due to our genetic inheritance,[60] born leaders are those who often organize our childhood friends in outdoor activities or elaborate on the rules of board games. Others develop leadership abilities through particularly challenging and diverse experiences.[61] Aneil would argue that much of his leadership ability evolved from facing various experiences early in life, such as raising his two brothers after his mom died when he was 12. This then gave him the confidence to assume leadership roles in student government in middle school and high school. Others of us develop leadership skills later in life, thanks to training and development opportunities that we receive through work or volunteering, especially when opportunities for practice and timely feedback arise.[62] For example, one of the board members of the homeless shelter for which Karen served as board president told her that community volunteering improved his leadership skills. We believe that although it helps to have a desire to lead and help others reach their potential, it is possible for anyone to become a better, more trustworthy leader—if they put their mind to it.

All of the leaders we've studied have found that regardless of their initial orientation toward leading others and creating change, they have refined their leadership style and capabilities through experiences and efforts to improve. This has required significant energy and determination to learn how to listen, give constructive feedback, set priorities, and establish rapport and trust with others. Courage, humility, and authenticity allowed these leaders to become more trustworthy and effective as change agents. With such leaders, change emerges in unique ways that are accessible to others who also desire to create lasting change. Each leader's courage prompted him or her to confront a status quo either to remedy an untenable situation or to significantly improve an unacceptable state of affairs. Humility encouraged these leaders to listen to others and act on their input, to patiently develop a collaborative approach with others and to learn from their mistakes and seek guidance. Authenticity motivated these individuals to learn how to lead others based on their experiences, but it also preserved their values and beliefs that were crucial in establishing trust where little existed before. Authentic leaders are guided by a set of end-values that represent an orientation toward doing what is right for their constituencies.[63]

Accelerating Change by Developing Your Own Trust Network

In our research, many leaders first created a circle of trust. They then used this sphere of influence to establish trust with other stakeholders.[64] Leaders' circles of trust typically consisted of individuals with whom the leader had worked to develop the norms and values that reinforced the ROCC of Trust, which the leader was intent on instituting throughout the organization. One of the leaders we profile, Bob Lintz (General Manager, General Motors' Parma, Ohio, plant), initially focused on building trust within his top management team. Often, very strong disagreements occurred among this team regarding how to turn around the plant's performance. Bob actually enjoyed surfacing these disagreements, because he felt it promoted more options to improve. Bob worked very hard to elicit a consensus agreement along with a commitment to speak with one voice to the thousands of plant employees when implementing the change strategy they had agreed upon. His goal was a cohesive and collaborative team which he believed could be created most effectively by establishing trust based initially on openness, and then by reinforcing the other components of the ROCC of Trust through joint decisions and actions. Bob then expanded his

Circle of Trust to include the plant's UAW leadership by sharing information openly and engaging in collaborative decision-making.

In a very different type of company, and initially led by women rather than men, the firm Two Men and a Truck, International also created a Circle of Trust. The Circle first encompassed a family of diverse individuals, which was then expanded to include employees who complemented the family members' abilities and talents. Today, with annual revenues of $220 million, the company still often refers to franchisees as strategic partners. The corporate office, its employees, and its franchisees work to be transparent in an effort to build trust and strengthen the brand. They build the ROCC of Trust with hundreds of thousands of customers throughout the U.S. and Canada, the UK and Ireland. They build the ROCC of Trust by creating industry-leading standards in reliable service, transparent pricing, moving goods at competitive prices, and by taking care of their customers based on the motto "treat everyone the way you would want your grandma to be treated."[65]

Sometimes a leader builds his or her Circle of Trust through experimentation and *active watching*. Whereas active *listening* is based on understanding another's point of view and asking clarifying questions to ensure understanding is accurate, *active watching* involves observing how others interact with one another to identify those who are most trusted within an organization. These trustworthy individuals are then included in the leader's circle of trust in order to quickly size up problems and opportunities. David Lassman, an operations executive and adjunct professor at Carnegie Mellon University, practiced active watching early in a new job at a manufacturing company in upstate New York. He identified key individuals who were able to help David fix a debacle by experimenting and innovating. Production yields, which had dropped from more than 75% to less than 25% following the company's purchase of another firm, were ultimately increased to levels higher than before the purchase.

Creating a Culture of Trust

Rensis Likert, the famous psychologist and sociologist and for whom the Likert scale is named, identified the leader's importance in creating a culture of trust. He called such leaders "linking pins," based on their job of linking people from one part of the organization with those in another.[66] Leaders' overlapping group membership allows them to share critical information and build relationships in an organization. Jack Gabarro, an emeritus professor at Harvard Business School, also stressed the importance of building a culture of trust if a leader is intent on creating change quickly and enduringly.[67]

Lenovo's Culture of Trust

Lewis Broadnax, Executive Director of web sales and marketing

The business management system that our CEO has put in place has ensured that all of the functional areas and regions have their say and their input into the entire process. It involves a senior leadership team which meets once a month to focus on a different area of the business.

The senior leadership steering committee is presented with issues or opportunities from all parts of the business. Our group, e-commerce, will present in May. We'll talk about our progress, where we're going to innovate, how we're going to beat our competition, what our barriers are, and what help is needed. The senior leadership team will listen to the issues and our proposals, and make a decision. Then a group works to resolve that problem. There's follow-up where the group comes back to present a status update and receive further guidance. All the functional areas of the company participate in this process. Every month a different function presents at different locations around the world.

I believe that the structure our CEO has put in place is really working. It has become a trusted structure because there's the ability for cross-functional teams to get together to work on an issue, and a management system that actually tracks all the problems, and then brings it back for closure. Now, more groups are reaching out to the extended organization for help, and extended teams are helping those groups to make sure that they are getting the support they need. So when someone says, "I'm working on this for our leadership team," everyone stops to find out what how they can help. It's become ingrained in the culture to pay attention and see where you can help out.

The leaders we've studied and worked with coupled their efforts to create a Circle of Trust with broader efforts to instill the ROCC of Trust throughout their organizations and with key stakeholders. To build trust through reliability, openness, competence, and compassion, leaders demonstrated their own trustworthiness, permitting their followers to reciprocate. Leaders demonstrated **reliability** by being accessible, keeping their promises, and being on time to meetings and important events. Leaders built a culture of trust based on **openness** by providing opportunities for their employees to talk with them without fear of reprisal, and by being transparent in their communications, often sharing sensitive information about company performance and other important issues. Leaders established **competence**-based trust throughout the organization by establishing high standards of excellence with clearly defined metrics. They also built trust through competence by hiring exceptionally bright. The leaders of Two Men and Truck International implemented this practice at the firm's inception and by insisting that anyone responsible for recruiting, selecting, developing, or retaining personnel adopt the "smarter than I am" approach to managing. Leaders also built **compassion**-based trust, the form of trust that takes the most time and is often the toughest component of the ROCC of Trust to build. Leaders demonstrated empathy in tangible and convincing ways by personally making symbolic and substantive sacrifices to advance the organization and by asking the same from their subordinates. Leaders building compassionate trust also develop innovative ways to save jobs during periods of organizational crisis or economic upheaval.

Two Men and a Truck, International established systemwide trust in terms of reliability and competence in many ways, including developing highly consistent work standards, industry-leading employee and franchisee training, and a franchise agreement that creates clear expectations for the franchisor, franchisees, and customers. Ted Castle (cofounder and president of Rhino Foods) established a culture of trust by sharing company financial information with all of his employees and then developing operating practices and metrics that have contributed to two decades of profitable growth. Bob Lintz (general manager, General Motors' Parma, Ohio, plant) quickly built trust in terms of openness by instituting an open-door policy with *all* of his 5,000 employees. He also expanded his effort to keep *all* employees current with information on performance to goals using his quarterly updates. He ran the business update meetings personally and would average 30 separate meetings over three shifts each quarter. He also eliminated many barriers (such as separate cafeterias and parking lots) between managers and the union-represented hourly employees, including by dispensing with suits and ties in the plant and adopting a sweater-and-slacks dress policy instead. The physicians we've studied have built trust in terms of compassion through their ability to listen before diagnosing and by sacrificing both time and money to provide patients with access to their expertise and healing efforts. Much like the leaders we've studied in other industries, these physician leaders created compassion-based trust by building strong relationships with their patients and staff members. Their efforts have been crucial to healing patients who are often some of the most vulnerable in healthcare.

Rebuilding Trust

A frequently repeated truism among both scholars and practitioners is that trust takes a long time to build, is fragile, and once broken is exceedingly hard to restore.[68] Indeed, our friend and physician leader once remarked, "Trust can be broken very quickly, but the repair, like a broken bone, can take a very long time to heal."[69] Often, the first step our leaders take to restore broken trust is to acknowledge the mistakes or wrongdoing that led to the lost trust and to apologize. The next step is to take immediate action to fix the mistakes or overcome the damage the wrongdoing has wrought. This action is essential to rebuilding trust, even when specific mistakes or instances of malfeasance led to the trust violations. For example, when ice cream and confections entrepreneur Ted Castle was forced to downsize his workforce because of cyclical changes in the economy or decreased demand, he did so creatively: He outsourced some of his best employees to local businesses that needed extra help. These employees volunteered for outsourcing because they believed Ted's promise to restore their jobs at Rhino Foods when his business rebounded—which he in fact did. He also built trust with other local businesses because he gave them his very *best* employees to meet their short-term employment needs. Dennis Quaintance of Quaintance-Weaver Restaurants & Hotels was forced to close one of his restaurants due to declining demand. Although restaurant failures are notoriously common, Dennis's had remained open for many years. He still felt it was necessary to preserve trust by being transparent in his decision to close the restaurant, being generous with employee severance, and offering laid-off employees opportunities to work for other restaurants that were part of his company. His humane and thoughtful approach to downsizing was critical to his ability to launch one of the most environmentally innovative hotels in the world using some of the same employees that worked for him for years in other parts of his business empire.[70]

Trust Leads to an Enlarged Sense of Purpose

Our research revealed that building and sustaining trust is both time-consuming and energy-intensive. Leaders can easily exhaust themselves and impair their capacity for building trust and fostering lasting change if they don't find ways to renew themselves regularly or enlarge their purpose for being. Noted management expert Charles Handy in a *Harvard Business Review* article, "What is business for?" recommended that businesses should "measure success in terms of outcomes for others as well as ourselves."[71] He noted that this philosophy would help not only create profits, but also make the world a better place.

Finally, we describe a variety of ways in which our leaders were able to renew themselves and in the process develop new challenges for themselves and their organizations. These new challenges enlarged the sense of purpose for the leaders themselves and for those around them. Mary Ellen Sheets, founder of Two Men and a Truck, International began enlarging her purpose 25 years ago using her first year's profits. She gave away the $1,000 in profits to 10 different nonprofit organizations in her community.

With this simple act, she created a culture of giving and caring in her organization that endures today and even has a name: "Movers Who Care."

The Reverend Jean Smith found a new purpose by taking her skills to a new arena, from a localized church to a global not-for-profit. Moving from her land-bound parish, she found a new calling among seafarers, ministering to them when they were homesick, in need of legal or financial assistance, and when their shipping companies went bankrupt and stranded them half a world away from their homes. These leaders courageously recognized their responsibility to the greater community, not just to their own organization or themselves. At a time when the morality of business is often questioned,[72] these leaders envisioned something better.

☐ Beginning the Journey

By developing trust, our leaders have achieved outcomes deemed exceedingly difficult if not impossible by their peers, academics, or industry experts. Leaders who read this book will be inspired to achieve similar accomplishments. Although trust has been diminished today, true leaders have an opportunity to build and rebuild trust and create lasting, positive change in their organizations and among the stakeholders who depend on them.

What Trust Is and Why It Matters

☐ Defining the ROCC of Trust

Most scholars define trust as a willingness to be vulnerable to another person or party based on some positive expectations regarding the other party's intentions or behavior.[1,2,3,4,5,6] Simply put, trust means you are willing to be vulnerable to others in the face of uncertainty. If you trust someone, you are more willing to become interdependent with that person, even though you can't be absolutely sure everything will turn out fine. The benefits we have discovered from building trust include deeper, more loyal relationships, stronger resiliency in the face of a crisis, and enhanced individual, team, and organizational performance. During the past two decades, through our research, teaching, coaching, and consulting work, we have identified four basic aspects in which individuals trust their leaders and one another: Reliability, Openness, Competence, and Compassion, which we call the **ROCC of Trust**. Several other scholars have articulated trust as a similar set of dimensions, including ability, integrity, and benevolence.[7,8] As do some scholars, we differentiate integrity into two separate dimensions: reliability and openness.[9]

The ROCC of Trust does *not* mean embracing blind faith. Several scholars distinguish among confidence, trust, and faith.[10,11,12] Confidence is the *general* expectation that you will not be harmed. Confidence can be expressed, for example, by someone who either does or does not lock their doors when they leave home or by someone who chooses to carry a gun for self-protection.[13] Blind faith, in contrast, means that the individual has no doubts that his or her choices will lead to a positive result or that the outcome is preordained or fated and should be welcomed. With blind faith,

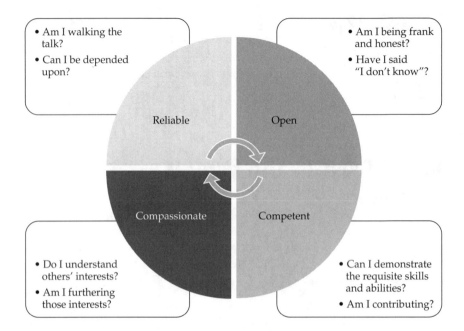

FIGURE 2.1   Explanation of the ROCC of Trust

negative consequences, as a whole, are removed.[14] When individuals have the ROCC of Trust in their leader, however, their actions and attitudes are based on repeated experiences that have been validated in a variety of situations. For example, John Gabarro (professor emeritus, Harvard Business School) said, "Judgments about trust in working relationships become specific based on the accumulation of interactions, specific incidents, problems, and events."[15] When a leader has developed the ROCC of Trust, it means that he or she has earned the privilege to be depended on when events go well and when they do not. Figure 2.1 elucidates what constitutes the ROCC of Trust.

Reliability

The ROCC of Trust starts with reliability. Trust in terms of reliability has been defined by other scholars as including consistency between one's words and actions.[16,17,18,19] In *The Leader's Edge: The Seven Keys to Leadership in a Turbulent World*, Burt Nanus wrote, "Nothing is noticed more quickly—and considered more significant—than a discrepancy between what executives preach and what they expect their associates to practice."[20] When someone can rely on us, we behave in a way that is even and consistent. We are dependable. As Brenda Bernstein, the founder of TheEssayExpert. com, told us,

> I find that I trust people when they are responsive, and I stop trusting them when they're not. I trust people who keep promises . . . deliver on commitments . . . pay on time! And I trust people who own up to their mistakes before I confront them myself. So, I really make an effort to respond in a timely manner to every communication. I do what I say I'm going to do. And if something happens on my end that could potentially break someone's trust, I immediately communicate upon realizing it, preferably before the other party has to bring it up

We remember events or obligations that are important to another person, and we become a source of stability in his or her life.

Reliability is the first component of the ROCC of Trust—without it, others will not give us a second chance. Dennis Quaintance (Quaintance-Weaver Enterprises) echoes these sentiments:

> I do not believe in contrived ways of building trust. If you just talk the talk and walk the walk, and make your own behavior consistent with the objectives and values of the organization, then folks will trust you. If you are a hypocrite, they will soon find that out as well. . . . Do what you say you're going to do when you say you're going to do it.

Openness

Openness is a willingness to be honest and forthright in dealing with others. It is the second piece of the ROCC of Trust. In describing Theory Z organizations, Ouchi discussed trust extensively in terms of openness.[21] Several other scholars have also defined trust in terms of this dimension.[22,23] Leaders who are trusted are more effective in acquiring skills, retaining and attracting followers, promoting change and innovation,[24] and facilitating coordination among departments.[25] An automotive executive, for example, expressed his trustworthiness and need to be open in this way:

> If they don't believe what I'm telling them, if they think it's all a bunch of bullshit, don't expect them to go out there and work a little

harder or work a little different. They're not going to be as receptive to change unless they understand and trust that the things that I'm talking about are, in fact, true.

If others believe we are honest, they will trust what we have to say to them. Our openness also encourages more openness from others. If we are honest with our neighbor, coworker, or family member, they become more willing to open up to us. Openness thus embodies a willingness to listen to new ideas and perspectives. This mutual exchange of information creates a more trusting relationship. Being open also includes being evenhanded in sharing information or perspectives. Greater openness may entail risks, however, as Pastor Jim Wenger of Faith Lutheran Church in Okemos, Michigan, shares,

> One of my favorite books is by Allan Loy McGinnis, *The Friendship Factor*. His strategy for building and sustaining friendships deals with disclosure; that is, sharing something about yourself. However, self-disclosure can be very risky. When we share something genuine about our true self, we risk being rejected or the information being misused. I have shared my inner life with some people I thought I could trust, and it was very disappointing. I have long worked to develop small groups where people could share their interior life with a few other trusted people. When it works it is a very satisfying and fulfilling experience. When it doesn't it can be a disaster.

Bob Lintz, the former General Motors plant manager, also shared some thoughts on openness and trust:

> You really have to have it in your inner soul or in your inner conscious about the type of person you are. Opening yourself up and displaying your weaknesses is not easy for a lot of people. If you're going to get people to trust you, you're going to have to open up to all of your strengths, weaknesses, and shortcomings and demonstrate a commitment to a change process to which you're trying to lead the organization. I just don't feel that you can fake it.

Competence

Competence is the third element of the ROCC of Trust. Competence includes the abilities, skills, and knowledge needed to achieve expected performance.[26] When we trust someone to be competent, we believe they have the abilities to perform their share of the workload.[27,28,29] We are more willing to be vulnerable and trust another person when we feel they are competent to do their job.[30] Notably, trust based on competence differs from power based on competence.

Indeed, individuals may be more powerful if they have knowledge, skills, and abilities, but they are not necessarily trusted unless the way they wield power is not simply for personal gain.[31,32] A 2010 article in *Communication Studies* addressing responses to deception in the workplace noted, "Expert power refers to a person's ability to *influence another* based on perceptions that the source is competent and knowledgeable within the organization."[33]

Leaders are characterized by how much their followers trust them to make competent decisions that affect the group or organization.[34,35] Even if we are viewed as reliable and honest, people will not be willing to trust us unless we can do the job for which we were hired. In certain circumstances, we use proxies for competence, such as a specific degree from a certain college. Still, direct experience with another person is a more convincing way to demonstrate competence. For instance, physicians almost always place their diplomas in their offices or examining rooms, but it is not until we spend time with them that we determine whether we can truly trust them. Interestingly, competence is perhaps the easiest piece of the ROCC of Trust to improve. If we are not as competent as we desire in a certain skill or subject, we can always improve our knowledge or abilities through education or practice. Research has shown, however, that if we are not competent, others are likely to terminate their relationship with us.[36]

When we asked one manager how his organization developed and maintained trust in the company, he stated,

> They've got to have some feeling that you're competent to lead them out of this mess. Because, they may like you a lot, but if they feel you're a bumbling idiot they say, "Shit! We can't trust what this guy tells us. He's gonna take us off the end of the cliff." I mean they have to be confident that you're competent. They've got to have some feeling that you know what the hell you're talking about. When you go out there to tell them to do something they've got to have some feeling that it will make a difference.[37]

Compassion

Compassion is the last piece of the ROCC of Trust. At a minimum, compassion means not taking unfair advantage of another party.[38, 39] Having compassion for others means that we must be willing to set aside our own concerns so that we can be truly empathetic toward others. It also means that we must place the interests of others at a level equal to or above our own. This is the last aspect of trust we find in others, because the other elements of the ROCC of Trust are easier qualities to develop or possess. Being a truly compassionate person, however, requires investing time and demonstrating empathy. Several examples of this dimension exist in the research literature. For example, managers can show that they can be trusted by caring about their employees' job security, welfare, and interests,[40,41] and employees can show they are trustworthy when they are concerned about the welfare of the entire organization.[42] Compassion is valued so highly as an aspect of trust because it involves furthering others' interests and not just your own. Bob Lintz, the former GM plant manager, told us many times, "You really have to be committed in your heart to doing what is right for the organization."

Rhino Foods has developed a culture of compassion in several ways, including its Employee Exchange program, which hires out employees to other businesses rather than laying them off in slack periods, which began in 1993.[43] In 2007, in partnership with the United Way of Chittenden County, Vermont, it began its Working Bridges Program,

> Working Bridges is a collaborative effort by progressive employers in Chittenden County, Vermont, to facilitate the development and implementation of innovative workplace practices to improve employee productivity, retention, advancement, and financial stability.
>
> Rhino Foods has assumed a leadership role in this collaboration—piloting several workplace practices under the Working Bridges concept that have been extremely successful. Several new programs have been created and implemented as a result of the project, including an Income Advance Loan program, Financial Literacy training, an onsite Resource Coordinator, and Bridges Out of Poverty™ training for supervisors.
>
> In partnership with North Country Federal Credit Union, a new Income Advance Loan program was developed and implemented, resulting in over $150,000 in short-term loans to employees, which have addressed various needs. Employees repay the loans through a payroll deduction. Once the loan is repaid, we don't turn off the deduction (unless the employee asks) and the deduction flows to a savings account. So the program has helped many employees transition from financial crisis to savings, and truly get on the path to building credit and improving their financial stability.[44]

☐ The ROCC of Trust

The four pieces or dimensions of trustworthiness—reliability, openness, competence, and compassion—together form the ROCC of Trust: A solid foundation on which we can put our trust in others. When a person embodies all four elements, we have *the ROCC of Trust* in another person. In contrast, when even one of the pieces of the ROCC is missing, we may not want to make ourselves vulnerable to that individual. As Sheldon Yellen, CEO of Belfor Holdings, told us,

> I met with a young guy earlier today applying for a job here. He said, "How do I know that Belfor's right for me?" I said, "If you have these six traits and characteristics, and you feel it in your heart, then it's the right place for you; if you're missing any of them, you probably shouldn't be here.
>
> "To build trust let these six ways of life speak for you:
> 1. Integrity: if you say it, you've got to mean it, really mean it!
> 2. Sincerity: if you mean it, let others feel it.
> 3. Humility: it's great to conquer, but don't triumph.
> 4. Courtesy: always, always in abundance
> 5. Wisdom: know enough to lead, but never leave anyone behind; and
> 6. Charity: you've got to have heart."
>
> I made him write those down: Those six traits are trust builders. If that's who you are as a person, you will gain the trust of others.
>
> I also believe that you let your life, your work, and your relationships speak for themselves. I tell my managers all the time, "Let your actions speak; talk less. Don't interrupt." When you do trust, verify. But, you've got to trust, but you've got to verify, too.[45]

Obviously, some pieces of the ROCC are more important in certain contexts than in others. When we deal with physicians, for example, we probably care about their compassion and their competence more than we care about these qualities when we deal with our dry cleaner. Even the same piece of the ROCC may carry more weight depending on the person we are trusting. For example, competence matters when dealing with both our physicians and dry cleaners. But our vulnerability is greater with the physician, who has the power to diagnose our illness such that we become either healthier or sicker. The dry cleaner, in contrast, only has the power to clean our clothes properly or shrink them.

Building Trust with His Team

Lewis Broadnax at Lenovo

To build trust, I always want to get to know the person and understand what it is they're trying to accomplish short-term and long-term. Then I want to make sure that we're setting that person up to be as successful as possible, and that they feel like they have all the tools they need to get to the next level. When you bring on someone, you know they're a good talent, but you want to make sure that they're learning what they need to get to the next step of their career.

Many people who started at IBM with me have stayed with me for extended periods of their career. As they've become managers and they've brought on their own new people, I can see that they're using some of the same principles.

More recently, we've gotten to a point where I think maybe we've done it a little too well, because people don't want to leave. They're driving great results for the business and learning new things along the way. This past year is the first year where our people are stacking up because they weren't leaving. The best thing for some of them was to get them promoted out into other parts of Lenovo.

They've done a great job. They're very, very loyal to the group. It's not that they're in their comfort zone and want to stay. It's just that they're loyal to the group, and they don't want to leave because they feel that that would leave the team high and dry, which is not the case.

We need to say, "You've done a great job. You deserve it. Go take the promotion. Go move on to your next phase of your career." I think it starts with empowering them, making sure that they feel like what they're doing is making a difference not only to themselves, but to the broader group.

The Bottom-Line Benefits of Trust

Leaders who develop trust with their subordinates and throughout their organizations create lasting, positive changes that are both significant in scale and broad in scope. Researchers have found that trust in leadership is positively related to a variety of outcomes, including job, organizational citizenship behaviors, organizational commitment, and job satisfaction, and is negatively related to intention to quit.[46,47] A 2011 survey of 10,000 people in the United States and 1,000 individuals in several other countries found that "employees who distrust their leaders are seven times more likely to report they are mentally and physically unwell, and almost half of employees who distrust their leaders are seriously considering leaving their employers."[48] Trust also has benefits that go beyond internal performance outcomes such as employee well-being and loyalty, to include firm competitiveness.[49] As Dr. Ranjay Gulati, the Jaime and Josefina Chua Ti-ampo Professor of Business Administration at Harvard Business School, told us,

> A key to enacting customer centricity within organizations is build-ing porous and collaborative silos within the organization that align quickly around shifting customer needs. Trust is a critical lubricant that enables greater collaboration within and between organizational silos. So, trust is not just a feel-good sentiment, but also something that can directly impact business success.[50]

In our own research, on which we will elaborate in subsequent chapters, we have found several compelling examples of leaders who have rescued failing organizations, created new companies that have grown and pros-pered for decades, and saved many lives as a result of their efforts to build trust.

In the 1980s, Bob Lintz, as a GM plant manager, built the ROCC of Trust with the local UAW union leadership and union employees of his stamp-ing plant in Parma, Ohio, a suburb of Cleveland. As a result, he saved a $250-million (annual revenue) plant. Prior to Bob's efforts, GM was con-templating a shutdown of the plant, because it was one of GM's worst plants in terms of quality, productivity, and efficiency. It also had one of the worst local labor agreements. Almost three decades later, it is one of the best stamping plants in world. Thousands of individuals kept their jobs, the plant now generates $1 billion in annual revenue, productivity

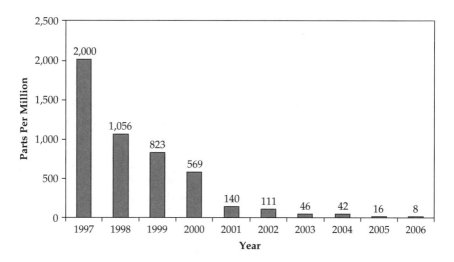

FIGURE 2.2   Decline in Parts per Million at Parma

has improved almost tenfold, and hundreds of millions of dollars in cost savings have been achieved. This is only one example of the results the Parma Plant has achieved; consider how much quality has improved even *after* Bob retired in 1999. The number of defects generated per million parts produced declined from 2,000 in 1997 to only 8 defects per million in 2006, as shown in Figure 2.2.

Ted Castle, a former University of Vermont college hockey player and assistant coach turned entrepreneur, also built the ROCC of Trust, particularly in terms of openness, at Rhino Foods. As a result, he grew his business from $8 million in annual revenue in the 1990s to $30 million today. He has also expanded employment to include providing jobs and job training to African and Bosnian refugees. Rhino Foods credits its Working Bridges Program with reducing employee turnover from 40% to only 15% and with helping improve the financial well-being and stability of its front-line employees.[51] The company also credits its Employee Exchange program with "saving thousands of dollars in staffing costs while retaining their skilled employees in the long term."[52]

Two Men and a Truck, International, the largest local moving company in the United States, grew from a $350 investment in a used truck in the mid-1980s in mid-Michigan to become a firm generating $220 million annually, with franchises throughout the United States as well as Canada and Ireland. The four family members who founded and lead this company credit their long-lasting success and industry-leading practices in

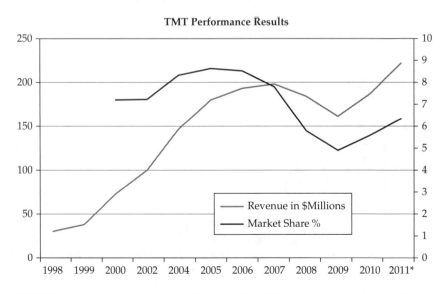

FIGURE 2.3 Performance Results from Two Men and a Truck International

part to building the ROCC of Trust with their employees, their 200 franchisees, and their tens of thousands of customers. Figure 2.3 shows how annual revenue has increased over the past 13 years. The average market share of its franchises has also generally increased, although it declined during the most recent recession and is now rebounding.

Kevin Lobdell, MD, was able to build the ROCC of Trust with his fellow physicians, nurses, respiratory therapists, and other staff members in a critical care unit of Carolinas HealthCare System based in Charlotte, North Carolina. As a result, he and his team improved the process for extubating cardiac surgery patients following their procedure by more than 100%. Now as high as 85% of patients are extubated within six hours post-op. Dr. Lobdell and his team also reduced mortality by nearly 50%, sepsis by 50%, and acute renal failure by 37.5%, while also improving operational efficiency by reducing ICU and hospital length of stay.[53]

The bottom line is that the presence of trust is more beneficial than its absence. Great results can happen when leaders are trustworthy and followers emulate that example.

Trust Tips

1. Being **reliable** means being dependable. Can others rely on you?
2. Being **open** means sharing information and being transparent. Do others believe you are fair and honest?
3. Being **competent** means being able to do the job. Do others have confidence in your abilities?
4. Being **compassionate** means caring about others' interests as much you care about your own. Do others feel you genuinely care?

Leaders Are Born *and* Made

For decades, we've been asked the same question over and over: Are leaders born or made? And, indeed, this question has been the subject of many scholarly studies. We argue that leaders have both inherent traits *and* learned abilities. In turn, we consistently answer this question by asserting that leaders are both born *and* made. By this we mean that although some individuals are naturally more inclined to become leaders based on early life experiences and, yes, even genetics,[1] all people have the capacity to *become* leaders if they first have the desire and second make the effort. Being an effective leader involves having certain traits with which a person might be born,[2] having the ability to learn specific skills and behaviors through developmental experiences, understanding one's personal orientation to learning (such as taking and analyzing the results of the Myers-Briggs Type Indicator), and receiving organizational support.[3,4,5,6] Some people are more empathetic than others, some are more energetic, and some are more engaging. Each person has a unique composition of talents, motives, and dreams that provide the raw material for getting the best out of everyone around. Everyone can draw on something in their background and experiences to become more effective at leading others if they really have the motivation to do so. Pastor James Wenger noted, "Leadership is learned, observed, practiced, and, through failure and repeated effort, developed until others recognize gifts of leadership in a person."[7]

Empirical research bears out the argument that both nature and nurture shape leadership development. Based on a study using the Minnesota Twin Registry, Richard Arvey and his colleagues found that 30% of the leadership behaviors and the leadership roles that people occupy can be attributed to genetic factors, while the remaining 70% result from environmental factors.[8] In a subsequent study, these researchers found that environmental factors such as socioeconomic status, perceived parental support, and perceived conflict with parents all moderate the influence of

29

genetic factors on whether a person occupies a leadership role.[9] Socioeconomic status and perceived parental support negatively moderate genetic factors, and perceived conflict with parents positively moderates those factors.[10] Stated more simply, the degree to which genetic factors influence whether one assumes a leadership role is reduced by socioeconomic status and parental support and enhanced by perceived conflict with one's parents. The authors of this study suggest that these results might be explained because more stimulating environments level the playing field, making one's genetic endowment for leadership less important, and conflict with parents, as a form of adversity, strengthens the role of genetics in predicting leadership roles.

On our blog, www.totaltrust.wordpress.com, we have been discussing the question of whether leaders are born or made for several years, and we urge our readers to share their perspectives. The family members who own Two Men and a Truck, International also contributed to this discussion with their thoughts. Mary Ellen Sheets (Founder, Two Men and a Truck, International) commented, "I think it's a combination of the traits you inherit from your parents and the situations you face that mold your life. High energy helps." Her daughter Melanie, company Chair, stated, "I strongly believe leadership is developed through circumstances people face. I agree with your students in that we are born with unique abilities. Circumstances in life may cause people with certain traits to be leaders." One of the original "two men," Brig, CEO of the company, wrote,

> My answer would be you can be born with a silver spoon in your mouth but not born with a "leader" gene! Leaders learn from life's school of hard knocks, watching others succeed and fail and surrounding themselves with successful people. You do not have to be smarter than the people you are leading in a certain field; you need to direct smarter people in tasks where their work pays off. In the service industry, you need to know how customers think (most adults have this experience) and you need to know how the frontline employees think. To do this you need to get your hands dirty and do the work. You now have some general guidelines to make operational decisions. With this information you can lead projects that may alter how the business is being performed. This, in turn, builds confidence others may have in you. This is what builds leadership.

Other readers weighed in on the discussion with insightful comments. One of Aneil's former Wake Forest University MBA students, Will Ford, described the relationship of a leader to others this way,

> I don't think leaders are born. I think leaders are people who are convinced. It's the willingness to believe in a group of people—to believe in their potential and then to risk part of yourself on that

belief. Leadership happens when the group realizes your sacrifice or willingness to sacrifice. I think of this as the transition point of leadership. What follows is a natural progression of believing in a group of people and those same people reciprocating. What keeps the relationship going is trust. I guess in some strange way, a leader isn't necessarily a person, but the willing interaction of a person and a group. Leadership is the relationship that happens.

Several physician leaders whom we profile in our chapter on healthcare leadership, believe that leaders are both. One of them, Dr. Brent Senior of the University of North Carolina at Chapel Hill Medical School, had this perspective,

> Leaders are never simply born! Vocal individuals may be born. Charismatic people may be born. But speaking and charisma only take the leader so far. Self-sacrificial, trustworthy leadership is something that goes against the natural bent of most individuals. It requires purposeful decision-making and introspection, and it can be "made."

Another physician leader, Dr. Kevin Lobdell of Carolinas HealthCare System, put it this way: "There are certainly people who have [innate] leadership qualities, but leadership development and practice are vital. I am a voracious consumer of leadership information. Leadership is lonely. I would recommend that leaders share with mentors, obtain coaching, and consider joining leadership groups."[9] Dr. Bruce Rubin of the Virginia Commonwealth Medical School also voiced the importance of seeking leadership development from mentoring and learning from others. "It is important to identify good leaders that can continue to be an inspiration. Call these mentors or role models or sounding boards or friends. Recognize that becoming a good leader takes time and effort and remaining a good leader is a continuous investment."[10] Dr. Rubin also argued that leadership is both innate and learned,

> I believe that leaders are born and made. I believe that the *desire* to lead is probably innate and appears in certain toddlers. I see young children who want to be the leaders just as I see adults who embrace leadership opportunities. I believe that the ability to lead is learned over time and experience, and requires a passion and a desire to lead well. Desire to lead is not sufficient alone, but the willingness to be a learner and to continually strive to be the best leader that one can—this takes work.[11]

A former Wake Forest MBA student of Aneil's and founder of a business intelligence software company, Doug Hoogervorst, wrote,

This is really not a one-or-the-other question. Yes, true leadership requires abilities such as charisma, accountability, and passion that some are born with in abundance. However, we all have these qualities, whether we admit it or not, and they are more or less developed by the experiences that have shaped us, plus nature's head start. Are leaders born? Yes, I think so. Some people are blessed with these qualities in abundance at birth. Can leaders be made? Absolutely. One of the primary qualities that separates humans from the rest of life is self-awareness and our ability to react, create, and shape our actions. We clearly can strengthen our weaknesses and play on our strengths. I, for one, was the antithesis of a leader in my 20s. Today I run a successful software company and think I have leadership skills.

Organizations largely agree with the assessment that leaders can be made; otherwise, they would not spend 21% of their training dollars or $12 billion per year on leadership development training.[12] This investment is applied to many forms of developing leaders, including classroom training, individual coaching, and action-learning. Scholars believe that the value of this leadership development training is that it builds both human capital (individual competencies) and social capital (relational competencies). Social capital is critical for building and maintaining trust.[13] Here, we assert that the way leaders build trust is a function of both their innate character and their learned abilities.

Based on our own direct collaborations with leaders, we believe leaders are both born and made, and that they have learned to build trust with others because of some qualities that may be innate, but also because of their experiences. They may have a greater propensity to trust others than the general population, although we haven't measured this specifically. Their experiences have directly shaped how they build trust with others. In general, they have demonstrated parts of the ROCC of Trust in accordance with the needs they perceived in their organization. For example, if transparency was lacking, they may have chosen to emphasize openness in their trust-building efforts.

The people with whom we've interacted behave both humbly and heroically, but they are not superhuman or unbelievable. They may be extraordinary leaders, but they are still ordinary people who rose to the challenge of creating transformational change by building the ROCC of Trust. Leaders are critical to building trust in organizations, and when followers trust their leaders, they have the potential to enjoy numerous benefits, including better job performance, greater organizational commitment, higher job satisfaction, and lower intention to quit.[14] Leaders who are trusted by their followers are also more easily able to effect change quickly in their organizations.[15] Of course, for change to take place in an organization, individuals must trust more than a single leader, and they will distinguish between trusting a leader at the top of the organization versus trusting their own immediate bosses or other managers.[16,17]

☐ Mastering the Three Levels of Change: Personal, Interpersonal, and Systemic

The leaders we've studied have recognized that in order to achieve lasting positive results in their organizations, they need to address three levels of change in their trust-building efforts: personal, interpersonal, and systemic.[18] The personal level constitutes the attitudes, values, and behaviors that individuals demonstrate that shape the capacity for influencing others. The interpersonal level constitutes the attitudes, values, and behaviors that individuals demonstrate toward one another that shape their collective action. The systemic level of change involves organization-wide or extra-organizational forces that enhance or impede organizational change, including organizational culture, structure, and external stakeholders. At the personal level, leaders need courage, humility, and authenticity to challenge the status quo, define excellence for others, and craft a compelling vision of the future. They also need the personal wherewithal to build trust, which includes physical stamina, emotional stability, and the ability to withstand repeated rejection. At the interpersonal level, leaders take the initiative to demonstrate the ROCC of Trust in order to build commitment and overcome followers' resistance to change, and encourage them to collaborate with one another to implement change.[19] This interpersonal trust encourages colleagues and employees to act in ways that lead to lasting change and better performance. At the systemic or broadest level, leaders build a culture of trust throughout an organization; institutionalize change efforts by focusing on processes, norms, rules, and reward systems; and build trust with external stakeholders, such as customers and suppliers.[20] These positive results then help to affirm the leaders' trustworthiness and trust-building efforts.[21] Of course, the ways in which a leader creates an organizational culture of trust will be influenced by the national culture within which the organization is situated.[22,23,24] We would expect that leaders in countries whose denizens value strong hierarchies are more likely to emphasize reliability and competence as ways to demonstrate their trustworthiness, rather than openness.

The current CEO of Lenovo, Yang Yuanqing, started to build trust with his staff by moving to the U.S. headquarters in Cary, North Carolina, to build relationships there. As Lewis Broadnax, executive director of web sales and marketing at Lenovo, told us,

When Lenovo bought the IBM ThinkPad division, the question was, How can Lenovo, which no one's ever heard of, come in and compete with the likes of Dell, Gateway, and HP? ThinkPad was the rock-solid brand with IBM. When people thought of ThinkPad, they didn't think, Chinese company. The two don't really match. How could Lenovo actually grow this business? How long would this really last?

The initial CEO of the company came over from IBM to make sure that the transition happened properly. Then Bill Amelio was brought in from Dell to start really driving this business hard, to get us in a position where we could compete with the likes of Dell. Yuanqing Yang, who is our current CEO (and was chairman of the board previously), then took over the reins, and his responsibility was really to take the company to the next level.

He's an incredible man; he's still not 50, and is thought of as one of the industry's great visionaries and leaders. His personality exudes confidence and trust. You see him around the local campus, and he greets you with a smile and asks you how you are doing. His demeanor, his thought process, and the way he approaches any issue are so calm and effective that I think everyone really just got behind him immediately.

The big turning point for me was Yuanqing's statement on culture within the company, what Lenovo was going to be, and how that was distributed throughout the entire organization. It was very clear early on that we were in this thing for the long haul. We were going to be a world class organization. We were going to be the best. It was clear that they were communicating to every employee, everyone that had anything to do with the company, what the culture was going to be, and making sure that everybody was on board with that. Everyone became focused on driving the company to those levels. Then, as the numbers started to come out, I think that comfort level with him just grew and grew. I think he's one of the few CEOs that really does want to empower you to go out and make the right decisions, make the right calls.

☐ Leading Through Courage, Humility, and Authenticity

We have found that the virtuous trust cycle often depends on three critical leadership characteristics: courage, humility, and authenticity.[25] Leaders exhibit personal courage by empowering employees or sharing critical information with them, both of which entail being vulnerable to others. When leaders also display humility, which, like courage, leaves them vulnerable to their followers, their subordinates may be more likely to be vulnerable and build trust with each other. Humble leaders can foster a sense of shared fate by acknowledging that they don't have all the answers and need help from their followers, especially in times of crisis. Authentic leaders are transparent in their motives and open in their values, and they act consistently with those motives and values. Authentic leaders thus have the capacity to encourage others to be vulnerable to them. Then their followers feel confident that they will not be exploited. Subsequently, they are more trusting of those leaders. Indeed, empirical research has found that a leader's level of transparency is positively related to followers' perceived trust and evaluations of the leader's effectiveness.[26]

A leader is courageous when he or she is willing to confront the status quo,[27] is confident about the future,[28] and is confident about his or her ability to make a difference. We believe that leaders who possess greater courage engage in greater trust-building efforts.[29] Research has found that leaders who are more self-confident are more trusting in general,[30] which in turn makes them more likely to build trust with others. For example, we all know it takes courage to admit mistakes. Leaders with greater courage will be more likely to admit to and repair mistakes by building trust with others. Leaders who are willing to confront the status quo are more likely to elicit cooperation from others, and this cooperation is enhanced by the trust the leader has built. When the leader has confidence in the future, he or she will want to develop the trust necessary to convince others to cocreate such a future together.

Leading Through Courage

One leader we have followed for many years who is clearly courageous is Mary Ellen Sheets (founder, Two Men and a Truck, International). Mary Ellen told us that she started Two Men and a Truck, international when she learned her bosses at the State of Michigan would never promote her. They had refused to promote her several times, assuming she would never leave because she was a woman. At the same time, her sons had been moving others' goods and furniture as a way to earn money for college during their summer holidays. When her sons returned to college, the phone kept ringing—people were calling and asking for moving services. Seeing an opportunity, Mary Ellen hired two guys, Joe and Elmer (see Figure 3.1), and she purchased a used truck to keep the business going. This side business supplemented her income as a data analyst. Despite her lack of formal training, she took on the bookkeeping, scheduling, customer relations, fleet management, hiring, and firing. She delegated the actual moving to

FIGURE 3.1   Mary Ellen, an Early Truck, and Joe (or Elmer)

Joe and Elmer. Eventually, she left her comfortable but stagnant government job to run the business as a full-time career. With abundant courage, and just a $350 initial investment in that truck, she created a franchise-based firm that now grosses more than $220 million annually, with 1,400 trucks operating in 37 states, Canada, Ireland, and the UK.

Leading Through Humility

A leader with humility is also more likely to build trust with others. Humility is defined as "a desirable personal quality reflecting the willingness to understand the self (identities, strengths, limitations), combined with perspective in the self's relationships with others (i.e., the perspective that one is not the center of the universe)."[31] Leaders who are humble are aware of their limitations and discuss them freely with others. This openness helps the leader ensure he or she is moving in the right direction.[32] Humble leaders are also aware of how others perceive them and make an effort to integrate these perceptions with their own self-perceptions.[33] Humble leaders are also more likely to build trust with others because they are open to feedback—which itself is a vulnerable and trusting act. Notably, humility is thought to be a trait that can be developed in leaders.[34] Based on the leaders we've worked with, we would argue that early developmental experiences and failures or mistakes are key sources of humility.

Bob Lintz, the former GM plant manager (see Figure 3.2), was just a college graduate in training when General Motors hired him. Soon after he was on the job, the general superintendent came to welcome him to the plant. He said, "Welcome, Robert," and asked him what he could do to help him. Bob said that none of his friends or family ever called him Robert and that he would like to be called Bob. The general superintendent looked scornfully and answered him, "Yes, Robert." This was a significant emotional event for Bob. He got the message loud and clear: We are not all the same, and rank matters. Bob vowed that from that day on he would insist that his subordinates call him Bob and he would treat everyone with dignity and respect, no matter what their position was in the organization. Over the next two decades as he advanced within GM, Bob eliminated other status barriers between management and labor, including discarding formal dress distinctions and the executive dining room. He made these efforts long before other GM plants adopted these practices.

By removing these and other barriers, Bob transformed the $250-million Parma, Ohio, stamping plant (scheduled to be shut down) into a

FIGURE 3.2   Bob (far left), his Wife Karen, and Two Friends with the Original *Ghostbusters* Vehicle

billion-dollar enterprise that has lasted more than 20 years after it was slated for closure. Achieving this long-term success began with the humble way that Bob dealt with everyone, including his own management team He said,

> What I learned about myself was that I was truly 100% committed to building trust with others and changing the organization. I learned how to handle all of the frustrations and letdowns that come along with a large change process.
>
> We had meeting agendas for my management team, and I couldn't wait to talk because I've got a lot of energy, and I want to sell my points. I recall times when I went into those meetings, well prepared, with seven items on the meeting agenda, and I would come out of the meeting zero for seven. In many cases I wasn't even close to having the best proposal. I walked out of there a lot of times thinking, "Why did I even open my mouth?" Going back to my office with my head down thinking, "Oh, they must think I'm a complete idiot." Then, to recapture my self-esteem, I would say to myself, "The good thing is that I lead and helped create an environment where we could talk openly, were every staff member was expected to contribute to make sure we made the best quality decisions." Especially since we were going to be impacting thousands of people in the plant and surrounding communities. I had the ability to admit to myself that I'm not as smart as I thought. Synergy really works and I was gifted with some very outstanding staff members.
>
> We had three or four staff meetings away from the plant to agree upon on how we would maximize our effectiveness in the decision-making process. One of the most important [results] was an agreement that once a consensus decision was reached, each member would support it 100%, no matter how hard he or she fought on an alternate approach. No whining or politicking after the meeting. Only a personal commitment to get out and make it happen. They NEVER let me or each other down.

Bob is too humble to say so, but we're also willing to bet that many others in his team also came in thinking that their ideas were the best of the bunch, but as a result of this trust-based team decision making, came out realizing that the collective ideas and the decisions that followed from them were better than their own individual ideas.

Leading Through Authenticity

Finally, an authentic leader is one who lives the values that he or she espouses. Authentic leaders have greater self-awareness, have an internalized moral perspective, relate transparently with others, and focus on positive self-development.[35,36] Authentic leaders are not perceived as being hypocritical, because no gaps or differences are discernible between their words and their actions.[37] They are also "perceived by others as being aware of their own and others' values or moral perspectives."[38] Of course, here we are assuming that the leader's values are consistent with the ROCC of Trust such that his or her authenticity is able to promote building trust. Clearly, a leader who is greedy, dishonest, or favors certain employees is unlikely to build trust with others, no matter how authentically these negative values are displayed.

Ted Castle (Rhino Foods; see Figure 3.3) coached collegiate hockey for the University of Vermont and had a small family ice-cream business on the side. Today, Rhino Foods adheres to the philosophy that life is a game to be won by playing fairly and honestly. "We try to bring a lot of what motivates people in a game, any kind of game, into our business," Castle noted. Early on, he realized that his employees would be more motivated if they knew the rules, were told the score, and could succeed through hard work. Ted's authentic actions paved the way for his employees to trust him.

To encourage his employees to think more like owners (although the firm was and is privately owned), he created a game that was consistent with what motivated him as hockey player or whenever he played board

FIGURE 3.3   Ted Castle Wearing the Rhino Foods Hat

games. He modeled it after games or contests in which there was a clear set of winners and losers, scores were kept, consistent rules were adopted, and rewards for success were fair. Ted opened his books to show his employees how to make the firm more profitable. Then, if his employees improved earnings, they were rewarded with profit-sharing. This built a great deal of trust with employees because he was being open about sharing sensitive financial information and demonstrating compassion for their well-being by sharing his company's success. In another effort, Rhino Foods worked with Ben & Jerry's to develop its Cookie Dough Ice Cream, which helped Ben & Jerry's become the first company to create such an ice cream product. Rhino Foods still supplies Ben & Jerry's with the cookie dough that goes into their ice cream. Rhino Foods now grosses more than $30 million annually.

We have found that courage, humility, and authenticity often coexist within leaders who have built trust and demonstrated trustworthiness effectively.[39,40,41] Other scholars have agreed, finding that "humility tempers other virtues, opens one to the influence and needs of others, and insists on reality rather than pretense."[42] Some researchers believe it is possible to develop the capacity to become an authentic leader while also developing other attributes, such as moral reasoning, confidence, hope, optimism, resiliency, and future-orientation.[43] Research has indeed found that authentic leaders are also courageous, in that they advance ahead of others when there is a risk in doing so.[44] As do courageous leaders, authentic leaders have high physical and mental energy,[45] persevere in the face of obstacles and difficulties, and analyze personal failures and setbacks as temporary—if not learning experiences—and view them as a one-time unique circumstance. Authentic leaders are easily motivated to work harder, are more satisfied, have high morale, have high levels of motivational aspiration, and set stretch goals. Moreover, authentic leaders have been found to enhance team performance through their effect on trust.[46]

Sheldon Yellen, CEO of Belfor Holdings (see Figure 3.4), a diversified building services company that owns Belfor Property Restoration, the world's largest property restoration company, provides a very compelling example of courage, humility, and authenticity as well as demonstrating the ROCC of Trust. His incredible success in building Belfor has clearly required a great deal of courage, *but because of his humility it took quite some time before we were able to convince him to be profiled in this book. Consistent with how we've worked with other leaders, however, once we established trust and respect with each other, he became willing to share his story with us.* The humility, openness, generosity, and authenticity we've witnessed in him have made it quite easy for us to learn how he became a great leader.

Sheldon, the oldest of four boys, had a very humble beginning. His father was in and out of hospitals for much of Sheldon's life, enduring nine

FIGURE 3.4   Sheldon Yellen (on the right)

operations for several serious stomach problems. As a result, his father was often out of work, necessitating that the family go on welfare. Sheldon courageously started working *full-time* at age 11 to support his family. He actually signed over his paychecks each week to his mother to help her make ends meet. He shined shoes, folded laundry, operated videogames and collected their quarters, and performed numerous other jobs to help his family. Sheldon missed graduating from high school by one credit because of his long work hours (he finally received his highschool diploma in 2011). After attending Michigan State University for one year (back in the mid-1970s, MSU obviously didn't check to see if high school was completed before allowing students to matriculate), he dropped out to continue supporting his family. At age 26, he joined his father-in-law and brothers-in-law in a Michigan awning company they owned, and Sheldon then built it into a $1.5-billion-a-year (revenue) business.

Sheldon chooses to reinforce his humility in several ways. As he reminded us during an interview for this book,

> You can't lead with titles. You can't lead with rules. You can't lead with words. You lead with trust, compassion, listening, and by example. I'm sorry for being repetitive, but you can't hide behind a title, behind an office, behind a structure.

You're going to give back more to others who will then follow and trust. I was not born the CEO of a $1.5-billion company. You know that. I had to gain the trust of people along the way, and I did it by implementing those six characteristics I mentioned earlier. I did it by not hiding behind my business card and title, and I did it by living what I espoused to my people.

I set the bar high for the company because I set the bar equally high for myself. To me, the responsibility to stay as close to the front-lines as possible is key. It's critical. I would never ask anybody that works with me to do something that I would not do myself, never.

To build a business, you've got to have humility; you've got to always be reminded of where you came from. "Back to the beginning"—my simple little way of reminding myself. Everybody can pick a different way of reminding themselves. I choose to keep my pictures on the floor, not on the walls, as you've seen yourself. Because in the beginning, as I remind myself every day, I didn't know if we'd make payroll. It's a lifelong effort to share with people your *insecurities*, and by letting somebody know your insecurities you're building trust.[47]

Sheldon's authenticity has been demonstrated to us in many ways. For example, he has remarked to us many times that he doesn't allow people to say they work "for him," but rather "with him." Each of the employees we've met has said the same. Indeed, his two executive assistants say they still get reprimanded by Sheldon any time they tell a visitor to Belfor that they work *for* Sheldon. Sheldon still personally signs every birthday card and writes notes in each one, even though Belfor now employs more than 6,000 people. When Sheldon was the subject of the CBS television show *Undercover Boss* in 2011, his compassion for his employees and his willingness to do any job given to him was completely consistent with the compassion and humility he's demonstrated in our time with him. Sheldon's authenticity comes in large part because of his willingness to give his most valuable asset, *his time*, to his employees and customers. It is because of his compassion for them,

I believe that a leader's role in building trust is to garner what I call *"all the time"* relationships [his emphasis]. Your business relationships, and not just your friendship relationships, have to be real. You've got to believe that life is all about people. If you believe that then you're halfway there.

So you have to *want* to go to a wedding. You have to *want* to go to a kid's graduation of one of your employees. You *feel a loss* when somebody dies. You *feel a joy and excitement* when somebody's born.

A retirement party should be as important to you as the person retiring. I call these "all the time" relationships, not what others think are just work relationships. I believe a leader's role in building trust is you have to feel that. "All the time" relationships are what are important. I think leaders are made based on the relationships with people that you have along the way.

As I shared with you before, I've been accused of "collecting people." I'm not sure I love that term, but in its proper context, if you're a person lucky enough to want to do that, "collect people," then you're a leader, because in your collecting people you're going to gain as much as you give.[48]

We think Sheldon will be in an excellent position to "collect more people" in the future. His episode of *Undercover Boss* was the highest rated in the series' three years, and more than 6,000 people applied to work at Belfor in the weeks following the episode.

☐ Building Trust According to Your Own Strengths

Consistent with others' work on leadership, we believe that leaders build the ROCC of Trust according to their individual talents and capabilities and focus on their strengths. Other scholars have argued that leaders should be helped to identify, develop, and leverage their unique strengths and talents. When leaders do so, they help others identify and nurture their strengths; they build awareness of possibilities, generate hope about the future, and encourage others to take courageous action to become their hoped-for possible selves.[49] They also can become more humble in the process, because properly focusing on one's own strengths requires acknowledging others' strengths, and just as importantly, recognizing one's own weaknesses. Sheldon Yellen told us that, on a recent conference call with all 140 heads of Belfor's business units worldwide, once all of them had assembled on the call, Sheldon got on the phone and simply said to the group, "Be humble or get humbled." After several seconds of silence, one of the executives asked, "Is that it?" Sheldon replied, "Yes," and hung up. He was making the point to his managers that Belfor's incredible success, including rapid growth in revenue and earnings even during the very tough economy since 2008, was no reason for them to become complacent. Sheldon's advice for leaders who need to become more humble is to recognize other's strengths,

You've got to start with the belief that you are "equal to," and not "better than." You were given certain skill sets and certain gifts. Use them appropriately. Laugh at yourself. Make fun of your shortcomings. Continue to remind yourself you're no better and be humble and grateful. Allow others to tell their story. That, to me, is the leader's role in building trust.

Leaders can properly identify their strengths through several vehicles, including the Reflected Best-Self Exercise,[50] a tool developed by researchers at the Center for Positive Organizational Scholarship at the University of Michigan Stephen M. Ross School of Business, and Strengthsfinder 2.0,[51] developed by Gallup. Both of these tools focus on a leader's strengths and not their weaknesses, arguing that it is better to focus on areas of contribution rather than areas of weakness. As Jon Sorber, one of the leaders/founders of Two Men and a Truck, International, told us, recognizing others' strengths is great for better teamwork in a top management team, and as our other leaders have told us, it really helps to remain humble,

What I think has been really cool about working with Melanie and Brig and our mom is that we all bring something different to the table. We all have our gifts and we all recognize that. I think Brig's strength is more on working with our franchises, and I'm more operational; that's my passion.

I think another thing, too, is that we've all stayed pretty humble. I mean this company's gotten bigger than we ever thought it would get. We all have more than we ever thought we would have. Brig has a saying that pigs get fat and hogs get slaughtered. And it's okay to be a piggy, but don't become a hog. We live by that. I mean every day in this business for us has been a blessing.

In looking at the ROCC of Trust and developing competencies in all four areas, we encourage leaders to first understand how they typically build trust with others. Some of our leaders built the ROCC of Trust by first demonstrating reliability, as Melanie Bergeron did when she joined Two Men and a Truck, International. She stipulated that franchisees adhere to their obligations and pay their contractual royalties on time. Ted Castle initially focused on building trust by demonstrating openness through his approach to the company's finances. Bob Lintz chose to emphasize competence by developing the common purpose of turning around the Parma stamping plant and saving several thousand union jobs. He did this by demonstrating that only world-class quality, productivity, and costs would keep the plant open. Mary Ellen Sheets built trust through her compassion for her employees, customers, and community by developing her employees, treating customers as if they were family, and donating significant money and time to local charities. Sheldon Yellen also chose to emphasize compassion in building trust with his employees and his customers, forgiving employees who he could have easily fired, and, on his very first restoration job, buying Christmas presents for the children and getting a hotel room for a family whose home had burned down right before Christmas, even though nobody had told him to do so.

The leaders profiled in this chapter have each faced adversity many, many times. Their courage, humility, and authenticity enabled them to build trust with key stakeholders, whether they were employees, union leaders, customers, or franchisees. Individuals in leadership positions or aspiring to be leaders must develop courage, humility, and authenticity so that they can find trustworthy others and build trust with them to become better leaders. In the next chapter, we focus on the interpersonal level of change and how leaders create a Circle of Trust.

Trust Tips

1. *Even if you don't feel like you were born a leader, you can still become one by improving your leadership skills and abilities.*
2. *Be courageous by having trust in others, admitting your mistakes, and having confidence in the future.*
3. *Demonstrate humility by understanding yourself and being* **open** *to feedback from others.*
4. *Others will know you are authentic when they see no difference between your words and actions.*

4
CHAPTER

Developing Your Own Trust Network

In our experience, leading others is a very *lonely* business. This is especially true when the environment is highly uncertain, which elevates the value of trust when individuals are deciding whether to cooperate with one another.[1] When we have led others, we have sometimes encountered significant resistance, even from people we least expected. Leaders whom we have studied, consulted for, and coached say they encounter resistance more often than enthusiasm when they try to implement change in their teams and organizations. Supporters *may* emerge from unexpected places, but it is more likely that resistors will rise to thwart the change effort. Robert Quinn of the University of Michigan Ross School of Business has argued that leaders encounter several typical responses as they work to transform their organizations: skepticism, laughter, or moral indignation.[2] People close to the leader are often skeptical of the leader's willingness to follow through on his or her commitments. In other words, they don't trust the leader's reliability. Would-be followers may simply laugh at the leader's claimed abilities to create lasting change. In other words, they don't trust the leader's competence. If skepticism or derision doesn't deter the leader, others may attempt to derail the efforts through moral indignation, arguing, "Who are *you* to say you have a vision for change?"[3] This implies not trusting the leader to be open about his or her agenda for change or not trusting the leader to be compassionate about who will be affected or whether the rewards from successful change will be allocated fairly. Because you will undoubtedly face significant resistance to change from at least some people affected by your initiatives, your efforts to lead others will be greatly aided by creating a foundation of trustworthy people who can help you. We call this the Trust Network.

☐ Your Trust Network and How It Helps You Lead Others

As you lead others using the ROCC of Trust, it is very important to develop a Trust Network, essentially a "merry band of brothers and sisters." These advocates can support your change effort through sound advice, regular encouragement, and tangible help. Trust involves both cognitive processes such as evaluating whether someone is reliable or competent, and also emotional agility, such as whether one feels another is open or compassionate. Indeed, many trust researchers have found that when people *feel* positively toward someone, they are more likely to trust that person.[4]

Your Trust Network helps strengthen the ROCC of Trust you are demonstrating to those in your organization and can help you avoid some of the pitfalls of leadership. Your advocates need not be physically proximate or even belong to your own organization. In fact, they can be useful to you if they *aren't* in your organization, because they are more likely to have different information or insights than your colleagues or people with whom you interact frequently.[5,6] Essential, however, is that they must trust you, be trustworthy themselves, and be motivated to help your change efforts and your leadership journey. Such supporters should not simply rubberstamp what you think or feel, but instead will have your back and your front. These are people who will provide a much-needed shot in the arm to immunize you against the inevitable assaults you'll face during your worthwhile leadership journey. They will also give you a shoulder to lean on or even a well-placed kick in the pants whenever you flag in your leadership efforts.

The number of individuals in your Trust Network must be manageable. This shouldn't be difficult, however, because you must choose your network members carefully. First, members of your network must possess the aforementioned qualities that your wider circle of friends will not. Second, your Trust Network size should depend on how many people to whom you can reciprocate by offering feedback, as well as moral and tangible support. Again, choose carefully those on whom you will depend, sometimes quite significantly, to keep your change efforts moving forward.

Your Trust Network helps you mobilize resources to facilitate positive change, especially when resources may be scarce or difficult to identify quickly. As homeland security specialist Eric Kutner told us,

> I've spent years building a network. I've been able to put people together—pieces of a puzzle together—by seeing how people fit together, seeing how people's interests or needs fit together, and build

relationships with them that are grounded in trust and credibility. The reason to network, the reason to build relationships, is because everything in business, everything in government or public policy, especially in Homeland Security or FEMA, indeed everything in life, is based on resources.

All these examples are based on resources—the word I use over and over again. People are resources, things are resources, and money is a resource. The only way to find resources that might be helpful to you or others is to have relationships with people who have those resources, are those resources, or know where those resources are. Because when something bad happens, say a crisis in one's company, or a family health emergency, that's not the time to start wondering, "Who do we know who knows people," or realize, "We don't really know anybody." That's when you want to be able to count on people you've built relationships with over the years.

Before discussing the specifics of whom to include in your Trust Network, how and where to start building it, and when you know it's functioning properly, let's look at a few examples. We have benefited greatly from our own Trust Networks in both our professional and personal lives. In contrast, we've made some of our greatest mistakes when we didn't possess such a network or failed to use our network members fully for guidance or assistance. By sharing these examples, our hope is that you will understand their relevance for effective leadership.

☐ Examples of Our Own Trust Networks

The first example relates to a much larger network than a personal Trust Network, and it consists of many networks based on trust and common identity. It has inspired our own efforts to build social capital among the current and former students we've taught at each of the universities where we've been professors.

☐ Doing Well by Doing Good at Princeton

Princeton's reputation as one of the world's truly great universities is due largely to its tremendous alumni loyalty. Routinely, about 60% of Princeton's alumni donate money with no strings attached through the university's Annual Giving Campaign, with totals averaging roughly $50 million. These unrestricted contributions are in addition to the millions of dollars in capital funds alumni and others donate each year, adding to an endowment that exceeded $17 billion as of 2011.[7] The university engenders such incredible loyalty from "birth," through its Freshman Week Orientation, including a mandatory fire safety presentation.[8] In addition to the stern lecture about the dangers of unapproved appliances, new students are also told that regardless of their financial aid, they are receiving a 50% scholarship. This is because it costs twice as much to provide the education they are about to receive as they are actually paying.[9] Students learn that this is possible due largely to the generosity of their forebears—alumni. Then, they are encouraged to pay it forward through hard work and dedication while matriculated at Princeton and when they graduate. Giving money, though, is just one measure of loyalty. Princeton's leaders emphasize this when students commit to annual giving as they graduate and become alumni.

Indeed, the stronger message alumni receive is that it is important to give of oneself in nonfinancial ways as much as, if not more than, financially. Alumni volunteer efforts enhance the social capital established as students and are a substantial complement to the financial capital they donate. Through the Alumni Schools Committee, Princeton alumni ensure that the vast majority of applicants are interviewed personally. Through its password-protected website TigerNet, Princeton alumni have forums that provide career networking and job opportunities and that help those who've moved to another city, state, or country; they also have resources such as parenting advice and even an Ultimate Frisbee discussion group. They can look up anyone worldwide who attended Princeton to make a connection. Alumni can find out who is working in a particular industry, job category, or part of the world in which they're interested. The social capital reinforces the trust Princetonians develop in one another based on friendships, common values, and a commitment to leaving their institution stronger than when they entered.

This Princeton example may smack of elitism and exclusivity, but we believe the school's practices apply to any institution interested in building long-term loyalty. The network has to be large enough, of course, to be useful. Similar alumni networks also exist in the corporate world. The consulting firm McKinsey is famous for celebrating its alumni (or former employees) as part of its larger family. Corporate alumni groups abound on LinkedIn.com, including Amazon, Apple, Applebee's, Best Buy, Dell, EDS, Lee Hecht Harrison, and IBM, to name just a few. Interestingly, in fact, Bain & Company has a global alumni network of more than 5,000 on LinkedIn, which is larger than the number of *employees* in Bain's LinkedIn group. Today's social networking groups host networking events and provide career advice, while their members even help each other find jobs. Again, access to these benefits is restricted to being a member of a specific alumni group.

☐ You Never Know When You're Going to Get *Really* Sick

One of the ways individuals become vulnerable is by falling ill. Placing oneself in the hands of a physician, though, represents one of the most significant forms of trust. When Aneil was diagnosed with thyroid cancer in 2002, he wanted to obtain input from several medical experts to ensure he received proper treatment and, thus, the best possible outcome. He not only wanted to be cured, but also wanted treatment and surgeries completed according to "gold standards," so that any possible complications were minimal.

Aneil didn't develop this orientation automatically, but achieved it after having a sinus surgery in 1999 that didn't go as planned. Having learned a painful lesson about trusting too much, Aneil first consulted his brother Allan, an orthopedic surgeon at Stanford Medical School, when he first learned his diagnosis. When Aneil met an endocrine surgeon, Dr. David Albertson of Wake Forest University, he asked the surgeon if he would be willing to partner with him; if he would consult with other experts who could share their expertise and opinions. Initially, this highly respected surgeon, who performed more than 150 thyroid surgeries a year, was taken aback. After Aneil shared his story about his failed sinus surgery and its aftermath, however, Dr. Albertson began to understand. Dr. Albertson himself had been hospitalized and had seen the medical system from the vantage point of a patient, not just as a physician and surgeon. Dr. Albertson became not only Aneil's surgeon, but also his advocate with many parts of the healthcare system during the several months Aneil was under his care.[10]

Aneil also consulted his best friend from college, Dr. John Gordon, who gave him the personal phone number of his uncle, Dr. Lewis Braverman of Boston University's School of Medicine, an internationally renowned endocrinologist and one of the world's experts on the thyroid.[11] Uncle Lew reviewed Aneil's case, confirmed that the proposed surgeries and radiation were appropriate, and told him he would be fine. Ten years later, Aneil remains cancer-free thanks to the dedication of his Trust Network—trustworthy physicians and friends who responded to his call for help and guidance.

☐ Making Important Decisions and Reinventing Yourself

At age 40, Karen wanted to return to graduate school and earn a PhD. Surprisingly, most of her friends, many of whom were moms, discouraged her. They didn't understand why she would uproot her life, move to another town, and go back to studying and taking tests, especially when it wasn't really necessary. They didn't understand why she would give up a "nice life," as one friend put it, for the rigors and sacrifices of graduate school. Karen, however, knew she needed to earn a doctorate. After conducting scholarly research and teaching for more than a decade with an MBA, she understood that advancing to a top-tier research and teaching institution would be essential to develop the necessary skills to conduct research and teach at the highest possible level. Working with world-class professors on their research projects, while also collaborating with them on classroom teaching, would give Karen the foundation to more fully integrate her research, writing, and teaching.

Through her Trust Network, Karen found support from those who understood her drive and who offered sound advice and important help. One was a good friend from her Ann Arbor days, Dr. Gretchen Spreitzer, who had earned her PhD in 1992. Gretchen was very supportive and wrote a letter of recommendation for Karen, because together they had coauthored a peer-reviewed article. Another member of Karen's trust network was one of her MBA professors, Dr. Kim Cameron, who had always been a great mentor and boundlessly encouraging. One of her colleagues at Wake Forest, the late Ed Easley, reached out to Karen and encouraged her despite his own battles with cancer. Another Wake Forest colleague, Dr. Kelly Mollica, who had taken a graduate seminar with Karen at Penn State, supported her as well. Although this group of supporters was small, it propelled Karen forward to make the deep change in her life she desired.

In another example, Aneil helped a member of his Trust Network, David Lassman, to reinvent his career several years ago. Although Aneil and David were college classmates, they didn't get to know each other until their 10th college reunion. As they sat together at one of the weekend's dinners, Aneil learned that David was a turnaround consultant with insights into leading change. Aneil invited David to be a guest speaker for one of his MBA classes. Aneil invited him back six more times over the next few years. Consequently, David discovered his passion for teaching and asked Aneil for guidance about becoming a part-time business school professor. Aneil introduced him to one of his mentors who was a management professor at Carnegie Mellon University (CMU), Dr. Denise Rousseau. Denise agreed to review David's resume and helped him land an initial teaching assignment in the executive education program at CMU. Today, David is an adjunct professor at CMU, teaching in its executive education and MBA programs, while also continuing his work as a manufacturing vice president in the Pittsburgh area.

☐ Launching Your Own Trust Network

Because each situation's circumstances will vary, and everyone has different talents and strengths, it is a good strategy to gather people from different backgrounds and capabilities into your Trust Network. Ideally, each member of your Trust Network will have talents and abilities that complement your own and one another's, have access to different resources, belong to different networks (e.g., work, school, professional associations, friends), and have time to help you. That should narrow the list of candidates significantly. As noted, you must also be willing and able to reciprocate. This should narrow the list even further. The selection of those who become members of your Trust Network will depend in part on the kinds of help you need. You will likely have members of an inner circle of trust on whom you call most frequently, particularly for sensitive or pressing issues. Your wider network will include those on whom you call from time to time, those you ask for information rather than advice, or those who help you with less significant issues.

Start building your Trust Network with friends who have regularly demonstrated the ROCC of Trust to you, *and* who have a history of reciprocating. We can't stress this second requirement enough. Your Trust Network will not be sustainable if you are the one who is always helping others. Not only is this exhausting, it is also a recipe for resenting those who professed they wanted to help you, but who then never follow through. It is also advisable to look for potential members of your Trust Network outside your regular place of work. Such individuals can provide objective advice and help, especially when you face a situation you would not be comfortable discussing with your colleagues or manager. Social networks such as LinkedIn may also provide a pool of candidates, especially if you seek to add members to your Trust Network beyond your functional area or industry. As you get to know people from these social networks better, you will be positioned to help them and ask for their help. Such opportunities will then help you decide whether to ask them to join your Trust Network. Indeed, based on our experience, only when you are really in need of assistance, i.e., you are vulnerable, will you know whether you should ask individuals to be part of your Trust Network based on whether they can and do offer assistance to you.

Your Trust Network has the potential to create a virtuous circle in which trustworthy individuals help one another become more trustworthy and, thus, more effective leaders. As our own Trust Network has grown, we have seen its members begin to refer to the network as an entity distinct from the two of us, with a set of common values. With repeated interactions, a network can evolve into a group that can provide a common identity for those in the network.[12] In an early and widely cited paper, Mark Granovetter wrote about embeddedness or "the ongoing networks of social relations between people [which] discourage malfeasance."[13] In other words, because links exist among people in the Trust Network, even if only through one person, others are likely to behave in a trustworthy way with other network members, because they know they will interact with one another at some point in the future. Indeed, we learn about one another's trustworthiness through repeated interactions.[14] If we treat one another in a trustworthy fashion, we will want to continue to include one another in our Trust Network. Of course, networks based on trust can also have negative results, for example, when nepotism or favoritism exclude worthy individuals from receiving the benefits that accrue within those networks. We would argue, however, that individuals within those kinds of networks are not demonstrating compassion, or are merely reserving it for a group that deliberately chooses to keep many people out.

☐ Is Your Trust Network Actually Working?

To evaluate the effectiveness of your Trust Network, consider whether you can call on several different members for advice when you need to make an important decision. Or, if you need to change jobs or careers, do you have people in your network who are able and willing to get your resume or marketing pitch *quickly* to individuals at organizations who have a job or business opportunity you would like to pursue? We have learned about the effectiveness of our Trust Networks in others ways, as well. For example, we have both received valuable and interesting consulting engagements based on recommendations from people in our Trust Network. As our networks have evolved, we have received leads from people who know people in our Trust Network.

One great illustration of your Trust Network's power is when people help one another without your intermediation. When we were completing an article for the *MIT Sloan Management Review* in 2009, we asked members of our Trust Network to share examples of fair and effective downsizing. Several members of our Trust Network sent us examples, a few of which we added to our article. Ben Holcomb, one of Aneil's former Wake Forest Evening MBA students, sent us an example from his current company.

Seeing that Ben had changed companies since his days as Aneil's student, Aneil followed up to inquire how Ben had landed at a new firm. Interestingly, Ted Budd, who had graduated from Wake Forest's Executive MBA program and was another of Aneil's former students, had hired Ben, even though the two did not know each other through their Wake Forest affiliation. It was through their mutual membership in Karen and Aneil's Trust Network that Ben and Ted had connected. Although Ted never asked Aneil about Ben, he interviewed and hired him for a CFO position.

The time to begin building your Trust Network is *now*. We have known some of the people in our Trust Network for decades; others for only a few years. Depending on your friends, acquaintances, and mentors, you may be able to begin building your Trust Network as early as high school. And, it is certainly a good idea to begin when you are in college or start a full-time job, whichever happens first. Every person you meet along the way has the potential to be helpful or influential to you in your leadership journey. And remember: Do not add anyone to your network unless you're prepared to help them as well. You should also be courageous enough to drop people from your network who ask you for help but stop helping you. Unless someone has special circumstances that prevent him or her from actually helping you for a certain period, it is better to move on and find others who can keep your Trust Network thriving.

Trust Tips

1. Keep in touch regularly with people who are important to you.
2. Be willing to share your concerns and opinions with those in your Trust Network.
3. Learn enough about your friend's issues to be a real help to them when they need you.
4. Support friends when they need you the most.

Building Trust Within Teams

☐ What Is a Team?

A team is "a small number of people with complementary skills who are committed to a common purpose, set of performance goals, and approach for which they hold themselves mutually accountable."[1] Work teams are composed of interdependent individuals who share responsibility for specific outcomes in their organizations. Such teams are influenced by the context in which they are working,[2,3] all while producing "something useful to an organization."[4,5] We spend most of our lives with teams of one type or another, whether it's families, athletic teams as a young child and young adult, teams in our careers, or volunteer teams outside of work. Despite such ubiquity, people may belong to work teams without having any formal preparation or training.

☐ Why Are Teams So Important?

People desire to associate with others for protection and to build identity, and teams are one way to accomplish both goals. To reduce their vulnerability to complex or challenging environments, people tend to associate with others who share similar traits, values, or interests. Teams are also the most typical way people in organizations come together to produce organizational outcomes. Indeed, if executed properly, teams can have a positive financial impact on the organization's bottom line.[6]

Greater collective effort is required as tasks and their results become more complex or require greater innovation. When people work together, however, conflicts inevitably arise about how and what to produce.

Interdependence among individuals within and across teams is essentially a form of vulnerability. As Patrick Lencioni, author of *The Five Dysfunctions of a Team*, wrote, "Trust lies at the heart of a functioning, cohesive team."[7] Thus, trust is essential for team behavior and continuing successful work,[8,9] but too much trust within a team may make it difficult for the team to monitor itself to ensure optimal performance.[10,11]

After we read online about his efforts to build trust in his teams at Microsoft, we were fortunate to interview Ross Smith, director of test. Ross explained how his team discovered that trust was important and the end results for his team,

> What we realized was that trust is a foundational component of innovative organizations. Businesses require freedom to fail, collaborate, take risks, and be transparent. A lot of those behaviors seem to be rooted in trust, and so we thought that if we as managers focused on building a high-trust organization, then people would have more autonomy, more freedom to experiment and apply their diverse skills in ways that we couldn't possibly think of ourselves. With Windows, where there's hundreds of millions of customers, it's not possible to fully represent the customer, so we really need diverse approaches in how we test the software. That's how we got started.
>
> What was also very interesting is that from a personal growth perspective, if people have more freedom to experiment, to learn new things and try new ways of testing, they're going to stick around, because they feel like they're growing. They have the opportunity to grow their skills and so they'll stick around—we see tremendous retention rates.
>
> As people stick around and stay in their technology area, they obviously get better at it. They get more technical. They understand more deeply how the software works, as well as building stronger relationships with their partner teams and their counterparts in other disciplines. Those relationships and the nature of work get smoother, because people have been doing it longer. So really we saw great increases in virtually all our traditional metrics.

☐ Building the ROCC of Trust Begins With the Team Leader

Trust begins with the team's leader,[12] and team leaders can influence team performance through team trust.[13] Moreover, a group leader's trust in other group members has been found to positively influence group members' trust in one another.[14] Leaders can influence many aspects of the team, including coordination, creativity, team learning, empowerment, commitment, team satisfaction, and performance.[15] Leaders also provide the group with vision, help set goals, and serve as the liaison or "linking pin"[16] to other parts of the organization. Moreover, leaders can create an open climate that supports employee involvement and teamwork.[17]

Most leaders focus on helping their teams with tasks and interpersonal relationships. Here, we will address how leaders can help their teams with the interpersonal work of building trust. Several experts on teams have emphasized the critical importance of first focusing on the interpersonal dynamics that build trust. Such trust can help overcome embedded conflict and gain commitment to a common set of goals and shared fate.[18]

In describing his approach to building trust with his top management team, Bob Lintz (General Motors) emphasized the essential importance of first addressing the interpersonal aspects of working together,

> To get my team involved and committed to the vision was really meant getting them to open up about their inner feelings and to voice their frustrations with the organization or with the politics or where they stood or where their career was headed—whether they were being listened to, how I really felt about them, or how they felt about their peers. Most of that is pretty well-guarded information, for fear of the consequences of speaking up. It was my role to get people to open up. I understood the consequences, and I also knew how difficult it was to open it up.
>
> I was able to get my immediate staff to agree to go out after work, on our own time, and really talk about these issues. To develop a relationship of openness and trust where we could really, really say how we feel without threat of reprisal. That took some time to do that, but once that was established, then that feeling of trust with one another just mushroomed.

Every leader has or should have a preferred style of building the ROCC of Trust with others. In general, our preferred way to build trust with others is to have conversations, but, admittedly, our conversational styles differ. One of the effective ways Aneil builds trust quickly is to share openly aspects of his background and experiences that he believes will establish common ground with those he is getting to know. He believes that everyone has goals, experiences, dreams, and frustrations that can be similar enough to build a common set of interests and expectations about what is important. For example, common goals can be about wanting to make a difference, enhancing one's career prospects, or simply eliminating long-standing problems. Aneil typically starts by sharing his own beliefs about what an ideal workplace should be. Importantly, these stories are not just theoretical or academic musings, but are based on his own great and ugly experiences working in organizations. He also shares any other background information that he thinks may be relevant to the specific person or group to whom he is speaking. This represents an effort to build openness-based trust. It also involves trusting the other parties with sometimes-sensitive information. He trusts that what he shares won't be misinterpreted. With some people, Aneil quickly relates his educational background and work achievements, and relates information that shows his expectations for excellence. With others, he may share his own success-ful battle with cancer or overcoming other personal challenges in his life. Aneil prefers to read people first before deciding what to share with them.

Karen, on the other hand, listens first when she is building trust with others. She asks questions about others and listens with genuine interest to what they have to say. She generally tries to make the other person feel as if no one else in the world matters when she is with him or her. She considers listening a gift to the other person—which she gives willingly and freely—because she is giving her time and attention to that person or group. This is a valuable gift when she probably has a million other things she could be doing at that moment.[19] Karen's style combines openness and compassion, because she is expressing her willingness to hear what others have to say (whether it is good or bad), and she is willing to listen to others' deepest hopes and fears. Once folks know they can trust Karen with their thoughts, beliefs, and experiences because she is a good listener, she demonstrates to them that she is also reliable and competent by following up with them. This may include sending a note based on the conversation. This "reflective listening" technique means Karen seeks to understand someone's ideas, then offers the ideas back to them to confirm she has understood correctly.

When you are dealing with larger groups, determining the best way to begin building trust can be more challenging. Ross Smith (Microsoft) found that each of his 80 team members had specific ideas about how trust should be built (see "Ross Smith, Microsoft" in this chapter). He also found that although he had built trust successfully with one team, he had to start from scratch when he began leading a new team. He noted, "People in my new team are still sort of assessing me, as well as each other, to see if our trust is really true when we're under pressure. They need all the same evidence and all the same steps, and they need the time and evidence to see that this is worth pursuing. It is almost more how they view me than the other way around."

☐ The Team Leader As Coach

In addition to the team leader's typical roles, another role the leader can play is that of a coach to the team. Team coaching is defined as "direct interaction with a team intended to help members make coordinated and task-appropriate use of their collective resources in accomplishing the team's work."[20] As a coach, the leader is responsible for helping the team identify team problems and consulting with the team about issues surrounding team processes and team problem solving.[21] Evidence has shown that a leader's team coaching leads to improved team satisfaction, empowerment, and improved relationships among team members.[22] Like the coach of a sports team, the leader can fill an important role in helping his or her team reach its full potential. This requires helping each team member develop his or her individual talents, as well as combining those talents to create collective team performance.

Coaching is effective in both one-on-one or group settings, sometimes both. The leader as a coach is an important role that helps team members use their individual talents to perform as their best selves. Just as an athletic coach brings out the best in his or her players, a team leader-coach helps his or her team members live up to their fullest potential. Potential will differ for each employee; some may have strong technical skills, whereas others will be talented with interpersonal skills. The leader-coach can also be an objective team player, noticing when one team member needs to be more accountable to the group, be a better listener, or sharpen his or her skills in a particular area to support the team more effectively.

☐ Making Team Members Accountable to the Organization and to One Another

Based on our experiences working with countless student teams at both the undergraduate and MBA levels, nothing is more demoralizing to a team than needing to compensate for a team member who either cannot or will not fix his or her individual weaknesses that undermine team performance. When Aneil was in charge of the full-time MBA program at Wake Forest University, one team in particular was struggling greatly. Over the course of many weeks, Aneil held several meetings with the team to determine why they were having difficulty completing assignments on time. He noticed their struggle based on the poor grades they were receiving for some of their team projects. Despite developing a written set of norms and rules that all team members formally agreed to follow, including showing up to team meetings on time and being prepared to discuss course materials, the difficulties persisted for the team. After several months, Aneil pinpointed one student in particular who was undermining the team. Aneil, the team, and even the problematic student agreed to divorce the student from the team. The divorced student was confident he could perform better on his own than with the team. Within a few weeks, however, the single student flunked out of the program because he failed to complete assignments in a timely and high-quality manner. The lesson the remaining team members and the entire first-year class learned was that team behaviors have real consequences for team trust and outcomes. Indeed, research confirms that trust is positively related with perceived task performance, team satisfaction, and relationship commitment, and negatively related with stress.[23,24,25]

We found that the same principle holds based on our experiences as team members ourselves, particularly Aneil's recent experiences leading a team of professionals and administrative assistants at Michigan State University (MSU). When Aneil was director of executive education for the School of Human Resources and Labor Relations at MSU, he found that his team consisted of individuals with deep-seated conflicts with one another, some of which had persisted for decades. For several months, Aneil simply did a great deal of listening to each team member's concerns. He also encouraged them to share previous experiences and results with one another, which helped build trust,[26] particularly in terms of reliability and competence. At the same time, he developed a financial management system that showed for the first time ever where the team was succeeding and where it was not, in terms of net revenue per program, marketing costs per participant, labor hours per program, and overall program profitability. Simply getting the team to learn what worked best and what needed to be improved or eliminated required significant time and commitment, but this approach was critical to getting the team to learn how to work together more effectively.[27] Aneil led the team to agree to eliminate roughly 40% of the programs being taught, because they were either not making money or were being delivered by other institutions more cost effectively. Aneil then restructured the team's tasks, based on market conditions. This also allowed him to retire one team member and move another team member to a different part of the school where the person's skills and talents could be used more effectively. Following this restructuring, the outcomes were compelling: The number and intensity of interpersonal conflicts in the team decreased significantly; the team members were empowered to work independently; program enrollments increased; and the team's net revenue increased by more than $200,000. All of these positive outcomes occurred with a team that was reduced from five members, including Aneil, to three.

☐ Building the ROCC of Trust Within Teams

In her article on trust in the *Harvard Management Update,* Judith Ross wrote, "Effective communications, goal attainment, and service attainment are possible only in an atmosphere of trust."[28] High mutual trust within teams enhances team performance by increasing members' engagement and focus on team tasks,[29] and compels members to assist one another when needed.[30] Trust is also important to developing shared goals, openly exchanging information, and sharing power among team members, all of which contribute to a team's performance.[31,32,33] Trust in the team leader can be enhanced when the team actually chooses its own leader at the outset or when the leader naturally arises in the team. Whether the team leader is assigned, is elected, or emerges over time, the leader is responsible for developing trust within the team. Although trust within a team may develop initially based on team members' general predispositions to trust others or their similarity toward one another,[34] the team leader should not assume this is the case. Indeed, these are poor bases for long-lived teams or teams with diverse member characteristics. In other words, the leader has the important role of building trust within a team,[35] particularly when teams are new and team members have no history with one another. Such trust helps the team to be more successful, including accomplishing its tasks.[36,37]

☐ Learning How to Listen

One key approach for building trust within teams is for team members to learn how to listen actively to one another. The team leader can demonstrate active listening by setting an example based on how he or she interacts with the team. Active listening is the process of giving nonjudgmental feedback to another by listening to the person and the message, and by decoding messages for their intended meaning.[38] This skill is not always easy, as words have more than one meaning, and sometimes the speaker might have difficulty expressing his or her thoughts. Active listening requires a higher level of patience and sensitivity than what we are accustomed to exerting during a typical workday. When we practice active listening, however, we are silent more than we speak. We also use three types of questions or phrases to help the speaker: we *ask questions to clarify* what the speaker is saying, such as, "what do you mean by that?"; we *paraphrase statements*, such as, "in other words . . . "; or we *summarize statements* (when someone is getting off track), such as, "now, summing up . . . "[39] All of these help the speaker explain him- or herself better when he or she might be getting frustrated or confused with the conversation.

Authors Gibson and Cohen noted, "Active listening is particularly helpful in teams when some members come from high-context organizations (strong cultures) and others come from low-context organizations (weak cultures)," because this listening technique allows greater clarification.[40] In one-to-one relationships, previous research has demonstrated that active listening builds trust in a variety of contexts, including salesperson–buyer[41,42] and physician–patient situations.[43] Research has also found that such listening builds trust within teams, both the virtual kind[44] and face-to-face teams. Most communication training we receive in school, however, relates to reading and writing.[45] Although we spend much of our time communicating in the form of listening, it is often not formally taught in college.[46] As adults, we spend most of our time talking and listening. It is thus important that we allocate team training time to listening skills in order to build trust in the team.

Trust within teams is far too important to be left to chance or trial-and-error learning. Very often, however, people are thrown together without any sort of formal training on how to work together effectively to be a cohesive team. In addition, organizations often establish reward systems at the individual level rather than the team level, further preventing team members from working together toward common goals. As a professor, Karen has found that her business-school student teams were thrown together without any training in how to be a team, and were rewarded largely individually rather than as a team. As a result, she became more proactive about ensuring that her teams learned how to function well together as they began their work. She started by analyzing each student's strengths before assigning each person to a particular team. Each team consequently included individuals with different strengths. She took this proactive approach rather than having students form teams on their own based on close friendships. This way, each team had the opportunity to draw on a variety of talents for the different tasks that the teams had to accomplish during the semester. In addition, she taught the students active listening skills, to give them tools for communicating more effectively and responding more patiently to one another. One senior student commented that Karen's approach was the best group experience she had been part of in her college career. Karen's focus was on strengths and talents and the opportunity to develop team processes and trust-building skills. And, Karen's approach is backed by empirical results. Studies show that team-building skills are most effective when directed at the team as a whole working together, rather than directed separately toward the individuals who comprise the team.[47,48]

Building the first piece of the ROCC of Trust, reliability, is essential to building the remaining pieces of the ROCC. Whether turning around a student project team or turning around a major revenue-generating team within an organization, it is crucial to establish the norms for how the team will work together and meet deadlines. Relatedly, it is critical to develop a process by which team members inform one another if tasks cannot be completed on time. The degree to which the leader involves the team in establishing norms and expectations will depend on the team members' experience and maturity, and how well they know one another. In Aneil's case, he had to work with a team that had not established clear norms and expectations. For those few norms that did exist, the team had not established clear consequences for violating them. Ultimately, Aneil recognized that the only way to develop team cohesiveness was to exit two of the team members.

Developing competence within the team requires the team leader to learn about the strengths and weaknesses of each team member. This process includes assessing the degree to which others can offset an individual's weaknesses within the team. Alternatively, if the weaknesses are detrimental, they will need to be remediated or the team member may need to be reassigned to a different team. It was easier for Aneil to determine who should remain on the team when one team member stated, "I don't like change," or when a team member and Aneil agreed that she was not sincerely interested in marketing the programs that she taught. Focusing on a clear set of goals and expectations, showcasing team members' accomplishments, and documenting learning and best practices[49] all build competence-based trust. Aneil first established a goal and then worked with the entire team to commit to that goal. The goal was that each program had to earn a profit or net revenue, which made it easier to eliminate unprofitable programs and restructure the unit accordingly.

The very positive results that Aneil and his team achieved also depended on Aneil building trust based on openness and compassion, trust both in him as a leader and among the individual team members. Leaders can build greater openness trust by providing ongoing feedback[50] and by providing opportunities for the team to share information with others. Sharing information is especially important with individuals who are new to the organization, when teams are forming or beginning a new project, or in virtual teams where team members work with one another across long distances.[51] As teams work together over time, they can build greater trust in terms of openness by making expectations more transparent, and by listening to each other, thereby increasing their cohesiveness in the process.[52] To build trust in him as a leader, Aneil also provided opportunities for his subordinates to provide feedback to him on his performance in leading the team. He listened carefully to that feedback, even when he didn't agree with it. One team member in particular was concerned that Aneil might use feedback as a basis for reprisal; importantly, Aneil had to demonstrate over several months that he would not do so. This also helped build the team's trust in him as compassionate. Aneil also practiced several symbolic and substantive approaches to building compassion-based trust in him, especially as he was a newcomer to the organization. One symbolic effort that demonstrated Aneil's compassionate nature was to provide some of his own personal funds to an administrative assistant to travel to a family funeral in Texas. Substantive approaches included spending significant time listening to the interpersonal, career, and professional concerns of all four of his subordinates. Some of these important concerns had been neglected for literally *years* before Aneil arrived. Partly as a result of these efforts, Aneil was able to secure a promotion for the administrative assistant in the team, something for which she had been waiting many years. He also empowered his team to take the initiative and make decisions that were best for the organization rather than waiting for him to make the decision. He regularly reassured team members that such initiatives would be praised rather than punished, because Aneil's predecessors had sometimes punished such efforts.

☐ Creating Opportunities to Build Trust

Building trust within a team takes significant time, using both informal and formal means of communication. Managers may not always appreciate the benefits of informal communication, however, because the results are not immediately apparent. For example, when Karen worked at Johnson Controls, the division's general manager once scolded her and others for lingering around the coffee pot. He didn't realize that such informal interaction was important for Karen to accomplish her job as pricing manager more effectively. During those times, she was building trust with the accounting employees, who had valuable knowledge to share with her. Indeed, research has shown that high-trust teams share knowledge, share power, and minimize power differentials, whereas low-trust teams engage in power battles, deal with each other through coercion, encounter many misunderstandings, and endure many conflicts of interest.[53] With the importance of effective communication for teams, training in listening and ways to communicate with different types of individuals is essential.[54] The leader can then build compassion-based trust by fostering a common identity through shared values and norms and by helping the team process emotional issues.[55,56]

When you are building trust with team members, first determine what piece of the ROCC works best for you and start there. Once you've established a bit of common ground with others, you will be able to build trust in other ways. As the team leader, it is important for you to make the first step in helping others identify their strengths and develop common ground with one another, and for you to ask team members how they need and want to build trust with each other. With these steps, you'll be on your way to building a trustworthy team.

Trust Tips

1. As the leader, help the team identify a common goal they are working toward.
2. Encourage the team to share their backgrounds and experiences with one another in order to get to know each other better.
3. Help the team members identify their individual strengths so that they can know how to rely on one another.
4. Give the team a common reward so that they want to work together to achieve that common goal.

Ross Smith, Microsoft

What were some of the key steps or actions you took to build trust?

We bought pizza and invited the team to brainstorm about behaviors that they felt influenced trust one way or the other. Then, we created a voting game to rank the importance of the behaviors (see www.defectprevention.org/trust). Basically, it just puts two choices side by side; you click the one that you feel is more relevant. From each person's answers, a collective ranking is created.

Our [initial] thought was we would generate the ranking, pick the top three, do those, and we'd be good. What we quickly realized was that the importance of the behaviors varied greatly by individual: A behavior that may be important to me may not be important to you, or something that I feel I do poorly may not matter to others. So, instead of determining which were the most important, we put all the behaviors into a wiki and had people contribute from there. We just put up the behaviors verbatim—in the language of the individuals that suggested them. I think this really helped because people could see that even though they might've been quite similar to others, everyone could see their own ideas represented and [that they] were valued as contributors. The wiki provided a kind of trust playbook for everybody to think about.

I think even almost more importantly, this exercise gave us a tangible framework [so] that people could start to *talk* about the behaviors. So when we would see someone doing something that was listed on the wiki, either positively or negatively, there was a context in which to comment on it. This outlet wouldn't have existed otherwise. So, for example, if someone was not being transparent or predictable, someone could say, "Hey, you know, by doing things that way you're not being as transparent as you could be."

As another example, someone wrote that one of the ways to show disrespect is to start doing email in the middle of a meeting. That then created awareness whenever someone pulled out a laptop. This is a good example of a behavior that some don't find as disrespectful as it might be to others. Not only did our Trust Wiki allow people to discuss these trust/distrust behaviors, but it also allowed us to go deeper into what *influences* these behaviors as well.

CHAPTER

6

Making Change Last by Creating a Culture of Trust

☐ Defining Organizational Trust

When we discuss organizational trust or a culture of trust, we are going beyond the trust that specific individuals have in one another. We are referring to the degree to which the members of an organization trust the organization as a whole, which includes the processes, norms, rules, and reward systems that reinforce the organization's collective trust.[1] Some degree of trust at the organizational level is essential for collective action to occur, including cooperation and collaboration.[2,3,4] Kouzes and Posner demonstrated the positive effects of leadership on firm performance and activities, which included human resource management practices.[5] Gould-Williams and Davies regarded trust as a critical component to an organization's climate that ultimately leads to positive exchanges.[6] A variety of organizational practices can foster, coexist with, or even inhibit developing organizational trust, and debate remains active as to whether and how informal and formal mechanisms actually work to build trust.[7] In fact, in some organizations, certain controls are in place that might inhibit developing organizational trust. Such controls might include employee monitoring mechanisms, rules, and procedures. These controls are in place, however, to maximize the organization's consistency and reliability to enhance performance. It is possible that control could develop into trust as relationships within and between organizations evolve.[8] If so, trust would evolve from personal knowledge with the controls established to deter untrustworthy behavior and toward trust based on common values or interests, with informal controls supplanting formal controls.[9]

Clearly, it is important for the leader to demonstrate the ROCC of Trust personally and interpersonally by identify other key individuals who can help reinforce the ROCC of Trust. It is equally essential for the leader to reinforce these efforts systemically by building a culture of trust throughout the organization. Building a culture of trust allows a leader to "leave a legacy" that outlasts the leader's tenure, providing benefits to the organization long after the leader has retired or moved on to face new challenges and opportunities. We define organizational culture as the "underlying values, beliefs, and principles that serve as a foundation for an organization's management system as well as the set of management practices and behaviors that both exemplify and reinforce those basic principles."[10]

This chapter does not attempt to delineate all the ways in which collective trust is developed and reinforced within organizations, or all of its benefits. We will, however, discuss many important ways leaders can develop and sustain collective trust within their organizations. These techniques are applied at three levels. At the personal level of change, leaders establish collective trust through their actions and by setting an example. At the interpersonal level, collective trust is established through norms and by identifying and selecting individuals to help build the ROCC of Trust. Finally, at the systemic level, collective trust is built by developing and implementing organization-wide information, measurement, and reward systems that reinforce the ROCC of Trust. After all, trust or distrust in the organization persists long after specific individuals depart. People can still trust or distrust an organization even after they have moved on to another employer.

☐ Positive Organizational Scholarship, Leadership, and Trust

The field of positive organizational scholarship (POS) includes many complements to organizational trust, because POS often incorporates many of the same leadership attributes (such as courage, humility, and authenticity), and several organizational characteristics that contribute to trust between individuals.[11] A positive organization is best exemplified by a belief in the human condition and its potential to result in positive performance[12] based on the key attribute of trust. Scholars in POS have focused on an individual's strengths to build performance rather than worrying about what the individual is lacking.[13] As one example, an individual's "best self" is used to build trust among an organization's members, which helps build a strong organizational culture and subsequently creates strong organizational performance.[14]

Leaders in positive organizations can create a culture that builds and sustains trust among organizational members, even as the organization faces adverse external circumstances or even crises. Leaders help create a positive culture by personally demonstrating compassion, forgiveness, and gratitude;[15] indeed, in the work context, these are not always easy traits to display. In our own research, consulting, and coaching, we have found that among the four pieces of the ROCC of Trust, compassion takes the longest amount of time to demonstrate, because it requires empathy to learn the needs and interests of others *and* a willingness to fulfill those needs and interests. In addition, having a forgiving attitude is not something that comes naturally in a business setting. People are often punished for mistakes, not normally forgiven for them. Finally, we do not always express gratitude for what others do; instead, we just expect others to do their jobs. When a leader helps create a positive culture, however, he or she paves the way for more compassion, forgiveness, and gratitude on the part of colleagues.

One of the most interesting themes in the television series *Undercover Boss* is how the leaders' sense of compassion for their employees develops. In this series, CEOs and other top executives disguise themselves as prospective employees to gain insights into the thinking and actions of rank-and-file employees. Two episodes in particular stand out to us. The bosses from Belfor and Great Wolf Lodge were moved to tears when they learned about the true trials and struggles their employees live with every day, while working hard at their often-demanding jobs. These bosses did not simply hear what their employees were saying and then return to their corner offices at headquarters. They actually listened carefully and responded compassionately by helping employees meet their individual needs and goals. One employee, after benefiting from such compassion, stated that she would give undying loyalty to her employer. The action that sparked her loyalty was receiving back pay based on a promotion she had received a year earlier but for which she had not been paid because of a corporate-wide freeze on pay increases. Even though this boss may not have acted out of compassion to earn loyalty, that is indeed what resulted. Many of the employees profiled on *Undercover Boss* who were at first surprised that the new employee was the head of their company not only expressed deep gratitude for the boss's actions, but also demonstrated, via follow-up television reporting, their strong loyalty and positive responses to the compassion provided to them. Although we are skeptical of reality television shows in general, and realize that leaders would be encouraged to be on their best behavior on such a show as *Undercover Boss*, our subsequent primary research on Sheldon Yellen and his company convinces us that at least he is the real deal.

A positive leader fosters strong interpersonal relationships among organizational members, which in turn strengthens the organizational culture.[16] Leaders can do this by creating positive networks within their organizations and focusing on developing their employees' strengths. The Gallup Organization has found that a focus on strengths energizes an individual to achieve better performance. Interestingly, however, the vast majority of organizations try to help employees fix their weaknesses rather than capitalizing on their strengths.[17] When employees feel as though they are appreciated for the strengths they can offer, they feel empowered to do their best job for that organization. Early in her post-MBA career, Karen had two completely different experiences within the same firm. In one assignment, her boss made Meryl Streep in *The Devil Wears Prada* look soft. This boss frequently criticized Karen, saying she was weaker than employees who were less senior in the department. She regularly told Karen she had to work harder and put in longer hours just to attain the same level of performance her colleagues achieved. Yet before Karen started her next job in a different department, her new boss, Bruce, recognized her strengths and communicated to her how much potential she had to contribute to the company. He encouraged her not only to do what she did best, but also to mentor a junior colleague to help another employee do her best, as well. Karen survived the first boss and truly thrived under the second boss. The difference was that one boss emphasized her weaknesses, and the other boss appreciated her strengths. Indeed, the two leaders used her talents quite differently. Karen ultimately received a major promotion to national account manager, in large part because of how her boss Bruce empowered her.

☐ Building Organizational Trust Through Open Communication

A positive leader also fosters a trust-based organizational culture through open communication.[18] Sharing positive information widely (rather than negative information) promotes team cohesion and increases trust in the organization. As Bob Lintz (General Motors) told us,

> I let them know that I didn't pretend to have all the answers. We had a complicated business, and getting them to listening to one another effectively and share their insights was the way we were going to prosper best. That took a lot of time. It was a process where the outcome would be something where they'd been involved, engaged, and empowered to help make the decisions happen.

Another way leaders build trust through open communication is by using positive meaning to strengthen the organization's culture. Positive meaning can be developed by helping employees understand how their work aligns with the organization's core values and how it contributes to the organization's long-term performance.[19] This also contributes to increased trust in the leader, and ultimately, trust throughout the organization. Again, Bob Lintz,

> Establishing trust with the union leaders required a different kind of an approach. It was more difficult to find the leaders among the union organization who demonstrated some thought to changing the way we did business, to changing management–union relationships. Those were the people that I went after.
>
> Bringing the union into a joint decision-making process was really critical. It was no different dealing with them than it was for me to get my management team to stop driving decision making from the top down. Helping the union understand where we needed to go as an organization, what kind of goals we needed to have, and what kind of hurdles and barriers we were going to have to overcome to make these things happen was critical.
>
> Momentum comes when you've got training systems, joint processes, and communications in place and things start to flow quite effectively. Once we got the joint process in place with the union leadership, and an ongoing calendar with them, change proceeded much more easily. They knew why we were making changes and were committed to help make it work. And, when the union leaders got pushback from the hourly employees, the union leadership was pushing back on them, using all of the reasons we were going in a particular direction.

In a very different, nonunionized context, CEO George Barrett described how Cardinal Health, a $100-billion-annual-revenue company, instills values throughout the firm, and how those values get reinforced through its performance measurement of employees,

> We do a lot of work to reinforce the authenticity of our core values, because this can't really be done in an isolated fashion. You have to have an integrated view of values. Reinforcing your values needs to be part of your formal messaging as a company, but it also needs to be part of the narrative of the company. It needs to be part of the stories and folklore that people tell. It needs to be included in the way you develop and train employees, and it needs to be part of the way you measure them.
>
> Just as an example, we try to make sure that in every town hall meeting we find a way to touch on our values. We will celebrate when someone demonstrates those values in a very clear way. Our values are expressed in our literature and notes that we send to employees.
>
> And as I mentioned, we build values into our talent management systems. We evaluate our people not just on "what," but on "how."

Someone who accomplishes things, but does so in a way that is not completely consistent with our values, is not a complete success story, right? So we actually give a significant weight to both the "what" and the "how."

When giving developmental feedback to employees about improving their "how," the approach varies. At the core, we make it transparent as to why we're giving feedback to the person. That's a hard thing to do, because value issues can be very sensitive. You have to use your language carefully when you discuss them with an employee. You just try to give examples, such as,

> "Okay, look. This is an area where we think that you need development. Here's one way to approach it. Let me give you an example of the way you approach something, and here's another way to approach it that would have demonstrated greater teamwork or greater collaboration or whatever it may be."

We just try to make sure that we're very specific with people about what we mean. I don't think there's a single way to address it. It varies by the employee; it varies according to their receptivity to feedback. Some employees are incredibly receptive to this, and some just throw up a wall. So we just try to make sure we're doing this in a most productive way.[20]

Ted Castle (Rhino Foods) understood that his employees would enjoy work and deliver their best performance if they understood the business better. He, therefore, shared private financial information with his employees. As a privately held company, he did not have to share information about the company's profitability, but he knew that if he wanted everyone to perform better and enjoy their jobs more, they needed to understand what was going on. By widely sharing this information, employees gained a sense of purpose and meaning, knowing that their efforts contributed to the company's health and success and ultimately their own personal financial success. Ted is a highly trusted leader because of his willingness to be open and honest and share information.

☐ Leaders As Linking Pins

Leaders who do not work at the top of the organization also play critical roles in developing organization-wide trust. Rensis Likert suggested that middle managers play a critical role in an organization because of what he called their "linking-pin" status.[21] That is, middle managers are not only a member of the team they manage, but are also members of the teams their bosses manage.[22] Middle managers are, thus, in positions that link one team to another by virtue of their membership in multiple teams. This creates opportunities to both gather and share information with their staff members,[23] while building security and trust within their teams.[24]

Middle managers represent the organization to their employees as much top managers do; ideally, they embody the organization's values and goals for their immediate subordinates. Often, rank-and-file employees do not have daily or even weekly contact with top management; therefore, they expect their immediate boss to be transparent about the organization's strategy and performance. Middle managers must also share important organizational changes, when they know about them, with their employees to avoid appearing to lack transparency. Indeed, direct supervisors are trusted more than CEOs, to the extent they communicate openly with their employees.[25] Thus, employees may or may not trust the organization based on their relationship with their immediate supervisors[26] and how they communicate. Referring to strategic communications, Tuck School of Business at Dartmouth Professor of Corporate Communication Paul Argenti noted, "Effective communications with employees, which is the basis for any internal communication effort, must start with how managers interact with other employees day-to-day."[27] This interaction should consist of "straight talk and truth-telling."[28]

Collective trust within an organization can be developed both interpersonally and through formal practices and procedures, especially ones that enhance consistent and transparent information.[29,30] Although leaders at the top of the hierarchy do not interact as frequently with employees as do the employees' supervisors, they can develop trust with their followers and throughout the organization through effective communications. Bob Lintz (General Motors) argues that his communication efforts were essential to building a culture of trust,

> Another significant effort we made was in organization-wide communications. We were unlike any other GM plant at the time that I was aware of with our business updates, our quarterly business meetings, or our diagonal slice meetings—communication practices that are now commonplace in GM. Those became very significant to our people to help them feel that they were getting the truth. Rumor mills typically run wild in a large organization like ours. For example, we would have rumors about what they thought I was worried about or what they thought I was going to do, or that the plant was going to close. I also found out how important body language was. If I was walking in the plant with my head tipped down

a little (my thinking position habit), I would often have people stop me and ask if everything was okay, as they perceived me to be worried. Our plantwide communication efforts were an excellent way of dealing with all these kinds of issues.

Getting first-hand information out to our people about what we were going to do or weren't going to do, and then having that information demonstrated in the ensuing days and weeks, started to build credibility and trust. If we then made a mistake, or if I made a comment that turned out to be contrary, I was very quick to correct that and to explain the reasons why something went differently than the way it was planned.

Leader member exchange (LMX) theory looks at the relationships between leaders and subordinates, how these relationships are formed, and how leaders differentiate among subordinates.[31] Leaders decide who is in the in-group favored by the leader and who is in the disfavored out-group.[32] This view of leadership differs from the view of a leader who shows no preferential treatment to any of his or her subordinates. High-LMX relationships are characterized by mutual trust, loyalty, and giving additional energy and effort beyond what is required by the job, whereas low-LMX relationships result in employees doing only what is expected of them.[33] The LMX theory of leadership and other interpersonal theories are not sufficient to explain how high levels of *organizational* trust develop, however. If an organization includes in-groups and out-groups, by definition the organization lacks trust, because intergroup rivalry would prevent true trust from developing. We argue that it is the extent to which *groups and other organizational subunits trust each other* that heavily influences how much and how quickly organizational trust develops. Given the inherent rivalry and conflict across groups in large organizations, often over scarce resources, it is critical that leaders find ways to foster collective trust across groups.

☐ Building Organizational Trust Through Systems, Processes, and Practices

One great example of developing trust in a large organization is how Two Men and a Truck, International fostered collective trust between its home office and its more than 200 franchises. They have established the ROCC of Trust through practices, systems, and programs over more than two decades. As Brig Sorber, the CEO, and Jon Sorber, the executive vice president, told us,

Before we started franchising, there were a lot of local moving companies out there already. But what we found is that when a lot of them got to five or six trucks, they started to seize up. They couldn't really grow anymore because of their lack of systems. I think where our value came in is with the software system that allowed our franchises to do bulk moving. Instead of six trucks and grossing half a million dollars, our franchises could grow to 15 trucks, 20 trucks, 30 trucks, grossing $4 million, $5 million, and close to $6 million for some of our franchises this year, so they see the value in that.

When we go to the International Franchise Association, there're a lot of franchise organizations that cannot believe that we share numbers across our system, and they say, "Wow, we wish we could do that, but our franchisees would never go for that." Because we've done it from day one, our franchisees don't know any differently. It works, they like it, but to change a whole system to that would be very difficult. But for us, if you're not sharing the numbers, if you're not sharing the information, you're missing the essence of franchising, because the whole reason to franchise is to learn from one another.

A lot of the franchises also don't know when to add management, don't know when to step out of a certain role and bring somebody in to do something else. At the home office, we typically know when a franchise is ready to go to the next level, or we know when they're flagging before they do. Our franchisees see the value in that, especially our closest franchises, typically the oldest, most mature franchises.

We have a mentoring program where new franchisees come in and are attached to our older, more mature franchisees that are in full compliance with their franchise agreement. They can visit their mentor or their mentor will come visit them. We also have a franchise leadership team representing our seven different areas of the country, as well franchise business consultants from [our] home office who not only ensure compliance but also provide assistance when requested. We also show our franchisees that our home office overhead generates results by reporting franchise royalties per home office employee. Even though we've grown over the years in terms of home office staff, our profitability has grown even faster.

[As a result], our other franchises in the middle will follow the big producers. Then, the "baby" franchises will do everything that you tell them because they're babies. So think of it as babies, teenagers, and then the 25-year-old that goes, "Yeah, I guess Dad and Mom did know what they were talking about after all." So that's another reason that they see the value of being in our system.

If our system is strong enough, our training is strong enough, and our measurements are strong enough, then there's no reason for them to do it on their own. If our system is strong enough, and they are following the steps, then are they profitable, are they gaining market share? If they are, they're going continue to follow our system, and that's what's been happening.

Formal systems, processes, and practices can complement the interpersonal mechanisms discussed above in several ways to foster intergroup and, thus, organization-wide trust. For example, after an organization has built trust by sharing information widely, it can expect that people will follow specific guidelines to create consistency in the way they provide service to customers. This is the case with Two Men and a Truck. Employees and groups understand that guidelines are in place to protect the reputation of the brand and will comply with the guidelines to both advance this goal and maintain their own trustworthiness with fellow employees. Employees, groups, and other organizational units will also be more willing to comply with control mechanisms if they believe that they are intended to improve the welfare of the entire organization. Consider another example from Two Men and a Truck, which changed its franchise arrangements more than a decade ago to improve customer satisfaction and the health of the franchise system,

One of the problems we had was that our "protected territories" system was not customer-friendly. Franchisees would decide which franchise would move the customer rather than the customer, which is not a good idea when we're heavily a referral business. For example [Brig starts drawing on a whiteboard], we have franchise "A" here; we've got franchise "B" here. These are protected territories. That means that only A is going to move in this area, and only B is going to move in that area. A's office is right here; B's office is right here. A customer in A's territory calls franchise B, because they see their trucks every day, and a customer in B's territory wants to use franchise A. Franchise B says you've got to call the A office. This used to happen all the time. Customer B would call franchise A and be told "Our office is X miles away from your home. We start charging from the time that we move, leave our office until we return, so your drive time's going cost you $75.00." Well, the customer says, "But B is right across the street. Why can't I just use them?" The answer is, "Because you're my customer."

Talk about an angry customer! Customers would call the home office and say, "I don't belong to anybody." Home office would say, "We don't know what you're talking about, ma'am." "A says I belong to them. I want to use this one right here. They won't let me.

Just so you know, I'm not going to use either one of them," and then the customer hangs up. How customer-friendly is that?

When we got rid of the protected territories, Jon, Melanie, and I traveled to speak with all the franchise groups and explained why we had to go to "marketing areas" instead. We brought franchise contract addendums with us, and about 80% of the franchisees signed the addendums right then and there. Ten percent of them said they would adopt the new system when they renewed their contracts the following year. Then there was the 10% that said, "I bought a protected territory; I'm keeping it." We said, "God bless you, except on your renewal, your agreement will be taken away." We didn't insert new franchises into a given franchisee's area, but allowed existing franchises to compete based on customer demands.

Now marketing works relatively still the same as when we had protected territories. B still can't target market into A's area, meaning they can't have a guy go over there and drop off leaflets, things like that. They could market using radio, TV, however, the bleed-over stuff. That's fine. Nobody can stop that.

Most of our franchises are now working together. They're pooling their marketing dollars to dominate the whole area. It gets really tricky when you get into a place like Atlanta, Georgia, where we have 10 franchises, but we have them all working together. There isn't one franchise right now that I think would want to go back to protected territories. Since our inception as a company, every single franchise has chosen to renew. The customers are happy. Home office is happy.

The leaders of Two Men and a Truck were thus able to institute an important organizational change that was ultimately trust-building instead of what easily could have been trust-destroying. They were able to do this because of the significant trust they had already established with their franchisees.

☐ Bob Lintz: Turning Around the Parma, Ohio, General Motors Plant

On a very personal level, Bob crafted his leadership vision based on his experiences at General Motors. His superiors reminded him regularly that the company had a strict, formal hierarchy, and that management and the UAW were to view one another as enemies or at least competitors. For example, many of bosses considered it inappropriate to address people by their first names, and rigid distinctions existed within even the management hierarchy. First-level supervisors wore ties, second-level supervisors added vests to their "uniforms," and higher-level managers wore ties, vests, and suit coats. Bob hated these and other distinctions. As Bob moved up the managerial ranks, he demonstrated courage, humility, and authenticity as he eliminated many of the distinctions between union and nonunion people and even among different levels of the managerial ranks. Many times, he courageously stood up against the status quo, humbly asked the local UAW leadership and his own direct reports for help, and authentically led the charge for a more egalitarian workplace. These efforts directly countered his own experiences as a first-line supervisor and lower-echelon manager.

Given Bob's early experiences at GM, it is not surprising that one simple but very important practical *and* symbolic example of his personal leadership has been sartorial. His preferred style of dress became a golf windbreaker over a button-down shirt and slacks. We've never actually seen Bob in either a tie or a suit in the two-plus decades we've known him. For many decades, what one wore in the workplace stood for one one's rank in the hierarchy and the respect and authority that went with that rank. Eliminating ties was a way to break down barriers between white- and blue-collar employees, which Bob did decades before it became commonplace at GM or any other large manufacturing organization. It was radical, to the say the least.

Interpersonally, Bob had to find others he could trust, both among the union leadership and from within his own management ranks. He had to confront any staff members who weren't giving 100% effort or seemed dubious about the direction they were taking. Through staff off-sites and other team-building efforts he felt he had everyone on board and that they would give their all. All except one, and it was the HR director. The director just could not convince himself that Bob and the team were taking the right approach. He could never imagine truly trusting the UAW. Bob rightly viewed this director as having a zero-sum perspective on working in a nontraditional way with the UAW, and after several unsuccessful efforts to change his mindset and behaviors, Bob finally asked GM to transfer the director to another location where they were not dealing with such a huge cultural change; GM agreed.

Bob built a culture of trust in many ways at the Parma plant. Bob worked hard to break down barriers between hourly and salaried employees, including eliminating separate cafeterias and parking lots, and removing the rigid dress code. More substantially, Bob secured and spent tens of millions of dollars for employee training for what became known as the Team Concept at Parma. This included not only teamwork among frontline salaried supervisors and UAW-represented subordinates, but also high-level teamwork between Parma's top managers and the local UAW leaders. This joint operating structure called the Floor Board involved biweekly meetings, joint decision making, and transparent communications within the group as it communicated to external constituents. Bob and his top managers were also able to negotiate the consolidation of eight unskilled job classifications into one general category, which empowered employees on the frontline to improve productivity and quality in a much more flexible way. The Team Concept, the Floor Board, and other decision-making structures and work practices reinforced norms of collaborative problem solving, open communication, and mutual respect. These were qualities shared not only among hourly employees and their supervisors, but also ultimately among all employees at Parma.

Although Bob could not change the pay and benefits for his hourly employees, as these were negotiated nationally, he did change the equally important reward system by which the Parma plant was allocated new business based on formal proposals to GM's top executives and the international UAW in Detroit. Rather than sending a team of managers and engineers to Detroit, Bob created *joint* teams of managers, engineers, and local union representatives, which worked together to develop proposals and then traveled together to present them. It was only when these joint teams failed in their initial proposals and were asked to develop more compelling pitches that the local union leaders became truly convinced that the plant needed to produce higher-quality products much more efficiently if Parma was to be allocated more business from Detroit.

Halfway through Parma's transformation, Bob had to demonstrate courage, humility, and authenticity by asking the union to give up a significant amount of overtime pay, which the labor contract obligated General Motors to pay them. This request also involved asking the union to evidence a great deal of trust, because union employees would be sacrificing current income for the possibility of future income. Overtime was no longer needed by 1998, because significant productivity and quality improvements had been achieved while revenues had grown to $750 million. The Parma plant was producing at this level with one-third fewer employees (3,175 versus 4,700 in 1990). Quality had also improved dramatically, as Parma became a preferred supplier within GM and achieved QS 9000 certification. The productivity and quality improvements were so significant that by 1998 the Parma plant had eliminated $20 million in annual overtime. At that time, it was labeled "bad overtime," because it had been used to make up for low productivity or poor quality. Giving up this overtime, however, resulted in the average hourly employee losing $10,000 in annual wages, with some skilled tradespeople losing as much as $25,000 annually. The way they could recoup these earnings was to succeed in acquiring new products to build from GM, which would result in additional work. The union's trust in the Parma leadership was such that they were willing to give up their "bad overtime" with the hope and potential for "good overtime" in the future.

The next decade's improvements proved to be even more dramatic. By 2004, Parma was rated GM's best stamping plant worldwide. It repeated this achievement in 2005, when Parma's revenues exceeded $1 billion, and it was named the best stamping plant, Japanese or American, in North America. In 2008, *nine years after Bob Lintz retired from GM*, Parma was still rated one of the best, most efficient stamping plants in the world, including its Japanese competitors operating in the United States.[34] The plant continued to take on large amounts of stamping work even as other GM stamping plants were being been shut down, and it currently processes more than 1,000 tons of steel daily and serves 40 different customers.[35] Today, it continues as one of the top stamping plants in the world, supplying parts for the new Chevy Cruze. Further, GM invested $60 million in the plant between 2008 and 2010, as it transferred work from other GM stamping plants.[36]

Clearly, the performance improvements Bob and the Parma plant achieved are impressive. They saved thousands of high-paying jobs that generate $25 million in annual payroll taxes alone[37] and provide billions of dollars in economic benefits to the greater Cleveland area over several decades. Personal examples abound that highlight the compelling transformation from an organization in which people distrusted one another—and even despised themselves—to an organization of mutual trust and respect. At one town hall meeting, an employee stood up and said Parma had changed not only how he communicated with his fellow employees, but also how he communicated with his loved ones. He told a room full of hundreds of people, "I love this plant. And, I love my wife. In 25 years, I haven't told her I love her. I'm going home tonight to tell her." On another occasion, Bob attended a funeral for an hourly employee. After the funeral, the late employee's wife showed him the briefcase this union employee had purchased and taken to work each day. She explained that for the first time in his life he felt respected and respectable enough to carry a briefcase. Inside the briefcase, he had only carried his sack lunch.

Beyond courage, humility, and authenticity, Bob possesses many personal qualities that allowed him to lead the transformation of the Parma organization. Perhaps at the core is his self-awareness, which motivated him to ask courageously and humbly for help from others in a way that was genuinely his own.

Trust Tips

1. *Be reliable*. Live by a set of commitments, such as an open-door policy.
2. *Be open* and honest. Share sensitive information with your employees that will help them do their jobs better.
3. *Be competent*. Help your employees find ways to do their jobs better by giving them the resources to do so and by living up to their expectations.
4. *Be compassionate*. Be willing to remove people from your team or organization who have a zero-sum mentality and thus are not willing to work on behalf of everyone's welfare. Truly listen to your employees' concerns about their job and their life so that they feel respected as human beings.

Trust and Innovation

☐ Innovation As a Leadership Imperative

A May 2010 IBM poll of 1,500 CEOs identified creativity as the number-one "leadership competency" of the future.[1,2] If this is true, how do we cultivate this competency in both current and future leaders? Here we must distinguish creativity from innovation. We thus define innovation as the ability to *implement* new ideas.[3] Still, creativity and innovation are inextricably linked. Of concern, however, is that the developmental foundations for creativity are not as strong as they used to be. In a series of creativity tasks developed for children by Dr. E. Paul Torrance, researchers were able to predict which children would achieve innovative accomplishments as adults.[4] Further, a recent *Newsweek* article titled "The Creativity Crisis" noted that children are not as creative as they used to be. In a creativity test in which children are asked, "How would you improve this toy to make it better and more fun to play with?" children gave fewer answers to this question than did children tested in 1990.[5] Perhaps this developmental change has occurred because we are not strongly encouraged to be creative in school, at work, or even in our leisure pursuits. Perhaps the increasing availability and sophistication of electronic entertainment has reduced the time and attractiveness of unstructured playtime. Whatever the reason, it may be harder for future leaders to foster innovation, if individuals have not been encouraged to be creative when they are younger.

As a result of these changes, business schools will need to emphasize innovation to a greater extent in their curricula in order to serve as a training ground for leaders who wish to foster innovation in their organizations. A 2010 report from the Association to Advance Collegiate Schools of Business (AACSB) on innovation in business schools states, "The role of business schools in supporting innovation remains under-developed, undervalued, and too-often unnoticed."[6] Yet the report also argues, "Business schools play a pivotal role by developing effective leaders and providing support for the engine driving sustainable growth in their communities and throughout the world." The AACSB report urges business schools to include innovation in their missions and sees business schools as a key link between the university setting and society in promoting innovation.

The purpose of this chapter is not to discuss how leaders themselves can become more creative, but rather to discuss how they can foster greater innovation in their organizations by building trust. Previous research has identified numerous organizational factors that foster greater levels of organizational innovation. A Babson College study, for example, found that innovation flourished in organizations when employees were rewarded for developing new ideas and bringing them to market.[7] Based on our research on downsizing, on which we will elaborate in Chapter 10,[8] we argue that a significant way organizations discourage innovation is by relentlessly emphasizing efficiency and reducing costs as a way to improve the bottom line. Instead, organizations could be providing resources and support for innovation that would improve both the top and bottom lines. The challenge for leaders is to stop emphasizing "doing more with less," instead enhancing innovation through deeper empowerment, broader information sharing, and greater collaboration regarding human, material, and financial recourses.[9]

Consultant and management educator Gary Hamel and his colleagues have thought deeply about the state of management and have developed a manifesto of sorts.[10] Hamel writes, "The aim of management 2.0 is to make every organization as genuinely human as the people who work there."[11] Among their 25 ideas for revolutionizing management, fully half focus on an organization becoming more innovative, whether through policies, practices, and empowering people or through becoming more creative. Our take on Hamel's concepts is that leadership is not just about managing people to get things done, but is also about unleashing individual and collective creativity to make work more fulfilling, and sharing information fully.[12] Hamel notes that these goals cannot be achieved unless a high-trust culture exists within an organization. As others have found in empirical research, "Trust is beneficial to all types of partnerships that face risk and require constant flexibility."[13]

☐ Mutual Trust Between Leaders and Followers Is Essential for Innovation

Mutual trust between leaders and followers is essential, moreover, for innovation to flourish. Leaders must want to empower their followers and these followers must want to accept responsibility and authority. Gretchen Spreitzer (University of Michigan Ross School of Business) noted,

> Trust is critical for leaders and managers to feel comfortable in empowering their people. Without trust, empowerment feels like too big of a risk for them to undertake. Subordinates also need to trust their bosses to feel comfortable acting in empowered ways. They need a sense that their manager trusts them and won't micromanage.

As Sheldon Yellen, CEO of Belfor Holdings, told us,

> Not everything comes from the top down. Some of the greatest ideas have come from the bottom up. As I've said many times to you, I innately believe that there's a little hero in everybody. Everybody's got a little good in them. Everybody's got a great idea in them. It takes a great leader to get that out of people.[14]

When asked for some recent examples of how employee empowerment at Belfor results in positive outcomes, Sheldon then shared these:

> We were having problems with gas expenditures throughout the company. We've got thousands of vehicles, and our gas bills are just climbing through the ceiling. One of the employees said, "Hey boss, why does everybody get to take a van home at night? Not everybody's on call." As you know, in our business we get calls at 1, 2, 3, 4 a.m. Our guys have got to go board up something, or suck water out of a home after a fire. They've got to have their vehicles with them. They can't get out of bed, drive to the shop, get a Belfor truck, and then also be there within an hour after the call, so we have people take vehicles home.
> So when the guy said, "Why don't we have on-call people?" I said to myself, Why didn't I think of that? So what we did was assign on-call people each week. Those on-call people take their vehicles with them, plus we keep two extra vehicles in every office. I can't tell you the exact reduction in gasoline expense for the year, but it was in the millions of dollars. Millions of dollars! Now, this idea came from a guy who was working a water truck.
> Another example was in our warehouses. We have a barcode system where you swipe your tools and materials in and out. There's a guy who's called a "cage guy" who sits there in the warehouse all day making sure that everything is swiped that comes out and it's locked up at night in the cage. The next day the cage is opened again. He swipes the equipment and barcodes it, and it goes out again and back, and so on and so forth.

One of our cage guys said, "Why am I sitting here all day? In the morning, I swipe everything. Everything goes out. At night, I wait for everybody to come back, and I put everything back. The next morning, I swipe it and it goes out. The next night, it comes back. I got 8, 10, 12 trucks lined up here waiting for me to get everything barcoded and swiped."

He said, "What if I worked nights, swiped everything at night, and in the morning I had two trucks going out to all the job sites and drop off all the materials and equipment they need to have. This way I don't have 12 people waiting to get out of here. I'm here by myself. That's one man-hour per hour instead of 13 man-hours per hour, right? What it will cost us to deliver to 12 job sites is less than 13 man hours in one hour." Simple math, right?

He was right, so we changed our whole delivery system. That came from a cage guy, a warehouse guy. He's more sophisticated than I am, I guess, because he thought of it, not me. We promoted him, and he's now a project manager running $9 million, $10 million, $12 million jobs.

Trust is also critical for individuals to share important information with one another, to exchange ideas, and to engage in problem-solving, especially under conditions of uncertainty.[15] Collaboration, especially when resources are scarce, also requires trust.[16] Trust also appears to enhance the development of new skills, knowledge, and expertise that are necessary for innovation. Under such conditions, employees are more likely to stay with the organization because they believe they can *grow and develop*. Innovation, employee growth, and retention beget further innovation in a virtuous cycle. As Ross Smith (Microsoft) told us,

In low-trust organizations, individuals are going to do what they think is going to provide them with the greatest individual reward. They're not going to necessarily take a bunch of risks, because failure is not rewarded, whereas in a high-trust organization, they're going to experiment, try new things, and try new techniques. They're going to learn new things. As a result, they're going to flush out more defects, more rapidly. Indeed, that's what we saw from our business metrics.

The challenge is that not everything that people try works every time. So, from an individual perspective, people are typically going to do what they think is going provide the most yield for what's rewarded. They're not going to necessarily take a bunch of risks, because failure is not typically rewarded. Whereas in a high-trust organization, they will experiment, try new things, and try new techniques. They're going to learn new things. As a result, they're going to flush out more defects more rapidly. That is indeed what we saw in our business metrics.

What was also very interesting is that from a personal growth perspective, if individuals have more freedom to experiment, learn new things, and try new ways of testing, they're going to stick around, because they feel like they are growing—they have the opportunity to grow their skills. We saw tremendous retention rates.

As people stick around and stay in their technology area, they obviously get better at it. They get more technical. They understand more deeply how the software works, as well as build stronger relationships with their partner teams and their counterparts in other disciplines. So those relationships and just the nature of work gets smoother, because people have been doing it longer. We really saw great increases in virtually all our traditional metrics.

☐ How Leaders Foster Innovative Cultures Through the ROCC of Trust

Returning to the three levels of change perspective introduced in Chapter 3, we have found that leaders of innovative organizations (1) regularly emphasize the importance of developing new or improved products, services, or processes through both their words and personal actions; (2) foster interpersonal trust among teams and collectives that promote risk-taking and collaboration; and (3) reinforce elements of the organization's culture or system that promote innovation, especially by balancing tensions between focusing on what customers want now and what they may want later.

☐ Innovation and Trust at the Personal Level of Change

As a leader trying to foster innovation, it is important to reflect on where you have been your most creative, or more generally, have been most successful in generating new ideas and getting them implemented. Each semester, Aneil told his students that his preferred working environment is one in which he feels "chronically inadequate, but nurtured." He also thrives when surrounded by bright, highly self-motivated individuals who are all clearly focused on achieving excellence in their endeavors, whether academic, professional, or athletic, and who also encourage and help one another as they pursue excellence. This type of environment spurs Aneil to "step up his game," to reach for and achieve excellence himself, and to work on continual self-improvement. When Aneil was being recruited by Princeton three decades ago, a student told him, "You may have heard that we work hard at Princeton. That's true, but we also *play* hard." Each leader must find and create his or her own optimal environment for innovation. At the personal level of change, the leader must be courageous enough to want to develop something unique and important, be humble enough to seek feedback from colleagues and customers (especially negative feedback to ensure that what is being created is truly different and valuable), and be authentic enough to change in ways that reflect the leader's particular combination of talents, values, and interests.

At the personal level of change, an innovative leader is also one who sees things that others do not. An innovative leader pursues what Schumpeter calls "creative destruction,"[17] a process that challenges the status quo. This concept embodies a leader's continual quest for innovation even in well-established companies and with well-established products—always seeing new ways to do things. Schumpeter noted that "expressions of energetic will" are found in the "strongest individuals" who will "create something new and destroy the old thing" to create a new enterprise.[18] Innovative leaders, therefore, are those who see new ways to do things, not just for themselves, but also for their organizations. In making a Schumpeterian reflection, Betta, Jones, and Latham noted, "The entrepreneur is the agent capable of combining people and opportunities into a productive organism."[19] Further, as Professor Jeff DeGraff of the University of Michigan Ross School of Business told us,

> I think the overarching issue of trust is that in innovation, unlike any other area, you're thinking about what doesn't exist yet. You're going someplace that you've never been before. You need to trust that the people you're working with are going to first look out for your safety and well-being and then make sure that you stand to gain like everybody else going on this voyage.

One of the best examples of creative destruction fostered by an entrepreneurial spirit is found in Mary Ellen Sheets, the founder of Two Men and a Truck, International. The business initially involved just her two sons, Brig and Jon, who moved household goods as a way to pay for college. She formally launched the company by investing $350 in a used truck. As the firm grew, she began selling franchises, expanding outside the state of Michigan, and growing the company to its present $220 million in annual revenues. Today, Two Men and a Truck has more than 200 franchisees in 37 states as well as Canada, Ireland, and the UK.

Mary Ellen is one of the most humble, courageous, and authentic leaders we have ever met. She simply saw an opportunity where others did not. In her view, although plenty of other moving companies operated in her area, she saw an opportunity for a new kind of moving company that would succeed by focusing on treating customers with compassion. Indeed, the company institutionalizes compassion in many ways, including the company motto ("movers who care"), its financial and material contributions to philanthropies, and in its annual Humanitarian Award given to a franchise "in recognition of actions of a purely philanthropic nature."[20] In fact, Mary Ellen gave away the company's first-year profits of $1,000 by writing $100 checks to 10 local not-for-profits. She has continued to donate to the same 10 charities every year since then,[21] and to date, Two Men and Truck has contributed more than $1 million to philanthropic concerns.[22]

From the beginning, Mary Ellen hired bright people who were, as she says, smarter than she is. She shares these employees' ideas through a monthly newsletter about how to improve the business and has subsequently watched her business grow exponentially. Her approach reinforces the trust her employees and her franchisees have for her on a personal level and her increasingly effective business model. Today, her three children run the business with one of the two original men, Brig, leading the company as CEO. The other of the two men, Jon, is the executive vice president, and Mary Ellen's daughter, Melanie, having taken her turn as CEO, is now board chair of the company. Mary Ellen not only created an entrepreneurial and innovative business model, but she also created a unique and innovative family business model for sharing leadership of a family-owned company.

☐ Innovation and Trust at the Interpersonal Level of Change

At the interpersonal level, innovation depends on the leader finding trustworthy individuals with whom to collaborate to use resources. Jeff DeGraff (University of Michigan) noted that when it comes to people working together to create innovation, "trust is also an issue of competency." When Karen and Aneil attended the University of Michigan Business School (now the Ross School of Business) to earn their MBA and PhD, respectively, they both benefited from the school's dean, the late Gilbert Whitaker, and his associate dean and eventual successor, B. Joseph White, who championed innovation and excellence in a variety of endeavors. Along with the then, associate dean for Executive Education, Thomas Kinnear, and others, these innovative leaders helped propel the school from being embedded within the top 10 in the *Business Week* biannual rankings of business schools to the number-two spot. They also increased the endowment by tens of millions of dollars and hired dozens of faculty from top institutions across the country, including globally respected thought leaders such as the late C. K. Prahalad, Karl Weick, and Richard Bagozzi. Gil, Joe, and Tom were very different individuals and very different leaders, but each found ways to build innovation into the school's culture. This is perhaps best exemplified by the school's Multidisciplinary Action Project (MAP), the first (and still unique) action-based, team field project for MBA students, which now involves 500 students working on 100 projects worldwide each year.[23]

☐ Innovation and Trust at the Systemic Level of Change

At the systemic level of change, innovation depends largely on an organizational culture, which either enhances or inhibits individuals' creativity, and cross-functional flexibility. It also includes awareness of the external environment, such as changing consumer preferences, technological developments, and economic trends. Indeed, the late Peter Drucker argued that entrepreneurial, innovative organizations perceive change as an opportunity rather than a threat.[24] Our own clients develop organizational cultures in which people are highly empowered and engaged to do what is best for the organization involved, have a clear sense of the organization's purpose, and can flexibly respond to changing circumstances. Leaders help reinforce their cultures' capability for innovation through several mechanisms, including metrics, reward systems, talent management systems, and socialization (e.g., onboarding), particularly in large organizations.[25] Leaders must also be willing to listen to junior people in the organization who have innovative and interesting ideas.[26] One key cultural element is the amount of *time* leaders allocate to developing innovations. Google is a well-known example; they have employees set aside 20% of their workweek to focus on innovation.[27] Another example is 3M, which has all employees devote 15% of their time to "pursue something they discovered through the usual course of work but didn't have time to follow up on."[28] Both of these companies are the exception, however, rather than the rule.

☐ Make Work a Game That All the Players Can Win

A great example of building trust at both the interpersonal and systemic levels of change is found in Ted Castle and Rhino Foods. Ted developed a management philosophy based on his hockey experiences in which he had learned that coaching was a better approach to managing people rather than monitoring or controlling them. He motivates his employees by having them set high standards for themselves and their work and then having them hold themselves accountable for those standards.

While coaching and playing hockey, Ted learned that playing a game—and winning—was a highly motivating way to achieve. He has, thus, adopted a team-based, game-oriented approach to running Rhino Foods. He noted, "I have a fundamental belief that most people like games, and they don't have to be football players or hockey players to enjoy games. People can like bridge, or checkers, or Risk, or Monopoly." He developed a list of things that people like about games,

> You know your opponent, you know the beginning and the end, there's usually a time frame, and you know the score. If you win, you usually celebrate. If you lose, you usually feel badly and try to figure out what to do next time. You meet and you prepare. What was there about Rhino Foods like that at the time? Nothing!
>
> Then I thought, wouldn't it be interesting to try to bring the elements of a game into our business? The score is making money. It initially sounded scary to share profit information with our people. But my colleague said, how would you feel if you played a game for three hours with scorekeepers and at the end of the game they blew the whistle, closed the scorekeeper book, and didn't share the score with you? That's when I decided to take a chance and open up our books to the 20–25 people we had back then. That's the how the Game really started.

In several ways, the management philosophy and approach that Ted developed not only demonstrated his trustworthiness in terms of the ROCC of Trust, but also demonstrated his trust in his employees. Rather than acting like a hall monitor, regularly checking on his employees to see if they were playing by the rules, working hard, and performing, he instead established an organizational structure, reward system, and culture that demonstrated the ROCC of Trust to his employees. In the process, these organizational characteristics enhanced his employees' willingness to take risks which resulted in a culture of innovation.

Ted first demonstrated openness by giving every employee access to the operating performance (e.g., expenses) of the company and demonstrated reliability by posting this information at Rhino Foods each day. He said, "The reason we did it daily is that we think that the most current, the most specific information is the best for people."[29] This information sharing also required some courage on his part. "My biggest fear was that people were going to think I was making myself rich. But, I knew I wasn't getting rich. We were making money, but at times I thought I could be making more money mowing lawns again. So, I said this issue should be easy. It comes down to whether you're willing to be open."

For example, before Ted's open-book management approach, employees thought that if they made four batches of fudge batter brownies, the company would sell that product for about $7,600 and that most of that was profit. By opening the books, however, Ted showed employees that half of this amount paid for the ingredients alone. He itemized all the costs for his employees and then showed them that the company also had to pay 40% in taxes on the amount that remained after all the costs had been paid. He showed them that the company would only be profitable if the employees completed all their work correctly. "I would remind them that last week we did it wrong and we had to throw it all away. I would then ask them what might have gone wrong with that job. So, we just started sharing information, and once you do this, you build confidence. It's contagious. If you want people to act like owners in your business, just tell them what you know."

☐ Talk Like Ted

Ted emphasizes that communicating in this way creates a fun environment in which to work. Through this fun, he also built the ROCC of Trust by demonstrating his humility, courage, and authenticity. As he told us, "It's our purpose and principles that we believe in that are important. We're trying to help people listen and respect each other, while engaging them by making it interesting. To a group of employees who just got off a seven-hour shift at 6:00 in the morning, I'm not going to show 20 Power-Point slides."

Creating fun-filled communication is also a serious business to Ted,

> We believe it's everybody's job to figure out how to engage people, so we look at it as a teacher does. There are good teachers, and there are bad teachers. The ones that usually are considered better engage their students. We take it really seriously that we need to be able to communicate in a way that grabs people's attention; having some fun along the way usually grabs people's attention.
>
> Sometimes, when we want to celebrate something, or when we report the first-time quality, the performance schedule, or our safety record, we have more fun by showing a picture of me with my Rhino hat on and either wearing a smile with my thumb up or a frown with my thumb down. It was our communications people who came up with that idea. It's not really about me; instead it's about how

our employees have chosen a way to engage with me and with one another in a way that they can laugh about.

This approach to communication, coupled with substantial job training and business education, enhances the reliability and competence of Rhino's employees, along with their innovative capability, by making it easier for Ted to delegate more decisions to his employees. "Personal responsibility is something we spend a fair amount of time talking about and figuring out how to make that happen,"[30] he explained. He created a reward system in which employees participate in a Bonus on Goals program where a payout is made if budgets are met, and once the company's capital investment requirements have been reached. This not only demonstrates compassion, but also increases employee trustworthiness by aligning their interests with the firm's. Employees improve their innovative capability by coming up with new ideas to improve the firm's work processes.

Another way Ted demonstrated trust in his employees and his compassion for them was by loaning his employees to other local firms that needed seasonal help when Rhino Foods endured a downturn. In fact, the idea of allowing employees to work at other firms came from the employees themselves. This idea emerged when more than half of the employees brainstormed over a period of three weeks on ways to avoid layoffs at Rhino. Ted asked his best employees to volunteer for the Employee Exchange Program to ensure its success, and Ben & Jerry's was one of the firms that participated in the program.[31] In exchange, Ted guaranteed employees their jobs once the market picked up. This innovative approach to downsizing and fluctuations in seasonal demand could only work if Ted had built a trusting relationship with his employees and Rhino Foods had credibility in the community. The program was successful, preserving the jobs of key employees who returned full-time to Rhino Foods when demand picked up, and the program has continued for the past 14 years.

As the business has grown, so has the need to change how Rhino Foods shares information with employees. The Game is now played differently in that performance is still measured daily, but rewards are now distributed every six months rather than weekly, so that longer-term performance based on innovations (e.g., capital investment decisions) can be properly assessed. As Ted recently told us, "We've continued to work hard at sharing information, helping people know what's critically important for our business." An annual planning process is now in place, with annual bonuses provided for achieving goals. With three shifts, the company now has three company meetings on the same day each month so that everyone can attend. Annual goals are reviewed, as well as any financial

information that employees want to discuss. Starting in 2007, four performance items "critical to the business" began being tracked: performance
to schedule, first-time quality, safety, and customer service levels. As Ted
put it, "The concept of looking at the business, seeing what's important,
sharing the information, tracking daily results, and getting people motivated to improve on those numbers has continued." The Game continues
to evolve from year to year, based on several factors. Ted recognized the
tradeoffs between familiarity with and complacency about performance
indicators and between flexibility and efficiency,

> How we do it each year is based on what's important and how savvy
> our workforce is. We tend to introduce new metrics carefully, be-
> cause we find that when we bring out a new metric it takes a while
> to gain some traction. So to be constantly changing things every year
> doesn't make sense. We've measured performance to schedule, first-
> time quality, and now we're measuring safety differently. We keep
> some of the old measures and then move some of the new in as we
> try to focus on different things. The reason we play the Game, how-
> ever, has not changed. We still believe it's important to have a daily
> focus on activities. In some parts of the organization, we're actually
> shortening the feedback time period. The production floor has an
> hourly performance worksheet. The three different lines they're run-
> ning know what they're supposed to make every hour, and they're
> measuring whether they did so, and if not, how can we fix it right
> away?

In further refining his approach to sharing information, Ted recognizes
the critical importance of providing feedback based on the nature of the
task and not using a "one size fits all" approach:

> The concept is to be identifying the most important things to the
> business, but also, what is the right amount of time to be tracking it,
> how can we be adjusting it? We've really gotten into this idea from
> Toyota: "plan and do, check, act." It's a continuous improvement
> methodology; we need to be picking the right plans to be tracking,
> how we go about checking on them, and how we go about adjusting
> them. If we make the problem so big that we never get to do it, then
> we're never going to get anywhere. So, the concept is, we're trying to
> keep getting better at little chunks.

As Ted has increased the level of trust throughout the organization,
he has fostered flexibility, creativity, and even patience, qualities that
are essential to any organization. At Rhino Foods, the need to reward
people every week based on their performance when the Game was

first developed then evolved into monthly bonuses and has now further evolved into bonuses after six months. Ted can even wait to share some of the performance information, although such information is still measured daily:

> We've combined our monthly bonuses into a six-month bonus, but we're still measuring our goals daily. We're still reporting progress on our goals at each monthly company meeting, but then rewarding our employees based on achieving these goals every six months. We continue to mature, grow, and figure out what works best for us, but the concept of sharing information, trying to get people to understand that they have a way to impact the results, is what is really important.

Rhino Foods' performance has proven the value of Ted's coaching philosophy. Rapid growth began in the 1990s based on selling inclusions, that is, brownie bites and cookie dough, to major ice cream manufacturers such as Häagen-Dazs and Ben & Jerry's. In addition to making and selling the Chessters ice-cream cookie sandwich, Rhino Foods also makes ice cream novelties and desserts for some of the largest food companies in the United States They have grown from $8 million in annual revenues and 40 employees in the early 1990s to just under $20 million a year and 75 employees at the end of 2011,[32] impressive given that the firm operates in a highly competitive segment of the food industry, one in which not all new ice cream products have long product life cycles (and not just because they melt!).

Ted and his wife, Anne, still own 100% of the business, but they are not running the business to go public or to sell it. As Ted expressed, "Instead, we are doing it because we still enjoy it, and because we're trying to create a really interesting work environment where people enjoy coming to work, where people are challenged, and where we are following our purpose, 'to impact the manner in which business is done.' "[33]

☐ Reinvigorating Your Innovative Culture Through Ongoing Reevaluation

When Two Men and a Truck, International was facing a negative impact on their revenues and profitability with the onset of the Great Recession of 2008, the firm's leadership felt it was necessary to assess all of their home office employees to determine who would be retained, how they would be evaluated, and how they should be rewarded. As part of this organizational reassessment, 30 employees were let go as roles, responsibilities, and reporting relationships were restructured. In addition, performance metrics and rewards evolved to encourage greater initiative and productivity. As Melanie told us in December 2011,

> By 2008, our double-digit-percentage growth slipped to single digits, then flat, then single-digit negative, then double-digit negative. Our new CFO, Jeff Wesley, really went to work. We were fat, so it was time for Jeff to cut the fat from the business. He had a lot of fat to cut. One of the many things we had to cut was the six-week sabbatical for employees. To go from lots of discretionary income at our firm to none so quickly is quite paralyzing. I admire that while we focused on ROI, Jeff did agree that "we can never let go of our core values and our customer satisfaction, but we also need to understand return on investment completely and have a return on investment for everything we do. Because this is what will keep us profitable and able to serve our customers going into the future." He was absolutely right. He kept us profitable through those tough years.
>
> Every person at TMT is now held accountable like you wouldn't believe. It needed to be done. Every single person at Two Men and a Truck needs to bring ROI to the bottom line. If they don't, they're perceived as not needed. Period. Well, how do you prove ROI, for example, for an administrative person or someone in training? Every person in every department now reports monthly to their boss, "the chief," and they have a MAP meeting—monthly accountability plan. We started this at the beginning of 2009.
>
> In that monthly accountability plan, employees have to show how they've made progress for that department. Take someone involved in training, for example. How many people got on that web-inar? How were the evaluations? These evaluations ask, "Is this going to help your business?" So the ROI rolls through the company in that way. They've got to be doing duties that bring dollars to the bottom line for the franchisees. Show results, loyalty, and trust. It's all about holding people more accountable. It's made a huge difference.
>
> Our people that speak with moving customers are currently called customer service reps; but they will probably be renamed customer sales reps, because they're closing the sale rather than being an order taker. With the new economy our tactics have changed. The TMT marketing department is teaching our customer service reps how to sell to the customer and strive for a commitment. Oftentimes the customer might say, "Well, I'll call you back when I talk to my spouse or I might check around." The customer service rep used to say, "Okay, that's fine." But not today. Now there's a closer at the end: "Would you like to move in the morning or the afternoon?" These are basic sales skills being taught that haven't been taught before.

In 2011, thankfully, we're having the best year we've ever had. This is even when housing is still down and customer confidence is still somewhat low. The blessing in this great year is that we are sharing the profits with our staff. In June of 2011, Brig did a surprise profit distribution to our staff. They were significant bonus dollars, up to 50% of some people's salary. We're doing another one in December. We're sharing the gain with everyone. This incentive is not only rewarding, everyone works harder and smarter.

Another thing that Brig does that I truly admire, and something he's very good at, is that he holds the "chiefs" accountable as well. He told each department chief, "You're going to get a chunk of cash based on how many people you have, based on the ROI of your department. Now give each employee in your department the share that they deserve based on the ROI, based on their MAPs."

The first time we did this, a couple of years ago, Brig said, "Oh my gosh, that's a lot of money." Brig said to each chief, "I want to see exactly what you're giving each person, because I do not want you to give every person in your department the same amount" (this is what our VPs did in the past). As Brig explained, "They don't deserve the same amount. Some work harder than others. You know, some have to put up with more. While they might have a menial job, it's demanding. But I do not want to see everyone getting the same amount."

Even after the first year or two, Brig still checks the bonuses. We looked at them last week. He looks at every single amount that each person's getting. There are a lot of big companies out there looking for great people. We don't want to lose our great people. So that's another reason we are giving bonuses based on profits. It's just the right thing to do.

In the process of instituting these changes, Two Men and a Truck's leadership retained elements of the organizational culture that had contributed to the firm's innovative nature and success, while eliminating elements that were no longer as important. Initially, everything was on the table. Again, Melanie,

We believe strongly in our core values. Prospects are brought in based on our core values. We hire and fire based on our core values. We're really, really happy and thankful to see these values at the forefront of everything we do.

With all the change and things we had to cut out at our corporate office (sabbaticals), a fun atmosphere has been maintained. For example, my office today is full of decorations. The departments are competing for best-decorated hallway. We'll have a big Christmas party in the office with games and prizes. We were able to take everyone to a Tiger game in chartered buses and we had a big "bring your family" picnic. It's about doing things together. The employee lunchroom is called the "Core Values Café." It has a flat-screen TV in it. The walls are all red. Almost every Friday there is a big potluck lunch in the Core Values Café. So there are a lot of fun, community-type activities going on within the home office.

We also have employee awards. Recognition, especially from peers, is so rewarding. These are given out at Brig's pizza luncheon, which is held every two months or so. The award is called the Great Blue Water Award, because many of Brig's analogies are about taking the ship away from the shore, taking it away from the safe harbor, getting into rough waters, facing discomfort head on, and enduring change. The chiefs also give department updates at these luncheons. It is a very festive and upbeat atmosphere.

Efforts to reevaluate and reinvigorate the culture have not been restricted to employees at the firm's home office, but have also been applied to the more than 200 franchisees that comprise Two Men and a Truck. Melanie continued,

And as far as living the core values, our whole awards program for the franchisees is based on the core values. We have a points system, and they get points for different areas, for living the core values. So our values are in the forefront. They're not like some words that we barely ever use. They're really, really used here, lived here, and enforced.

Our franchisees are changing their cultures as well. They are hiring real managers with experience rather than maybe their brother-in-law or a cousin or a good mover being promoted as a manager. Many of our managers now have college degrees. Our franchisees are also replacing their customer service reps with salespeople. So, it really makes everything more efficient for the customer, because it's helping them make a decision.

In addition to people practices reinvigorating the firm's core culture, significant financial investments also improved the franchisees' human capital and technological capabilities. Some of these investments are paid for by Two Men and a Truck as the franchisor and some of them are paid for by the franchisees. Melanie explained,

You should see our Stick Man University (which is our training center). The home office just put $370,000 into an upgrade. It is absolutely beautiful. Another big investment we have as a system is an

IT upgrade, which is costing about \$3.4 million per year. In the beginning of a huge IT project, it's all behind-the-scenes work. You can't see the fruits of the labor for sometimes up to two years. Two Men and a Truck Corporate has already put hundreds of thousands into it, but going forward our franchisees are investing into it as well. The franchisees make monthly payments toward it, one percent of their gross monthly income, with a minimum monthly payment of \$1,500. The IT fee will never be treated as a profit center where corporate makes money off the franchisees from this IT investment. Now that they understand, they're paying for it even though they haven't seen the results yet. So you have to have really difficult and transparent conversations with the franchisees to get them to understand. IT can be hard to understand regardless! This takes trust. These changes will help us to better serve our customers. Our goal is to become the premier moving company in the world . . . IT will be instrumental in helping us get there.

At Two Men and a Truck we're all really fair, firm, and transparent. The key word for Two Men and a Truck I would say is transparency. I think it's our transparency that's brought us trust. First, because we share all the franchisees' numbers with one another. No one can pretend to be something they're not. Sharing of the numbers causes people to communicate and mentor each other.

From the corporate standpoint, Brig explains everything thoroughly. He is very transparent. You can approach him at any time. He'll stand up on a stage with the franchisees and say, "Okay, ask me questions. I know you're mad. Ask me." If no one asks the questions, he'll say, "Okay, here's the question you're all afraid to ask." He'll just bring it up.

I was speaking recently to a group and an attorney said, "Well, that's nice that your franchisees are transparent, but do they see corporate headquarters as being transparent with them?" I thought that was a great question. I then repeated what I just told you about Brig being very transparent, how franchisees can ask him questions at any time. We also use a third-party source to evaluate our franchisees every year. This is a confidential evaluation. Franchisees feel safe to share what they are thinking. We also have a Franchisee Advisory Board made up of franchisees. We meet with them at least quarterly face-to-face. Transparency breeds trust.

As does Ted Castle of Rhino Foods, the leaders of Two Men and a Truck exemplify the ROCC of Trust and institutionalize it in ways that foster innovation and growth through sharing information, collaboration, and risk-taking.

Trust Tips

1. Demonstrate *reliability* by sharing details to get things done.
2. Demonstrate *openness* by encouraging new ideas.
3. Demonstrate *competence* by taking on a new challenge.
4. Demonstrate *compassion* by not punishing one-time mistakes that lead to learning.

Interview with the "Dean of Innovation," Professor Jeff DeGraff of the University of Michigan Ross School of Business

What is the leader's role in fostering innovation?

The leader has really three essential roles. So right off the bat, the first challenge of the leader is to properly diagnose what's going on or at least to make sense of it and help the group make sense of it.

The second role of the leader is to make sure that they have available to them the culture and competencies required to succeed in that situation.

Third, and this is the hardest one, is synchronization. Value isn't created in any one of the quadrants. It's created in the hand-off between the oppositional quadrants. So the challenge the leader has is to coordinate or integrate these opposing practices and opposing views.

Trust Across Borders

Increasingly, work is conducted across both organizational boundaries and geographic borders. Three decades ago, books such as *The Virtual Corporation*[1] and *The Boundaryless Organization*[2] extolled the benefits of breaking down hierarchical and geographic boundaries to create more flexible organizational structures and promote greater effectiveness. Back then, as today, organizations' employees, customers, suppliers, and markets were increasingly global. Competition, which is driven by innovating, continuing to reduce costs, and executing plans more quickly, has forced organizations to identify the best ideas, regardless of their physical location. Furthermore, organizations must develop these best ideas for the most receptive markets, whether they are domestic or global. As Professor Ranjay Gulati of the Harvard Business School told us,

> Trust is equally important across organizational boundaries. Firms are increasingly operating in an interdependent world where they are "shrinking their core" and partnering extensively. As firms increasingly rely upon partners for tasks that were once close to their core, trust becomes the catalyst for success. Learning how to engender trust becomes a critical success factor for such firms.[3]

Further accelerating these competitive forces are both free-trade agreements and ever-advancing information technologies (IT). Notably, IT tends to follow Moore's Law of Capacity, which estimates that processing speed, memory capacity, and sensors double roughly every two years.

Individuals have become much like organizations in obliterating boundaries. Human capital is following the example of financial capital by seeking the best opportunities to earn high rates of return, whether locally or distantly. Indeed, 15 years ago, *Fast Company* declared the United States to be "Free Agent Nation," defining free agents as the

103

self-employed, independent contractors, and temporary workers, and estimating this population to be 16% of the American workforce in 1997.[4] And that trend has continued. A 2011 survey conducted by Kelly Services estimated that 25% of the U.S. workforce was self-employed. Interestingly, 90% of these mavericks surveyed wanted to be self-employed. This was up from 19% just two years before in a 2009 survey.[5] Moreover, this is hardly an American phenomenon. For example, in 2011, India's population of self-employed is estimated to be 51% of its total workforce.[6] Once again, information technology is expected to accelerate this trend toward a world without boundaries. Social media platforms such as LinkedIn, Facebook, Twitter, and others only enhance free agency. Importantly, trust is the essence of this new way of working. In this environment, trust is essential; it's required for knowing who to contact about new career opportunities, who will be a great employer, or whether to remain in your current job.

At the personal level, the leader must demonstrate courage, humility, and authenticity to break down organizational boundaries. A great example of all three qualities is Peter Löscher, president and CEO of Siemens AG. Adam Bryant, author of *The Corner Office*, recently interviewed Peter. When asked how he creates a trusting team culture, Peter replied, "I'm always telling people, 'Look, I make a mistake every day, but hopefully I'm not making the same mistake twice.'"[7] The ability to admit having made mistakes is a rare quality for a CEO, but is one that enables him or her to be open to feedback and that encourages others to try new things without fear of making a fatal mistake.

☐ Virtual Teams and Trust

Boundaries take on another meaning when individuals band together into teams and begin to work together across geographic boundaries, either within the same company or across firms. When team members are based in different places, they are called a virtual team. Previous research has shown that leadership behavior is very important to trust and commitment within virtual teams.[8] One study found that having a shared vision, such as a customer focus, rather than emphasizing who has the most power in the group, helped the virtual team achieve higher levels of trust.[9] This same study found that high-trust groups shared power within the group based on the knowledge that each individual brought to the group. Finally, those high-trust groups functioned well if they had a facilitator who reinforced and encouraged the shared vision.

When creating virtual teams, it is critical to begin with a face-to-face meeting[10] so that members can meet each other. When this is not possible, avatars or photos can be used to help team members get to know one another virtually. Research on the factors that help virtual teams function effectively points out that one of the difficulties with such teams is that individuals who work together in person often rely on nonverbal communication.[11] When those nonverbal cues are absent, as is the case in a virtual team, group members do not exchange feedback as quickly. Because feedback on performance takes longer to receive in a virtual setting, trust develops more slowly in virtual teams, but it does, indeed, develop.

One positive factor of the ability of a virtual team to build trust is the extent to which members contribute to conversations.[12] In addition, when team members stick to deadlines, they are considered more trustworthy.[13] Both of these findings demonstrate the importance of openness and reliability-based trust. Rules for building trust more quickly and for greater effectiveness in virtual teams include getting started on tasks promptly, communicating frequently, overtly acknowledging that one another's messages have been read, being explicit, and setting deadlines and sticking to them.[14]

We have coached virtual cross-functional teams at a leading global bank as part of the Leadership Development Program at Duke University. Karen's team included members from Hong Kong and Malaysia, who were natives of Hong Kong, Malaysia, and India. Aneil's team consisted of team members from the UK and the United States We each held an initial meeting at Duke University in Durham, North Carolina, so that everyone had the opportunity to meet face-to-face. At that time, teams were given their tasks and were told to set up future meetings and objectives. The goal was to return to Durham in six months to present their completed project. After the teams left Durham, we held conference calls and exchanged emails for the next six months at all times of the day (and night) to review the teams' objectives, set new goals as parameters changed, and ensure the teams were sticking to the timetables they themselves had established. The teams were extremely busy because their members had full-time jobs in addition to their extra team projects. Despite their demanding schedules, the teams continued to meet over the six-month period. Karen's team returned to Durham to present an outstanding project to the other Leadership Development Program groups. The team's boss called to thank Karen for the outstanding results his team accomplished.

In contrast, Aneil's team, despite having fewer cultural and geographic barriers, had more difficulty developing cohesiveness and commitment to a clear set of goals. The key difference between the two teams based on our observations and expertise was the much lower level of initial trust that Aneil's team had in its leader and the subsequent trust they developed with one another. In addition, Karen's team exhibited several features of a strong team in general, such as sharing team leadership from meeting to meeting and having a strong, shared vision of their ultimate goal.

☐ Trust Across Organizations

On an external level, companies pursue interorganizational arrangements such as joint ventures and strategic alliances when they believe they can gain access to a market or industry more quickly by collaborating than if they invest in it by themselves. A recent survey by Bain & Company revealed that approximately 50% of the companies surveyed were participating in strategic alliances,[15] making it one of the top 10 management tools leading companies used.

The ROCC of Trust also exists at the interorganizational level. Openness-based trust between customers and supplier organizations was a key differentiator between Japanese automotive firms and their suppliers versus European or U.S. automotive firms in the 1980s and 1990s.[16] Competence-based trust has been discussed extensively in research examining the auto industry, contributing to a reduced need for inspections (monitoring), for example.[17,18] In terms of compassion, not behaving opportunistically or selfishly in pursuing the firm's objectives has been found to contribute to interorganizational trust,[19,20,21] and such trust has been found to be positively related to firm profitability.[22] Interorganizational trust has also been found to be a positive influence on whether partners will invest more in an alliance and to its effective functioning.[23,24,25,26,27] Governance structures, that is, how organizations choose to operate in a joint venture, strategic alliance, or some other organizational form, will influence how and to what extent trust develops between the organizations.[28] One study, for example, examined the effect of preexisting trust on the governance of the new relationship. This study found that preexisting interorganizational trust is both a complement to and a substitute for formal governance modes and can greatly enhance exchange performance.[29] There are also scholars who have argued that trust can substitute for contracts at the organizational level and that the actual presence of a contract can signal distrust.[30]

One interorganizational partnership in which Karen participated was with Pepsi, when she was the account manager for a $75-million account at a plastic bottle manufacturer, Johnson Controls. As the account manager, Karen was the key liaison between her company (the manufacturer) and Pepsi, playing a role as an advocate. She felt that it was her responsibility to help each side work for the other's best interests. Thanks to Karen's ability to build trust with Pepsi, they invited her to participate in an internal team to evaluate their delivery process from Karen's company to filled-bottle delivery at the store level. Karen was the Johnson Controls representative working with Pepsi employees as they sat in a conference room, full of yellow Post-It notes, and mapped out the delivery process from beginning to end, identifying every moment of truth and trying to find ways to make the process more efficient and effective. By being a member of Pepsi's internal team, Karen was able to create a stronger partnership between her company and Pepsi. Pepsi in fact formally requested that Karen be promoted to the position of account manager representing Johnson Controls for all of Pepsi's U.S. business.

☐ Trust Across National Borders

Building trust across borders is an area of trust research that needs to be explored further, as more and more multinational companies have teams that work together across borders which are geographic, ethnic, cultural, and language boundaries. One study has found that individuals' propensity to trust varies across countries, depending on whether they belong to individualist or collectivist cultures.[31] Many business practitioners have emphasized the importance of developing global leaders, which includes an ability to listen and understand the cultures they live and work in.[32] As one senior executive commented, "We have hired and trained people to work in silos. We need to identify future leaders who can operate in a globally integrated company, and train them to think and work globally."[33]

Lenovo's e-commerce business has had experience building trust between its office in Morrisville, North Carolina, and employees in Argentina. As Lewis Broadnax, the executive director of web sales and marketing at Lenovo, explained,

> Development for the [Lenovo] website traditionally has been here in the Research Triangle with our core team. When we hit the downturn in the economy, we let a lot of those people go and added resources to low-cost areas of the world. Buenos Aires was one of the places that we went. At the time we were able to hire three people for the price of one developer here in the U.S. So for the business at that point it made sense. We had to ensure that we were getting the maximum resource for the investment we were making.
>
> Immediately we found that productivity dropped and the people that remained in the U.S. were all overworked. We had bottlenecks. No one would reach out to the Argentina team to do any work. When we tried to force the work down to Argentina, the work that was moved was very, very menial. The team here did not want to send anything of importance down to the Argentina team because we just let a lot of people go. They thought, "Now I'm training my replacement. In two months I'm going to be gone. So I'm not going to send anything that's worthwhile down there."

That was the fear, even though all of the organizational changes that needed to be made had been made. The people that were staying were people that we wanted to stay. Now all of a sudden the people that we really want to stay feel like they have to do everything to save their job. They don't want to let anything go, even though they're working 60, 70, 80 hours a week. The tasks and workflow are slowing down, and in Argentina we've got really smart people that are being given these menial jobs. We went through this for a couple of quarters.

Phase two involved having some teleconferences to make sure that we are working better together as a team, and can now start shifting work between the two locations. However, we still had a language barrier, poor phone lines, and little clarity on who was responsible for which tasks. The tasks were dumped off at the last minute, so there's little effort to make it work. The Argentines really don't understand what their responsibilities are because they're brought in at the last minute, and they send back work that is really not good because they haven't had proper clarity on it. The Argentines are frustrated because they didn't understand what the request was, and they weren't given a deadline. They're sending back things that they think are creative, but don't fit the brand or strategy, because no one really told them what they need to do. The U.S. team says, "We told you. These guys can't do anything."

Phase three involved getting both teams together face-to-face for three or four days. Now they're in a room working on a project together. There's enough time for them to be able to understand what each other are saying, and really understand where people's strengths and weaknesses are. They're collaborating on the project. Each of them is bringing their own talents to the project. That's what really made the change.

Now the guys from the U.S. come back and they now understand what is needed to actually communicate with the remote teams what prep work needs to be done. The language barrier is still there, but they now know that they have to deal with that, so they figure out a way to make sure that the calls are longer, that they're using a very good phone. That they're talking clearly. That they're asking the guys, "Can you understand what we're saying?" Follow-up notes after the meeting. Immediately, productivity goes through the roof.

On top of that, now the employees in Argentina are feeling more empowered. They create an entirely new tool for the team to use. They learn the scripting language that was about to be deployed on the site, and they become experts before the team of people in the U.S. Now we're flying them from Argentina back here to train the rest of the team here. All this happens over the course of a quarter and a half—very fast!

One way that trust is being explored across borders is through a global network of scholars interested in the topic of trust. The First International Network of Trust (FINT) is an international network of scholars and practitioners interested in the topic of trust. They meet each year to discuss theories and practices surrounding the topic of trust. We asked the president of FINT, Professor Dr. Antoinette Weibel (see sidebar), about her perspective on the current state of trust research. "Trust is essential for human interactions, and where it is missing, self-interest and conflicts prevail. In times like ours, we need to understand how to restore trust and deepen trust, or otherwise, what we call in the Germanic countries 'social peace' is at risk."

Trust Tips

1. **Reliability:** Set clear expectations for how the members of the partnership should work together, as well as clear goals, objectives, and metrics.
2. **Openness:** Develop a common language, terms, and references so that the partners can communicate openly.
3. **Competence:** Rotate leadership of the partnership regularly to take advantage of all the talents.
4. **Compassion:** Make sure that everyone agrees as to how rewards for the partnership's success should be shared, and then stick to the formula.

Interview with FINT President Professor Dr. Antoinette Weibel

1. **How has your definition of trust changed since you began examining it?**
   I started to make the core construct of trust—the "willingness to be vulnerable"—more central to my thoughts on trust and trusting. Recent events have brought this state, which I believe to be a rather unpleasant one, to the fore, but at the same time we have not paid much scholarly attention to vulnerability, for example how it is perceived and felt.
2. **How has trust changed in importance for the welfare of individuals and organizations over the past decade?**
   We now understand better what the consequences are if trust is lost—and trust loss seems to have occurred in all our important institutions, be it firms, regulatory bodies, or politics.
3. **What do you think accounts for the erosion of trust by members of society in our various institutions?**
   I cannot answer that for all institutions. When we look at companies, however, the prevailing assumption of modern economics that companies need only to maximize shareholder value, and that monetary incentives

are the prime way to motivate leaders to do so, are the root cause of many problems.

4. **What are some necessary or important first steps leaders can take or should take when attempting to repair trust violations?**

   Change of incentives systems—intrinsic engagement and integrity should be valued, and in some instances input control and a common binding cause are much better ways to govern a company than by means of bonus systems and other types of piece-rate wages.

5. **To what extent are leaders born or made based on your own research and experience?**

   First, I believe that a good leader has a tendency to trust, as such a tendency is infectious. Second, such a tendency arises from two characteristics: a psychological disposition to trust and learned trust. So to some amount, trust-inducing leaders are "born" as they have experienced very early in their life nurturing relationships and thus have a high proposition to trust. But to some amount, leaders are also made, as trust is also an outcome of a learning process, and this can be influenced by companies' processes and structures and by training measures.

6. **What are some ways in which leaders can institutionalize their interpersonal trust-building efforts within their organizations (e.g., practices, processes, reward systems, contracts)?**

   Trust-inspiring control processes—that is, control which is learning and development-oriented, allows for participation, and is not tied to pay-for-performance. Emphasis on social competences and individual virtues when selecting new employees and promoting employees. Decency, virtuousness, and abiding by the golden rule when leading the company.

Antoinette Weibel, president, has been a First International Network on Trust (FINT) member from the first hours. She has organized and co-organized various subtracks at FINT and the European Group for Organizational Studies (EGOS) and FINT-affiliated symposia at Academy of Management. Antoinette is full professor of management at the University of Konstanz, in Germany. Her current research interest is on regulations and trust in systems, stakeholder trust in organizations, rewards and trust, and rules and happiness.

CHAPTER

Trust and Healthcare

☐ Why Focus on Healthcare Leadership?

In this chapter, we focus on leadership in the healthcare context, specifically leaders responsible for guiding teams of healthcare professionals. Trust in healthcare settings is particularly salient to the ROCC of Trust for several reasons. First, healthcare represents a significant portion of the U.S. economy. In 2011, healthcare expenditures represented 18.2% of GDP,[1] and they are expected to reach 19.6% of GDP by 2019, according to the U.S. Centers for Medicare and Medicaid Services.[2] Second, vulnerability is at the core of trust; indeed, when we are sick we are often at our most vulnerable.[3] Third, healthcare is an exceedingly complex context, in which many different actors shape organizational change efforts, patient outcomes, and bottom-line results. Fourth, beyond rapidly rising costs and lack of access, the healthcare system faces many other challenges. In the next 15 years, we could see a shortage of up to 150,000 physicians because current medical schools will not be able to keep up with the demand for them. This will be especially true for primary care physicians who work on the front lines of implementing the healthcare reform bill in the United States.[4] In short, healthcare provides a perfect context for examining how trust influences a leader's ability to effect lasting, positive change, both among individuals and in the institutions where they work. George Barrett, CEO of Cardinal Health, the $100-billion healthcare firm based in Ohio, told us,

> Healthcare is a very personal issue. The stakes are great, both for individuals and society. We believe that all Americans should have access to healthcare, but providing affordable access has been a real problem. Using the legislative arena to ensure affordable access poses enormous challenges. Our healthcare system has been characterized by significant misalignment among consumers, providers, and

payers, and information transparency has been low. This requires some structural change, but legislation requires scoring, and scoring structural change is a huge challenge.[5]

As we will discuss in this chapter, building the ROCC of Trust is essential for a healthcare leader to effect change, both in patients and in healthcare organizations, in an industry that is desperate for real reform within both its costs and practices. Reform is necessary not only because of the unsustainable growth in healthcare expenditures, but also as a result of the challenges that healthcare has seen over the past 15 to 20 years,[6] including structural changes in information technology, the focus on the business aspect of healthcare, demands from patients, regulatory burdens, and changes in reimbursements.

Both positive and negative examples can be drawn from trust relationships in the context of healthcare. In general, patients trust their doctors to a large degree.[7] In fact, they trust their doctors more than they do insurers, the government, and employers to protect their health information, but they remain wary of electronic medical records and the potential for loss of privacy.[8] Not all is well with respect to patient–physician trust, however. Lower-income patients report trusting their physicians less in terms of medical decision-making and quality of their care. Lack of trust in quality of care relates more specifically to doctors' not referring patients to specialists and performing unnecessary tests.[9] Unfortunately, physicians only have themselves to blame, to the extent that they don't act in a trustworthy manner. In an article published in the peer-reviewed journal *Health Affairs* in 2012, "10 percent of physicians admitted to telling patients something that was not true, . . . nearly 20 percent of physicians said they had not fully disclosed an error to a patient in the previous year because they feared the admission would trigger a malpractice case, . . . [and] more than 55 percent of physicians said they often or sometimes described a patient's prognosis in a more positive manner than the facts might support."[10]

☐ The Changing Nature of Physician–Patient Relationships and Implications for Trust

The foundations for the physician–patient relationship, and thus also trust, are changing. Dr. Kevin Lobdell, director of quality and program director of cardiothoracic surgery at the Sanger Heart and Vascular Institute and Carolinas HealthCare System, put it this way: "As care becomes more patient-centered and we live in a more transparent society, the need to focus on patients, their families, and needs is ever increasing."[11] Dr. Brent Senior is an otolaryngologist (an ear-nose-throat [ENT] surgeon), the Nathaniel and Shelia Harris Distinguished Professor, and vice chair of academic affairs at the University of North Carolina (UNC) at Chapel Hill Medical School, and another physician leader with whom we've worked for several years; he echoed Dr. Lobdell's views and expanded on today's challenges in healthcare,

> Frankly, the relationship between doctors and patients is under constant attack. The cynical person in me says that those who want to hijack healthcare for their own purposes realize that the relationship, with its key element of trust, is at the center of healthcare. This is why you see Blue Cross Blue Shield commercials that emphasize relationship. Here is the crux: It is always present in healthcare, whether it is provided by the doctor or not. Hence if the doctor–patient relationship can be eroded, then that opens the door for other forces to insert themselves and subsume that relationship in order to manipulate patients for their own benefits.
>
> That is the problem—all of these forces/institutions/individuals have at their center not what is best for patients, but what saves/makes the most money. These can be governmental forces, insurance carriers, and, not to be minimized, attorneys. But, can the patient really have a productive relationship that results in health with a company? Does a company or for that matter a government agency really have at its core the health of the patient?
>
> Ultimately, though, I believe that with the erosion in the doctor–patient relationship comes erosion in doctor–patient trust. With erosion in trust comes erosion in actual health. With erosion in the doctor–patient relationship, outside forces believe that they can achieve health from a cookbook or an online manual. Doctors become 'healthcare providers' and health becomes a point on a scattergram.[12]

Dr. Bruce Rubin, physician-in-chief of the Children's Hospital of Richmond and chair of the department of pediatrics at Virginia Commonwealth University's Medical School, is another physician leader with whom we've worked for more than a decade. He discussed how insurers' increasing monitoring and financial control over physicians' use of medical tests and prescribing behavior have interfered with physician–patient relationships,

> There is an increasingly greater burden placed on physicians if we need to obtain tests or begin medications that we believe are essential for our patients. I care for complex patients who often require the

---

The Patient's Viewpoint: Cancer Survivor

Andy Fleischmann

In what ways have your relationships with your physicians changed generally over the past few years?
Doctors are more hurried than they have ever been—and that's a problem that will likely worsen in the coming years. In my experience, this time pressure means that, unless you as a patient are ready to ask questions and be your own advocate—even when the physician looks like he wants to get to the door—you won't be able to build much of a relationship at all.

How do you personally build trust with your doctors?
By asking clear questions and making it explicit that I want replies that involve full disclosure of all information—no "sugarcoating" to make things "easier" for me.

What is important for you to do at the outset of the relationship?
Make sure that the physician I am meeting with matches the references and descriptions I've gotten. And, if I have concerns, raising them early and clearly.

How does building trust with your doctors require personal sacrifices on your part?
I have found that many specialists are focused on their science, not their patients, unfortunately. (Primary care physicians are more patient-focused—but also, sad to say, people whom you see much less of when a health crisis arises.) So, typically, building any sort of bond requires extra effort from the patient—since the doctor is seeking to meet with his or her next patient as quickly as possible.

---

use of medications off label or medications or devices that are not normally used for children. Invariably, these requests are denied initially by insurance carriers. It takes hours of phone calls to increasingly senior administrator physicians until I am able to convince powers-that-be that my recommendations are not only good for the patient but probably cost-effective for their company.

It is frustrating when my efforts are unsuccessful. When this happens, the senior-level administrator at the insurance company invariably tells me that I am free to prescribe whatever I consider important for my patient, but the insurance company has no obligation to pay for this care. This is always difficult to explain to the patients and their families. Even when I've spent hours on the phone I go away from this feeling that I have not tried hard enough.[13]

More generally, patients' trust in the healthcare system overall remains in short supply,[14] and distrust between doctors and managed care, between nurses and doctors, between doctors and hospitals, and between patients and managed care is on the rise. In a *Harvard Business*

Review article titled "Turning Doctors into Leaders," Thomas Lee wrote, "At many hospitals relationships between doctors and administrators are downright antagonistic, and financial interests are poorly aligned or even in direct conflict."[15] Morale among physicians is low due to the limited time they are allotted with patients, the lack of autonomy they have in making decisions about patient care, and the quality of health-care they are able to provide.[16] These structural changes have resulted in reduced trust in the healthcare system.[17] Importantly, the erosion of trust compromises medical outcomes by endangering "patients' lives and well-being."[18]

☐ The Challenges to Building Trust in Healthcare Contexts

A number of physician leaders discussed with us several forces that have combined to hinder their ability to build trust with their patients. One such force is the role that insurance companies play. As Dr. Senior noted,

> Insurance carriers require more and more approvals for care that I provide. I must fill out forms for the prescribing of medicines, the determination of the need for surgery, the determination of the need for a CT scan. A faceless individual then looks at those forms and based on the boxes I check, determines whether what I have sug-gested for the benefit of the patient over, in some cases, hours of interactions, is really appropriate or not.[19]

Dr. Rubin also commented:

> One of the big changes in medical practice is that we have much less time to talk [with] and to listen to what our patients have to tell us. The time spent talking to patients, listening to them, building a rela-tionship, and understanding their concerns are incredibly important. This is important today, but we have much less time for this because of the increasing burden of documentation in the electronic medical record. Third-party payers demand extensive documentation with the belief that what is not documented has not been done. I only see this increasing, in the guise of either accountable care organizations or increased measurement and monitoring of outcomes.[20]

Both Dr. Senior and Dr. Rubin bemoaned the unintended negative con-sequences for trust-building with the shift to electronic medical records. As Dr. Senior stated,

Government mandates "quality." The government has mandated that all practices begin using electronic medical records. In the past, doctors hand-wrote the critical information about a patient on a piece of paper and seconds after reading these concise documents, we knew the issues of concern. With the higher-quality electronic medical record, we now have to literally wade through multiple pages of gibberish and unnecessary "documenting" that fulfills mandates, but does nothing for care.[21]

Dr. Rubin concurred, saying,

Because of changes in healthcare and increasing demands for complex electronic medical record documentation, much more of my time is spent staring at a computer screen than examining and talking with the patient. I'm distressed to see that the residents spend far more time staring at a computer screen in their workroom than at patients' bedside. Of course, when the patients don't see us they can assume that they are not receiving care, out of sight, out of mind. All of this conspires to make it more difficult to gain and sustain trust.[22]

Dr. Senior and Dr. Rubin also both discussed how new work rules for residents have reduced physician–patient contact time, further eroding trust. Here, Dr. Rubin and then Dr. Senior elaborated in emails to us,

Work-hour restrictions for residents have negatively affected our ability to build trust with our patients! "How?" you ask. Resident duty-hour restrictions, where residents now literally have to always keep an eye on the clock in order to avoid being in violation, have resulted in a generation of doctors being trained to believe that doctoring is time-limited shift work. The sense of medicine being a "calling" has been lost, further eroding the doctor–patient relationship. This has further eroded the confidence of the public in doctors in general, resulting in acceptance by the public of greater insertion by other forces into that relationship. "Sorry that you are bleeding, Mrs. Jones, but I must leave now, because my shift is up." This is unacceptable in anyone's eyes; however, the response to solving the problem is vastly different among different groups. "Old-fashioned" doctors respond by saying you stay and solve the problem for the patient. But government agencies respond by establishing rules about how to pass off patients to new doctors. Which response results in greater trust by the patient?[23]

   With the introduction of resident work-hour requirements, residents-in-training are not allowed to stay and provide continuity of care for their patients. Once they've reached their mandated work hours, they are required to leave and sign out of the hospital, even if they choose to stay on, and even if they have had adequate rest. I recall becoming extremely involved in the care of patients and felt it was my duty and honor to remain with them during critical moments of their illness and care. Work-hour rules make this difficult, if not impossible, for residents-in-training today.[24]

Sometimes, conflicting messages that patients receive from other physicians before they see a specialist interferes with trust-building, including when the stakes are particularly high. In these situations, transparent communication to build trust in terms of openness and compassion becomes critically important. Dr. John Gordon is codirector of Dominion Fertility in Arlington, Virginia. He is also a clinical faculty member of the George Washington University Department of Obstetrics and Gynecology and the Medical College of Virginia/Virginia Commonwealth University School of Medicine. As Dr. Gordon told us,

> As a physician practicing in the field of reproductive medicine, trust is absolutely critical to all aspects of my interactions with my patients. Although some patients do have insurance coverage for fertility treatment, over half or more of the patients ultimately will have to pay out-of-pocket if they pursue advanced reproductive technologies such as in vitro fertilization. This lack of insurance coverage has the advantage of completely engaging the patient in their healthcare decisions. Suddenly every dollar spent is a dollar out of their pocket, and their approach to decision making, I believe, is far different than if a third-party entity, such as an insurance company, is footing the bill. My goal is to present the options to the couple in a light which allows them, with my direction, to make an informed decision. When considering these treatments, which cost from $2,000 to $30,000 an attempt, these discussions are very important. A couple who pursues six months of treatment, at $5,000 a cycle, could easily run through the resources that they have put aside for family building.
>
> So when patients initially present for discussion of their fertility treatment options, building trust with them is crucial. It is crucial because if they believe that you do not have their best interest at heart, and are simply pursuing economic gain, they will quickly abandon not only your clinic but also possibly their attempts at family building (which could be unfortunate as the majority of our patients ultimately do obtain success).
>
> I am also faced with dealing with preconceived ideas. In their well-meaning way, an OB/GYN generalist will pronounce that they see absolutely no barrier to a patient conceiving and not to worry, in spite of the fact that fertility in women markedly declines

after the age of 35. Week after week, I am forced to tell professional women over the age of 43 that their chances for a successful pregnancy and delivery with their own eggs is vanishingly small, even though just a week before their doctor shared with them platitudes such as, "I am sure you have the eggs of a 20-year-old." Unfortunately, unless that physician has invented some sort of time machine, that patient's eggs have been around since the day she was born, and if she is 45 at this point, then so are her eggs. The monthly chance of pregnancy at age 45 is less than 1%, with a 50% rate of pregnancy loss (compared with peak human fertility, which is 25% pregnancy rate per month, with a 10–12% pregnancy-loss rate).

Our patients are also extremely motivated and spend hours on the internet researching their condition, which can make my job difficult, as anybody with good HTML programming skills can make a very impressive website and claim to be an expert in fertility. This has led to the phenomenon of certain laypersons becoming self-proclaimed fertility coaches and Internet chat room bullies. They readily criticize the plans that have been initiated by a patient's own physician, claiming superior medical knowledge and often directing patients to their own physician who, by some miracle, has overcome all odds in delivering them a baby when no other physician in the country was willing to treat them. This story plays out day after day, and in building trust I must overcome many preconceived notions and misinformation that has been nurtured through hours of web surfing.

So in building trust with my patients, I seek to explain to them normal physiology and discuss with them the results of previous tests. I explain why certain tests are appropriate and then from there review with them a range of treatment options based upon the test results.[25]

☐ The Benefits of Trust in Healthcare Providers

Trust in physicians is related to several healthcare outcomes. First, trust is highly correlated with patient satisfaction,[26,27] even though trust is forward-looking and satisfaction is based on past experiences.[28] Second, trust in physicians is positively related to patient loyalty.[29,30,31] Healing itself depends on patients being willing to work together with their healthcare providers, which in turn is based on mutual trust. Patients who trust their physicians visit them often,[32] and the more they trust their healthcare providers, the more they are interested and willing to actively improve their own health.[33] As Dr. Senior observed,

> Trust is a two-way street. Just as they need to trust me, I need to trust them. So just as I hope to offer reliability, openness, competence, and compassion, all of which take time, I need the same from my patients. Trust of a patient in me is good, but trust in each other is a relationship. Trust is necessary for healing. It is unlikely in my world that patients will get better if there is no trust.[34]

☐ Building Trust in Healthcare at the Personal Level of Change

At the individual level, courage, humility, and authenticity are once again essential foundations for a healthcare leader to build trust with others and be an effective change agent in the long term. Consistent with leaders in other contexts, physician leaders will be more effective in motivating their followers if they can learn to be servant leaders.[35,36] Physicians can learn to be servant leaders if they first learn to be good followers. By learning what they like and don't like in other leaders when they occupy subordinate positions as residents and fellows, they will be more effective at modeling their behavior accordingly when they move into leadership positions. Followership occurs naturally when individuals are trained in medical school, residencies, and fellowships, yet physicians-in-training often don't realize they will be working in *teams* once they finish their medical education.[37] Indeed, a new breed of leader is needed to manage complexities in the healthcare context that demand teamwork.[38] Not only is this new breed of leader a team player, but he or she is someone who must communicate effectively with colleagues, and who works hard to effect positive change in processes to achieve better patient outcomes. Dr. Lobdell shared his own approach to medical teamwork and some of its challenges and rewards,

> With respect to building trust with patients, I try to lead with transparency and honesty. We have more information about the work we do and how we manage it than ever before. I try to share this information with our patients, their families, and the medical team in order to provide care that we all envision. It takes longer to relate information through a team basis to our patients, but it will pay dividends in the long term.
>
> We work continuously at building trust: working our way through conflict, getting committed, holding ourselves accountable,

and producing results. These are the fundamentals of teamwork and we've reinforced them through our daily work and regular meetings.

Our approach to teamwork, with trust as a foundation, has helped us perform at a high level, as evidenced by the Society of Thoracic Surgeons three-star rating for two programs under our auspices.[39] The three-star rating by the Society of Thoracic Surgeons is achieved by only the top 15% of adult cardiac surgery programs in the United States.[40]

This new breed of leader might be developed through efforts such as the multiple-mini interview that has emerged at eight medical schools in the United States.[41] This technique is similar to speed dating, in that prospective medical school applicants are subjected to a series of interviews to demonstrate their social skills. These medical schools have found that whereas physicians may be competent technically, they are not always socially competent, which can risk quality patient care. Bob Lintz (retired plant manager, General Motors) has served on the board of trustees of the Cleveland Clinic for many years and is now helping lead the Clinic's quality improvement strategy. He told us,

> The Cleveland Clinic is pursuing the same kind of cultural efforts like the one I led with the General Motors Parma plant. They are pursuing a very similar approach, realizing full well that with approximately 42,000 people, having a common culture that focuses on initiatives to improve the patient's experience is key to being the best. The objective is winning together as a total unit and sharing best practices. They are developing a culture that creates an understanding that every employee in one way or another is a caregiver and impacts the patient experience. These are the same kinds of cultural issues we integrated at General Motors . . . efforts to engage all employees with safety and quality as the overriding priorities. It's kind of déjà vu, quite honestly. But, we're dealing with a very different kind of a structure than we have in General Motors.
>
> They have very gifted groups of leaders in both the medical and administration communities at each hospital. To maximize the synergy of all that talent and work as "one unit" they have developed common performance measurements under an umbrella of transparency, mutual respect, and trust.
>
> While all employees are involved in the change process to maximize the patient experience, it has become obvious how important the doctor's role is in meeting their goals. We are in a world now where patients expect that their doctors have a good bedside manner. However, physicians are not formally educated in interpersonal

people skills or communication skills when dealing with the patient. The clinic is identifying those physicians that have weaknesses in these areas and training is being provided to improve their performance.

From my own personal viewpoint, what I love seeing at the Cleveland Clinic Hospitals is that they are creating an atmosphere where some ongoing historical problems associated with providing healthcare are now looked upon as an opportunity for improvement . . . using the same type of employee engagement and problem-solving techniques we utilize at GM to improve our dedication to the customer.

At the interpersonal level, the healthcare context is unique in that a wide variety of stakeholders directly impact the ultimate customer—the patient. Healthcare leaders must not only build trust among their colleagues, but must also build trust with their patients. Indeed, increasing demands for outcome-based performance[42] require building trust with patients. Patient trust is critical to numerous healthcare outcomes, including patient compliance, as well as lower rates of morbidity, mortality. A 2006 article appearing in the *European Journal of Public Health* noted, "Trust has traditionally been considered a cornerstone of effective doctor–patient relationships."[43] Seventy-five percent of patients believe their physicians to be the most trustworthy sources of healthcare information, but 50% still look to sources other than a doctor for information about their health.[44] Moreover, when it comes to actually making the right decisions about their healthcare, only 43% of individuals trust their physicians, 44% trust their nurses, 22% trust their hospitals, 13% trust their pharmaceutical companies, and only 8% trust their managed care plans.[45]

☐ Building Trust in Healthcare at the Interpersonal Level of Change

As with other leaders, physicians must be able to demonstrate each of the four components of the ROCC of Trust. At the outset of their interactions with physicians and other healthcare practitioners, patients demand reliability. In particular, increasingly, they are fed up with being unable to see their physicians at the appointed time and with the associated excessive waiting times. In a recent survey, nearly half of 3,200 respondents said that patients should receive a discount on their bill if they are kept waiting.[46] Physicians must also, of course, be considered competent, not only by their patients but also by their staff members.[47,48,49] Although patients may find it difficult to assess competence *ex ante*, they trust their physicians in part to the extent they actually demonstrate such competence.[50,51,52,53] Patients also trust physicians based on how open and honest they are,[54,55] whether they demonstrate respect for the patient's views,[56] and whether they convey compassion.[57] Indeed, physician caring and empathy was rated as the most important attribute in a 2004 study. This is demonstrated when patients feel "they are treated as distinct and valuable persons."[58]

What follows are some examples from our own extensive experience with physicians and nurses who have demonstrated the ROCC of Trust consistently over many years.[59] They all take as much time as necessary to listen carefully to our symptoms and concerns so that they can develop a complete diagnosis and treatment plan. In these efforts, they collaborate with teams of nurses, physician fellows, and others who assist in diagnosis and follow-up. Ultimately, we are assured that they have our best interests at heart and are providing us with sound and competent care. Our physicians who have demonstrated the ROCC of Trust have exceptional listening skills, which have been found to be critical for trust between physicians and patients.[60] They take sufficient time to ensure that we are included fully in any treatment plan, involving us in decisions about our options. This approach is also important for creating a sense of partnership and trust between patients and physicians.[61] The doctors explain,

> Because I am in a quality-of-life profession, I think it is essential for me to understand what it is that is bothering the patient. That requires listening. (Dr. Brent Senior, UNC–Chapel Hill Medical School)
>
> I build trust with my patients, both the children and their caregivers, by taking the time to really listen and understand what their concerns are. And I do my best to make sure they know I understand this and will do my best to answer them. As a pediatrician, my patient is not only the child but also the family and caregivers. It is important to address what concerns the parents or the caretakers have, but equally important is to learn the child's understanding and their concerns, as this can be quite different. Also, the magic doesn't hurt![62]
>
> At the start of the doctor–patient relationship, I tell them that I truly want to understand and try and find answers for their concerns, but there are many things that I do not know and cannot determine. I want to be honest with them, even when I don't have the answers that they hope for. I also make them aware that I care for other patients; thus, when I am spending time with them, I need to focus on their care, but I need to do the same for the other patients under my care as well. They need to know that they—and others—can count on me.

I find it helps for the patients to understand my limitations, limitations in knowledge and in time. In my position, with "Physician-in-Chief" embroidered on my coat and referrals from around the world, I don't have to prove competence as much as I need to remind my patients of the limitations of our—my—knowledge.

Building trust with my patients does not require a great deal of sacrifice on my part. It is part of what I do. In the long run, I believe it makes communication in patient care better. (Dr. Bruce Rubin, Virginia Commonwealth Medical School)

Dr. David Pawsat is the founder and physician leader of the Center for Optimal Health, a Lansing, Michigan, integrative medicine practice (www.cfohealth.com). We learned about him through a member of our own Trust Network, Melanie Bergeron (chair, Two Men and a Truck, International). Our teenage daughter, Maggie, has suffered from chronic sinus infections and side effects from several courses of antibiotics and steroids. We were anxious to find a real solution to Maggie's health issues. When we visited Dr. Pawsat, he explained his own journey from emergency-room physician to integrative medicine specialist as a result of his own health issues, which are also chronicled on the center's website,

What he did not realize, at the time, was his energy, progressive fatigue, and 40-pound weight gain was also due to an undiagnosed thyroid condition. After initiating conventional medical therapy with minimal improvement, it became apparent that health goes far beyond one pill a day.

After this realization, Dr. Pawsat began to study the fields of Alternative, Integrative and Anti-Aging Medicine. It quickly became apparent how far-reaching the research and evidence had become that prevention and healing begins with a sound physiologic balance of nutrition and hormonal balance. He found a prevalent part of the medical community in Europe, Asia, and even the West Coast of the United States used scientifically sound methods for creating physiologically sound healing.[63]

Dr. Pawsat courageously left his career in emergency medicine to launch a medical practice that integrated Eastern and Western philosophies, focused on the whole person, and aimed at treating not symptoms but their underlying causes. Dr. Pawsat's humility emanates from overcoming his own health struggles, and in recognizing that as an ER physician, he had only really treated symptoms for the chronically ill patients. His authenticity is based on working with his patients to improve their health holistically, using the same approaches he has used on himself.

The most important step Dr. Pawsat took for Maggie was to remove inflammatory foods from her diet, including wheat, eggs, soy, dairy, and peanuts. A blood test confirmed that she was, indeed, allergic to wheat. Eliminating wheat alone resulted in a dramatic improvement in Maggie's allergy and sinus symptoms and her overall health. Dr. Pawsat then worked with Maggie to eliminate other chronic health problems stemming from her use of antibiotics and steroids. Every step of the way, Dr. Pawsat provided hope for Maggie that she would recover her health completely, and she has made a dramatic improvement.

Neurologist Alan Finkel, one of the founding physicians of the Carolina Headache Institute (www.carolinaheadacheinstitute.com), routinely spends two hours with each new patient as a standard practice. For him to understand the complexities of migraines and other headaches from which his patients suffer, he not only asks his patients about their medical history, but also about their personal histories. He does this to understand how environmental, family history, and other factors may have contributed to the patient's current symptoms. As part of his initial evaluation, Dr. Finkel spends significant time explaining how headaches can develop, and he then provides a range of options on which he and the patient both agree before medical treatment commences.

Dr. Brent Senior often receives referrals to his ENT practice from other surgeons and physicians who have exhausted their own range of solutions and ideas for treating chronic sinusitis and related medical problems. This is how we came to know him, after Aneil had seen more than a half dozen ENT specialists, including one at the Mayo Clinic following sinus surgery in 1999. Although he did not cause any of Aneil's problems, Dr. Senior was more than willing to work with him in a highly collaborative fashion and was willing to consult with other medical experts with whom Aneil had worked as part of his efforts to heal. This included collaborating with Dr. Rubin and Dr. Finkel, who was providing treatment for Aneil's sinus pain and headaches. A decade later, Dr. Senior continues to work on finding a long-term treatment for Aneil's symptoms, now recognized as "empty nose syndrome," which afflicts thousands of other patients.

Assuming that the physician has the requisite competence, reliability, and openness, perhaps the most crucial dimension of trust for these professionals is compassion. Behaviors that demonstrate caring and empathy include eye contact, body language facing the patient, active listening, and an ability to explain information such that the patient understands. Dr. Rubin personally demonstrated his compassion for Aneil when he agreed to take him on as a patient beginning in 2000. This may not be remarkable except for the fact that Dr. Rubin's practice specializes in pediatrics (although adults clearly also benefit from his research into effective treatments for cystic fibrosis). He recognized that Aneil had exhausted other avenues for help, and he felt called to help Aneil in any possible way. Dr. Rubin's compassion extends to *all* of his patients. As a physician at

Wake Forest University, he was not compensated for any of his clinical time, which was extensive. His research grant money paid his entire salary and benefits, as well as that of his research team. More than a decade later, he continues to see Aneil as a patient and is building a medical research team to find successful treatments for empty nose syndrome and related symptoms. Demonstrating his compassion, Dr. Senior travels to Vietnam every year using his own money and that from philanthropic donations so that he can train ENTs in that country and provide *pro bono* care. And, Dr. Finkel has started an initiative to help soldiers at Fort Bragg, North Carolina, to help them with their headaches related to post-traumatic stress disorder. All of these physicians care for their patients, wherever they may find them, with deep compassion.

Chris Morton, MD

Dr. Morton is a pediatrician with Chapel Hill Pediatrics and Adolescents in North Carolina who has been our children's primary care physician since 2004. He is one of the most dedicated, thoughtful, and caring healers we know. Dr. Morton always takes the time to listen to *both* our children and us. One of the reasons our teenagers like him is that he talks *to* them, not *at* them. *They* are his patients and he wants to know how they are feeling, and what they think about his treatment options. They feel respected by him and so they respect him and follow his directions. It is not always easy to get an appointment with him because so many families love Dr. Morton, but when we have the option of waiting for him for a check-up, our kids always ask for him. He is conservative in his treatments while being open to new approaches, and he closely collaborates with his fellow physicians in their practice so that our kids will always be taken care of.

☐ Building Trust in Healthcare at the Systemic Level of Change

At the systemic level of change, trusted leaders involve others in decision making to create effective teams, communicate openly, create a culture of inclusiveness that values people and their efforts, and eliminate bureaucracy with human resource management policies that promote trust.[64] However, considering the difficulty in developing trust within and across teams we've discussed in previous chapters, we would argue that Cardinal Health's innovative approaches to developing bridges across various interdependent elements in healthcare is helping to develop systemic trust in the healthcare industry. George Barrett, CEO of Cardinal Health, provided us with several examples. One example is disseminating best practices in cancer treatment,

> We try to play an informed, knowledgeable advisor who has a clear understanding of the integration of the system, or the poor integration, or at least the interdependent views of the systems. We also recognize that there are places that we don't really influence this.
>
> I'll give you an example of one where we do. We just recently acquired a company that is now part of Cardinal Health Specialty Solutions. This business focuses on specialty disease areas, with an initial focus on oncology. Much of our work is about integrating the interdependent healthcare elements.
>
> So Cardinal Health Specialty Solution works with oncologists to provide a number of services and tools to help them run their practices. At the same time, we also work with them to analyze their clinical outcomes data.
>
> From that data, we can help them define the optimal clinical pathways for treating a particular cancer.
>
> It sounds like that should be obvious, in that every physician practice would do that. The truth is that there is plenty of literature around best practices, but compliance with these best practices tends to be uneven. It's helpful for us to be able to assist physician practices with using their own clinical data to inform decisions around standardization.
>
> This is also of interest to those who are paying for the treatment—who see the inefficiency of poor adherence to clinical pathways. We help the community oncologists work with payers to better align incentives to encourage adherence.
>
> So, in this way we've been able to serve as a bridge between the payer and the physician—working to improve outcomes, while at the same time increasing efficiency of the system and decreasing cost.[65]

This innovative approach also helps physician leaders keep up to date with the exploding amount of new medical knowledge that can inform and disseminate best practices. Cardinal Health also helps to improve efficiency in another major segment of the healthcare sector, pharmaceuticals. Again, George Barrett,

> We can also improve the overall efficiency of the system by helping pharmacies evaluate generic alternatives. This is very important since 75% of prescriptions in the U.S. are filled with generic pharmaceuticals. A pharmacist may not readily have all the information on which drugs are available generically.

By building formularies of these generic products that are available and can be appropriately substituted, providing that information to pharmacies, taking advantage of our scale, and aggregating demand, we help pharmacists run their pharmacies most efficiently by giving them opportunity to access drugs at a lower cost. We are able to do so because we are aggregating the demand over many, many thousands of pharmacies.[66]

A third area in which Cardinal Health also helps to improve efficiency in healthcare is in the hospital arena. George Barrett described the company's approach,

As a hypothetical example, a hospital might use many different sizes, weights, and colors of gauze across the various departments. While it makes sense to stock a certain number of gauze products according to clinical needs, there is likely some product redundancy. Take a sterile six-ply gauze pad of a specific size for instance. If one department likes the round pad, another department likes the square pad, and a third department likes the beige color versus white, etc., then there is inefficiency associated with ordering, stocking, and handling all those product versions when there is no real clinical differentiation. The hospital may not even realize the duplication. That requires access to information, and a perspective that really is about cost effectiveness and getting quality outcomes in the most efficient way.

Hospitals and hospital systems increasingly understand that in order for them to thrive and to deliver quality care, they have to be very efficient. We can be enormously helpful to these big institutions—to help them run the "business" of delivering care.[67]

To build trust with others, physicians must also learn how to be good team members, learn how to communicate and disagree in a healthy manner, and take time to listen to each other.[68] An excellent example of this approach is when Dr. Bruce Rubin of Virginia Commonwealth University (VCU) was involved in the merger of two medical organizations. He explained:

Soon after arriving at VCU, the department of pediatrics began a merger process with the Children's Hospital of Richmond, a chronic care and rehabilitation facility. This merger strengthened the continuum of care that we provide and increased opportunities to provide better care for the children in the region. However, change is always viewed with suspicion by some—including employees at both places and, surprisingly, by some pediatricians in the community.

I was fortunate that I could spend many Fridays during my first six months meeting with community pediatricians in their offices, discussing problems and things that we were doing right at VCU, and hearing their concerns about this merger.

I also began to care for patients at the Children's Hospital site on a regular basis, which really let me see the inner workings of this great hospital and a culture that put children first. This was something we had not been able to do as a children's hospital within a hospital at a large and busy academic medical center. To the satisfaction of the nurses and other staff, I established that I was not just an administrator but also a competent physician.

The merger has been successful for everybody and, most importantly, for the children of Virginia. We continue to grow and to build.[69]

Another physician leader with whom we have worked for several years, Dr. Kevin Lobdell of Carolinas HealthCare System, has created systemic-level change. Dr. Lobdell began a quality improvement program in 2004 to advance cardiac surgery outcomes. He and his medical team focused on extubating heart patients sooner following surgery in order to improve their morbidity and mortality outcomes, and enhance the operational efficiency of the critical care unit. As Figure 9.1 shows, the percentage of patients who suffered mortality declined from approximately 4% to far less than 1%, and those who had to be on a ventilator for a prolonged period of time decreased from 14% to less than 4% following the changes instituted by Dr. Lobdell and his team.

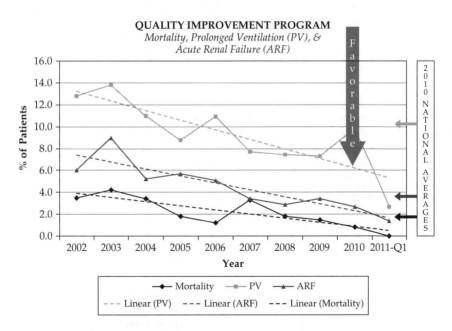

FIGURE 9.1 Quality Improvements in Patient Care

At the personal level of change, Dr. Lobdell developed and demonstrated courage, humility, and authenticity. Courage was necessary to challenge the status quo of patient outcomes, which were not improving substantially over time, and practices that needed to be changed to improve those outcomes. Some of his humility resulted from an automobile accident, which left him unable to continue his surgical specialty as a pediatric cardiovascular surgeon. The accident, in fact, required him to reinvent his career. His authenticity was developed over time through several executive education programs and executive coaching, which helped him identify his leadership strengths. By developing trust-based relationships among physicians, nurses, and other specialists, Dr. Lobdell and his team have changed the way they work together and how their unit is perceived within the hospital system. Equally important, they have achieved significant improvements in extubation times, acute renal failure

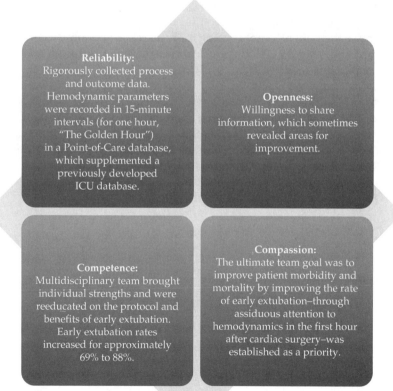

FIGURE 9.2   The ROCC of Trust at Carolinas Healthcare

rates, and mortality rates that have been sustained over several years and that are several times better than national averages. As he and coauthors note in one of their peer-reviewed articles, "The importance of trust in the change process cannot be underestimated. Trust should be considered the foundation for a cohesive and effective team. Only with trust can a team deal with conflict, become committed, be held accountable, and focus on results."[70] Dr. Lobdell and his colleagues built the ROCC first with one another and subsequently were able to do so with their patients. The ways in which each of the pieces of the ROCC of Trust were built are described in Figure 9.2.

An area for ongoing research is the degree to which physicians need to trust their patients in order to achieve positive medical outcomes. Although it may seem like common sense that mutual trust is essential between physician and patient for them to collaborate and achieve enhanced patient compliance, this is not an area we have formally investigated yet. Research has found that physicians who have greater trust in their patients create an atmosphere of open communication,[71] which is critical to collaboration, and reduces the need for the physician and his or her staff to monitor the patient. Another area for research is how physician leaders develop other leaders. As one physician has noted, "As a leader, your job is to create other leaders."[72]

As this chapter has shown, trust between physicians and patients is critical as healthcare changes and evolves. As patients, we have less time with our physicians due to managed healthcare; consequently, we want to trust that our physicians will remember us and our medical issues in that short amount of time. When physicians have less time with their patients due to managed healthcare, they, too, want to trust that their patients will do what they have suggested. For both patient and physician alike, the goal is to become healthier and stay healthy.

Trust Tips

1. **Reliability:** *Ensure that the actions you take are consistent with the best evidence-based medical practices known.*
2. **Openness:** *One of the most important things a physician can learn to do is to listen to his or her patient. Help him or her feel that no one else is more important in the moments you have with that patient.*
3. **Competence:** *Act in ways that reinforce the professionalism that your credentials claim.*
4. **Compassion:** *Help your patients and staff see that you have their best interests at heart—that you truly care about others.*

Rebuilding Trust

☐ Trust Takes Time to Build, and Rebuilding Trust Takes Longer

It is more than ironic that we were working on this chapter when Aneil received a phone call out of the blue from a leading talent management firm with which he had been developing a strategic partnership for more than a year. Aneil's Human Resources Executive Education unit at Michigan State University (MSU) and this firm were planning to launch an innovative program for senior HR leaders, with only four months before launch. The program had taken months to develop and Aneil had spent hundreds and hundreds of hours developing the program and marketing strategies. It represented a significant fraction of his responsibilities, and he had staked his reputation on the program's success. Several people at the firm had reassured him many times that it was very important for the program to succeed. As such, he was then taken completely by surprise when one of the firm's senior partners, an individual who had originally started the program, said,

> I've been tasked to deliver some bad news. The new executive in charge of leadership development programs has decided to focus on custom programs and e-learning and to put the program and the relationship with MSU on indefinite hold, which means to end it. The people at the top asked me to deliver the bad news, because they didn't have the guts to do it themselves.

After he hung up the phone, Aneil felt as if he'd been punched in the stomach. He realized once again that promises can be broken quite easily, and that the reality of others' self-interest can trump their rhetoric of partnership. Over the next several weeks, he sought to find a way to salvage the program he had worked so hard to develop. He reached out to other talent management firms and MSU alumni who had already started helping him market the program. Some of the individuals Aneil contacted were actually glad the talent management firm had said goodbye, although they were disturbed by the way the news had been delivered. These individuals, who were from competitor firms, would now be in a position to help Aneil to a greater extent than prior to this highly distasteful incident.

It is more than our personal experiences, however, that have motivated us to write about trust violations and rebuilding trust. The importance of understanding how to rebuild trust was also apparent when Karen presented our research on teams and trust at a conference at the University of Michigan. When she asked the group whether there was something about the topic that still needed to be discussed, several people—nearly simultaneously—asked, "How do you rebuild trust? Can you ever fix broken trust?" These professionals, who were charged with building strong teams at the University of Michigan, Michigan State University, and Wayne State University, were all frustrated in their attempts to mend broken relationships. They felt there was no easy way to do this.

Trust is built over time, as we share experiences with others. Over time, we weigh our level of trust with others based on our experiences with them.[1] Positive experiences reinforce our trusting beliefs, and trust grows. With negative experiences, our level of trust is typically reevaluated. We either decrease trust in specific areas or decrease our overall level of trust.[2,3] Distrust, then, is not the absence of trust, but rather an expectation that another will not act in a trustworthy manner, based on our previous interactions with that party.[4] Some scholars have argued that only certain dimensions of trustworthiness are involved when it comes to distrusting others.[5,6] Before trust can actually be violated, some distrust may begin to pervade a relationship, because the other party fails to reciprocate when we first attempt to build trust with that person.[7,8] Given that distrust can be triggered by suspicion,[9] and that some people are predisposed to be suspicious,[10] it is not surprising that distrust can develop so easily.

Based on our research, consulting, and coaching, and that of others, we don't believe it is important to distinguish loss of trust versus distrust or to argue that losing trust is based on certain dimensions and distrust is based on other dimensions. In the examples we discuss here, you will learn about behaviors that contribute to building trust and see that the opposite of these behaviors destroys that trust. What really matters, then, is how you work to rebuild trust, repair trust violations, and/or overcome distrust. We use these phrases synonymously. How long it actually takes to rebuild/repair/overcome, and how much effort it takes, may be a function of which dimension has been violated. Rebuilding trust is a function, moreover, of how frequently violations have occurred, how much is at stake, and how much emotion is involved.

☐ Rebuilding Trust at the Personal and Interpersonal Levels of Change

Unlike building trust, in which an individual can act unilaterally to build trust with someone else, rebuilding trust requires the other party to interact with us—both people involved in an exchange must deliberately choose to repair the broken relationship. We define trust repair as a "willingness to be vulnerable to the other party following a decline in that willingness."[11] Courage, humility, and authenticity are all involved, on the part of either the trust violator, the one whose trust has been violated, or both.

First, if our trust has been violated, it takes courage and openness to share this difficult information. Trust can be violated and the other person may not realize an infringement has occurred. It is difficult to tell someone that you don't trust them anymore, or that you trust them less than you used to trust them. It is a difficult thing to think and an even more difficult thing to tell. If we value the relationship, however, we will tell the person they have acted in an untrustworthy way. Only then can you take steps to repair the relationship. Second, the trust violator, in turn, must be humble enough to acknowledge what has happened and take the time to understand both your message and the emotional aspects involved. Third, the person must then actually apologize for violating the other's trust, and the sooner the better.[12,13,14,15,16] Apologizing obviously requires humility. Research has found that apologies work best if the trust breach appears to be an isolated event.[17] The person must acknowledge the wrongdoing or mistake, apologize for it, and promise that it will be corrected. If the person is a leader, all of this must be done in a visible, even public, fashion. This initial act may begin repairing and rebuilding trust.[18] As Dr. Kevin Lobdell told us, "It is imperative that we explain completely and quickly when we make mistakes or trust is eroded. We need to be authentic and genuine in the process."[19] Apologies are not necessarily easy, however. As Pastor Jim Wenger (Faith Lutheran Church in Okemos, Michigan) shared,

> The maturity to say we are truly sorry and to take responsibility for our own mistakes doesn't come easily. The temptation to save face and blame someone else or to blame circumstances is an easy way out. But if there is a misunderstanding, if there have been hard feelings,

taking ownership of how our own actions may have contributed to the misunderstanding immediately lessens the defensiveness that leaves people divided and on opposite sides.

Apologies are not sufficient for trust repair, however.[20] Following any apology, the behavior of the trust violator obviously should be consistent with the apology.[21] To truly repair trust, the violator must understand how trust came to be violated in the first place.[22] This requires the violator to ask the victim what is necessary from their perspective to repair the trust. Asking "How can I make this up to you?" is a good start. This requires the violator to be authentic, because it involves recognizing that there has been a breach between the violator's espoused values or behavior and the actual ones. By listening to the victim, the trust violator must acknowledge that he or she did not live up to the expectations of the one who was trusting, and then find ways to repair the damage. If the victim lets the violator begin to undertake a repair, then he or she is granting forgiveness and allowing the relationship to begin to be reinstated.[23] The violator then needs to follow through so that repair can begin. Importantly, the violator must also find ways to demonstrate trustworthiness in the future to reassure the victim that providing the violator with an opportunity for repairing the broken trust was justified. For reconciliation to actually take place, victims must evaluate several criteria, including whether they can live with the personal ramifications of the betrayal, whether they can live with the impact of the betrayal, and if the betrayer has learned from the mistake and will not cause harm again.[24]

Sometimes, repairing trust is not possible, and the only option is to exit the relationship. This might be because common ground no longer exists between the parties to come together, or because the rift between them is too vast. Further, the violation may be so emotionally hurtful that there appears to be no way to mend such a violation. Finally, if either party has no interest in repairing the breach, then exit is the only solution. As Brenda Bernstein (founder, TheEssayExpert.com) told us,

> I recently had two parents of college essay clients tell me they were dissatisfied with the services of one of my consultants. Unfortunately they did not tell me there was a problem until it was too late to give them the level of service they were very reasonably requesting. I asked them what they thought was fair in terms of a refund, and both of them came up with very fair arrangements. I refunded them immediately and let them know that the consultant would no longer be working with me. I lost not only their business, but also the business of the referrals they did not make. I learned some lessons.
>
> One of those lessons was about being up front with asking for complaints! There is a line in my terms of agreement that directs clients to

inform me immediately of any problems. However I have not been writing this in a welcome letter. My welcome letter now states,

> Please read our Terms of Agreement if you haven't already: http://www.theessayexpert.com/terms_of_agreement.html   From my perspective, the most important part of the agreement is that if at any time you are dissatisfied for any reason, please contact me immediately and I will do everything possible to address your concerns. The Essay Expert is committed to excellence and will not stand for anything else.

The other lesson is that I need to be very clear with my consultants that I want them to give specific, detailed, and involved feedback to clients. This consultant, though very qualified, had a different threshold than mine at which she felt she was doing too much to intervene with the students' writing. She no longer works with me. Rebuilding trust means putting integrity back in where it was out.

When Aneil turned down an offer to join the Management and Organizations Department at Columbia Business School just out of graduate school in 1992, several faculty members perceived he had violated their trust, because he had not indicated he was having second thoughts during the weekend he was considering three job offers from three leading universities. He simply informed one of his friends on the faculty that his decision was to accept another institution's offer. He then sent a formal follow-up letter to Columbia. When he learned they were upset, he called his friend in person to apologize. At the annual conference of management faculty that took place several months after his decision, one very senior member of the Columbia faculty pointedly told Aneil that he continued to be surprised and upset by Aneil's decision. What Aneil didn't know, but discovered later, was that for the second year in a row, their first-choice candidate had turned down this department. This contributed to the faculty being upset.

Aneil continued to feel badly about how he had handled the decision, and he didn't want any of the Columbia faculty to continue to harbor negative feelings toward him. Consequently, he reached out to one of the other senior members of the department's faculty. He asked if he could have a few minutes of his time during the conference to explain his decision. The faculty member agreed, and over the course of 15 minutes, Aneil apologized for the way that he had handled the decision, explained his thought process, and then said he hoped someday that this person would be able to accept his apology and possibly share it with others on the Columbia faculty. The faculty member responded that what Aneil had just done had taken a lot of guts, and thanked him for the apology.

Aneil subsequently invited this faculty member to serve on a panel discussion at an annual conference, and his invitation was accepted. The faculty member went on to provide helpful feedback on manuscripts Aneil wrote, and the two coauthored an article that was published in a top-ranked research journal several years later. Clearly, trust was restored. Of course, whether someone can repair a trust violation depends on whether the person whose trust has been violated is willing to continue in the relationship and not walk away.[25] Aneil benefited from the Columbia faculty member being willing to talk with Aneil, which gave Aneil an opportunity to repair the relationship's trust.

Trust repair involves both parties "as they attempt to resolve discrepancies in their beliefs."[26] If both parties are not willing to repair the broken trust, then it simply will not happen. If both parties are willing to repair the trust violation, however, then it is more likely that a direct confrontation will occur that will lead to trust repair.[27] What helps influence whether the person whose trust has been violated allows trust repair to occur depends on several factors, including whether the violation is considered deliberate, whether it has happened repeatedly, how severe it is, and how important the relationship is to the victim. The more deliberate, frequent, and severe the violation, the more likely that a negative emotional response such as anger or fear will emerge, which makes it more difficult for violated trust to be rebuilt.[28,29,30] The more important the relationship is to both parties, the more likely it is that trust repair can occur, perhaps because the person whose trust has been violated might give the

---

To me, trust is something (a gift) we give to ourselves. I say ourselves, because if we do not trust others, we begin to see ourselves as unworthy of trust.

The people, events, and circumstances that annoy us most indicate those areas within ourselves that we need to evaluate. If we see another as likely to cheat us in a given circumstance, it's because the thought of cheating has crossed our own minds in a similar circumstance, or perhaps we have cheated in those conditions. If someone calls us a parakeet, however, it's unlikely we would get upset, because we do not believe we remotely resemble such a bird.

The things we dislike most about others are the very things we dislike most in ourselves. This is why we dislike those things in the first place. Personally, when I have found the need to rebuild trust, it always starts with me understanding the other person's frame of reference. Rebuilding trust then starts with going within and seeing the other person as no different from me in this situation, which helps us offer the gift of forgiveness. In that way, we are really forgiving ourselves.

—*One of Aneil's Executive Education participants*

other party the benefit of the doubt. It may still prove very difficult, however, for trust repair to occur.

☐ The Challenge Leaders Face When Rebuilding Trust

The challenge of rebuilding trust is especially important for leaders. First, negative events are more salient and weigh more heavily than positive events, contributing to trust's fragility.[31] A leader's behavior that violates another's trust will have a greater impact than will trustworthy behaviors.[32] The prominence of any given untrustworthy behavior by the leader will be greater than for subordinates, because the leader has power over his or her them. Further, greater vulnerability makes "trust concerns more salient,"[33] which means that subordinates are more likely to remember their superior's violations. Subordinates, however, may be less likely to bring up trust violations involving their superiors because of dependence issues. The implication of this is that when the leader violates subordinates' trust, it is likely that subordinates will hold on to these trust violations rather than voice their concerns. They then may choose to exit the organization if the violation is significant enough.

At the teams and trust conference at which Karen presented, a university administrator asked Karen how to repair trust with her subordinate after she had promised her a raise. After budget cuts at her university, the administrator was forced to postpone the planned increase. She was embarrassed and had not yet talked to her subordinate face-to-face about going back on this promise. She was not sure how to proceed.

In this case, the situation was not a deliberate breach on the supervisor's part, but one of unfortunate timing. She wanted to give her subordinate a raise, but budgetary constraints would not permit it—at that time. She felt as if she was betraying her subordinate, with whom she had a wonderful relationship, but had not even apologized weeks later. Karen suggested that the first thing to do was to acknowledge the breach and apologize. Even if she could not control university budgets, she could acknowledge that she had made a promise, had to go back on that promise, and in doing so hurt the relationship. This alone would go a long way toward healing the relationship. Then, as Karen suggested, she could promise her subordinate that she would keep her informed about when and how she would be able to deliver on her promise and obtain that raise. This would eliminate any uncertainty or anxiety that this delay may have caused. Some leaders prefer secrecy in order to maintain a feeling of power, but research has shown that "rebuilding trust occurs in work environments where information is shared openly."[34]

☐ Bridging the Interpersonal and Systemic Levels of Change: Rebuilding Trust in Teams

In an ongoing project on trust and teams at Microsoft, Ross Smith and the 80 employees who work together on his team have identified numerous behaviors that build trust.[35] Independently, they each developed a list of behaviors they felt would lead them to trust others. They then voted on the most important of the behaviors presented and agreed to abide by them as a group. The top 10 behaviors Ross's group identified comprise our ROCC of Trust. The number following each behavior indicates the behavior's position in the group's list. Four behaviors focus on honesty or openness: be honest (1); have transparency in decision-making and actions (4); encourage open discussion (6); and be open and authentic (6). Three emphasize reliability: be a role model—have integrity (2); demonstrate integrity (3); and do what you say you are going to do (9). One deals with competence: model accountability by acknowledging mistakes and the lessons to be learned from it (10). And one encompasses compassion: respect the dignity of every person and role (5). A final behavior addresses listening: listen before you speak. Understand, diagnose (7). In our interview with Ross, he said that his method for addressing ways to prevent team members from distrusting one another was to simply invert the wording of each behavior, and then have team members identify aloud whenever a team member engaged in that negative behavior. Indeed, a recent study found that the most common ways trust is broken are quite similar to the negative behaviors that the Microsoft team identified, including poor communication, unwillingness to acknowledge mistakes, performance issues, inconsistency between words and behaviors, and disrespectful behavior.[36] What Ross's team did at Microsoft was to give each team member permission to highlight distrusting behaviors by first agreeing that they all wanted to live up to mutually identified trusting behaviors.

☐ Rebuilding Trust at the Systemic Level: Organizational Downsizing and Responding to Crisis

In our two decades researching organizational downsizing, we've learned that whether downsizing is a proactive strategy to improve the organization's competitiveness or is done reactively in response to change in the larger economic environment, it calls into question the trustworthiness of the organization's leadership.[37] This is the case for no other reason than it violates the compassion dimension of the ROCC of Trust. Some of the key findings we've made about downsizing and trust were achieved in the context of an industry-wide crisis in the early 1990s, which questioned the survival of hundreds of organizations in the U.S. automotive industry.[38] Since then, we've studied downsizing in various industry contexts and in periods of economic growth and recession. The way leaders act during the downsizing effort influences whether trust is preserved or destroyed. Before delineating those actions, let's consider how *not* to downsize someone, as a friend relayed to us in a recent interview,

On Monday, May 3, I drove to the Ann Arbor office and arrived at 8:45 a.m. On the way to my desk, I stopped at the cube across from mine. Crystal (finance), Pat (engineering), and Greg (my boss) were putting the final touches on the bid package that was due that day. I told them that I would organize the data and put it in presentation format.

Then my phone rang, and Greg said he needed to meet with me. I passed him on his way to the copier, and he said to meet him in the conference room. This was odd. When I arrived at the conference room, Nancy (VP of North America HR) was in the room. I knew something was up. Greg started telling me that my position had been eliminated, and that they had a letter for me to sign. While [I was] in a state of shock, Nancy took me through the letter. Then she left the room to get the outplacement person. While she was gone I asked Greg if there were any other options. He said no, it was a business decision, and he was not allowed to tell me any more. He had to follow the script.

Then the outplacement guy came in and gave me his card and said to call him tomorrow. Nancy then proceeded to take my cell phone, computer, and corporate credit card. She told me she'd get my purse and coat and showed me the door. On the way out, I told the receptionist, Kelly, goodbye and that it was nice working with her. Kelly was in shock, too.

I could not even call my husband because I did not have a phone. I had to drive to Warren, and when I saw his face, I broke down and cried. When I watched the movie *Up In the Air*, I could totally relate to the people being fired. This experience was one of the most humiliating in my life. I was treated like a common criminal and was not allowed to say goodbye to anyone. They gave no regard to my 20 years of experience. I could have been moved to a number of different positions; I had done so in the past without complaining.

Only a handful of people have reached out to me to see how I am doing. No one has tried to repair the broken trust. It is similar to having a cancer: "If we contact her, we could lose our jobs, too." To me, it has been like cutting off the past 20 years of my life.

Their initial offer was for one month of benefits and one month pay. Nancy, the VP of HR, said that she really liked me as a person, but this was the best the company could do. I hired a lawyer to get a better severance package and was able to get six months of pay and six months of benefits in the end.

My attitude about companies has permanently changed. I totally understand that business is business and that each employee is a cog in the wheel. Large organizations act like this. I need work and am willing to do anything. I do not have the luxury right now to find the dream job; I just need something to keep the roof over our head.

Although our friend's experience is all too common, based on our own research, consulting, and coaching, we've found that leaders may be able to maintain trust among the organization's key stakeholders during down-sizing—depending on their actions. They will consequently accrue several benefits that follow from such trust, including preserving employee morale, loyalty, and organizational reputation and even the capacity for innovation.

The first way we have encouraged leaders to preserve trust during downsizing is to maintain open communication with all stakeholders, including employees, about the process and the rationale for the pending downsizing.[39] By ambushing our friend at the last moment, her company did a great disservice to her, her colleagues, and itself as an organization. Not only did our friend lose trust in this company, but also now her co-workers are looking over their shoulders, wondering when one of them will be called into the conference room for a talk with the VP of HR.

In this example, our friend's boss could have been a "linking pin" between her and top management, which probably made this decision.[40] Our friend previously trusted her boss, Greg, to look out for her best interests, but he abdicated his responsibilities when he turned her over to the VP of HR. We suggest that by training managers in interpersonal communication skills, they will be better equipped to maintain the trust that has been built between themselves and their employees in times of crisis such as the one we've profiled.

Communicating and implementing the downsizing decision also provides an opportunity to sustain or destroy trust. Leaders can help preserve trust by communicating a credible vision of the future while also instilling hope, particularly as to how the organization will prevail through this crisis and even emerge stronger.[41] This requires the leader to foster a culture of innovation and creativity and to enhance organizational flexibility. Indeed, when managed properly, downsizing can be an opportunity for the organization's talent to be empowered and encouraged to innovate.[42]

Sometimes, the need to rebuild trust includes not only the entire organization, but also entails the organization's external stakeholders. Such is the case when an organization faces a crisis. Organizations encounter crises of all kinds, some of their own doing and some over which they have no control. Trust with stakeholders is important for an organization to move through a crisis and remain intact. It is critical, therefore, to think about trust before a crisis situation hits and hope that you don't have to rebuild trust and deal with the crisis simultaneously. Here, we are defining an organizational crisis as a major threat to system survival that leaves little time to respond, in which the situation is ambiguous, and in which resources are inadequate to cope with the situation easily.[43,44,45,46] The leader's first role in a crisis is to preserve, if possible, and restore, if necessary, an environment of trust[47] in order to conserve the organization's reputation and viability.[48] Previous research has shown that stakeholders are more likely to forgive an organization that already possesses a high level of trustworthiness with its stakeholders.[49]

Hurricane Katrina and its aftermath provided a clear context in which organizations could demonstrate their trustworthiness when individuals were at their most vulnerable. Homeland security specialist Eric Kutner shared two particularly compelling examples,

> When Craig Fugate was the director of the Florida Division of Emergency Management, he decided to provide whatever help was needed by people in *other* states after Hurricane Katrina. He said, "We're going to send the resources and worry about the paperwork later." He trusted that he would get paid by whatever state, local, or federal government entity for whatever aid Florida sent to the other states. In order to help people and build trust with them, he didn't wait until all the i's were dotted and t's were crossed to send aid. Now that Fugate heads the Federal Emergency Management Agency, I think the attitude has also been to send the help first, and then dot the i's and cross the t's. He's telling people to give others the benefit of the doubt because it might save somebody or help somebody. It's bought him a lot of credibility, a lot of trust from many other people.
>
> Another example of trust-building during Hurricane Katrina comes from the private sector. Hancock Bank reopened the day after Katrina went through New Orleans, and with their bank building damaged, it set up temporary "branches" using Winnebagos and folding tables. The bank handed out at least $200 to anybody who came to the bank needing money, regardless of whether they were actual customers of the bank. In essence, the bank trusted the community.[50]

The bank didn't have any formal way of recording the loans, and so they relied upon simple IOUs written on pieces of paper that it stored in cardboard boxes. Out of the several million dollars they lent to people in the community, they lost only $280,000[51]. However, five months after the storm, Hancock bank also opened 13,000 new accounts with individuals who were not previously customers of the bank. Customers said, "You were here when I needed you, and this is going to be my bank in the future."[52] As former bank president and CEO George Schloegel said, "The need for one another builds a special culture about how we face the future. I think the moral fiber of this community is much, much stronger because of coming through [Hurricane] Camille, or coming through Katrina 30 years later."[53]

The effort to rebuild consumer trust and reputation by McNeil Consumer Products, a division of Johnson & Johnson, following the poisoning of some of its Tylenol products in 1982 has been well documented. Our interview with Peter Smith, who was a top executive of McNeil Consumer Products during the Tylenol crisis, however, holds timeless lessons for Johnson & Johnson that it would do well to remember and reapply in the present.

As McNeil's director of international marketing, my job at the time was to help expand Tylenol-brand products into overseas markets working with Johnson & Johnson's worldwide system of 150 affiliate companies. We had been hard at it for two years, making good progress, when the news broke in September 1982 that cyanide-doctored Tylenol capsules had killed seven people in suburban Chicago. Even as we struggled individually with our own initial shock, the corporation and company shifted into crisis management mode.

Communication was our preoccupation 24/7 for the next several weeks. Internationally, our marketing group just kept relaying to the world of J&J the latest news and what we were doing in response, step-by-step. We updated, explained, answered questions, provided more details, and held hands. Slowly but surely, our persistent flow of trusted information helped calm the waters and restore a semblance of order. Full restoration of the Tylenol business at home and abroad would take months and require major new investments and initiatives. But, the critical success factor was already in place: absolute dedication to clear, consistent, and complete communications.

An example I will remember forever occurred during the first three days of the crisis. Media worldwide had begun to ask if McNeil had cyanide on premise at its headquarters or manufacturing facilities. One of several theories at the time was that a disgruntled current or former employee had committed the crimes. The top management crisis team asked the director of research and development to investigate. Later the same day, he returned to the meeting to report that his lab kept a small amount of cyanide under lock and key to use in a proscribed ingredient quality test every few months. J&J's chairman, Jim Burke, who had taken personal charge of the crisis from the moment it broke, made an instant decision. We would call a press conference immediately and confirm we kept cyanide in our lab at headquarters and explain why—the truth, the whole truth. He then added: "The public will be fair."

And so we did, and the public was fair. So was the media. I won't deny many of us swallowed hard at the time. It was not easy to confess to the world we had "cut down that cherry tree." But, we did and never had to look back. The fundamental principle reflected in that decision sustained us throughout the Tylenol comeback. Just like J&J's corporate credo said (paraphrased): "our first responsibility is to the consumers and users and beneficiaries of our products . . . if we do that right, our shareholders will also be well-served." Flash forward 18 months and Tylenol had reassumed leadership of its market segment in the United States and was once again launching new Tylenol businesses abroad.

Johnson & Johnson's more recent history demonstrates the need for constant vigilance in order to minimize losses in trust and reputation and to restore them quickly. In 2010, Johnson & Johnson failed to recall contaminated cold medicine products until 20 months after it initially received complaints from consumers, and then was issued a warning letter by the Food and Drug Administration to promptly address significant violations of regulations involving "current good manufacturing practices" for pharmaceuticals.[54] In contrast to the Tylenol crisis of three decades earlier, J&J's reputation and trustworthiness suffered due to a lack of quality controls and other factors that are the direct responsibility of Johnson & Johnson. Then on February 17, 2012, J&J announced another recall, this time of infants' Tylenol,

Johnson & Johnson recalled its entire U.S. supply of infants' Tylenol— about 574,000 bottles—due to a design flaw that hasn't caused harm but sets back the health-products giant's efforts to regain sales following a string of earlier recalls.

The move Friday involved bottles of grape-flavored infants' Tylenol, which had only just returned to shelves in November, one of the few recalled consumer products J&J had put back on the market.

The recall, in the wake of a management shake-up in J&J's consumer group, of which the McNeil unit is a part, suggests J&J still has a ways to go to resolve its quality problems and regain consumer loyalty.

U.S. sales at McNeil were $1.4 billion last year, 55% off the peak in 2008, the year before the recalls, according to Wells Fargo Securities. The recalls also damaged the company's reputation. Among over-the-counter pain medicines, Tylenol ranks eighth in loyalty, after trailing only Advil in 2009, according to the most recent survey of 49,000 adults by marketing consultant Brand Keys Inc.

J&J executives have expressed confidence recently that the worst is over. "We feel positive about where our consumer business is headed in 2012," Chief Executive William Weldon said during an earnings call last month.

In a statement on Friday, Mr. Weldon called the latest Tylenol recall "clearly disappointing after all the progress that McNeil has been making to ensure its products meet the highest level of quality and consumer satisfaction."

J&J may have forgotten or neglected tough lessons learned and principles embedded in previous decades which need to be reapplied today.

For an organization facing a crisis, then, the first step its leaders should take to preserve trust and reputation is to be reliable by clearly following through on any commitments made during the crisis. Next, someone in the organization must be responsible for maintaining openness (communication) with all stakeholders during the crisis. Open and honest communication serves to reduce uncertainty about the many concerns stakeholders have during the crisis.[55] The organization must also appear to be handling the crisis in a competent manner. Stakeholders want to have as much information as possible about the way in which the organization is solving the crisis.[56] Finally, it is important for the organization to show compassion to any victims of the crisis. Those victims might be outside the organization or people within the organization. This includes asking for forgiveness and demonstrating how it will prevent such mishaps in the future. Overall, consistent information is the most important aspect of getting through a crisis with as much trust and credibility intact as possible.[57]

The truth about broken trust is that we do not really know if we have trust with another person or an organization until we are truly vulnerable and that trust is exploited. Only in the most vulnerable of situations do we know what it is like to have our trust violated. Broken trust most definitely includes an emotional component, because if the relationship is a close one, we are devastated and possibly even harmed, emotionally or financially. Rebuilding trust, then, is not just an academic exercise, but a difficult and challenging pursuit. As we've noted, rebuilding trust is a two-way street. If you want to repair trust with another party, they must be willing to meet you halfway. If you are fortunate enough that the other party agrees that this relationship is worthy of keeping and repairing, then we hope the ROCC of Trust will be useful to you as you rebuild trust.

Trust Tips

1. Be **reliable** by following through on your commitments.
2. Be **open** by admitting that you made a mistake.
3. Be **competent** by fixing your mistake(s).
4. Be **compassionate** by forgiving others when they make a mistake and apologizing when you make one.

CHAPTER

Making Trust Last by Enlarging Your Purpose

Leaders are often criticized for selfish gains and taking large profits at the expense of the general public or even their own employees. Charles Handy, management scholar, author, and founder of the London Business School,[1] has noted that business leaders are not fundamentally greedy, but are just playing by the rules that Wall Street asks them to play.[2] The leaders we have profiled here, however, live by a different set of values and rules, enlarging their purpose to one that goes beyond just returning profits to stakeholders. These leaders have enlarged their purpose by "associating with a cause in order to give purpose to [their] lives,"[3] drawing on communities of stakeholders for inspiration.

☐ Create a Cause Larger Than Life

Dr. Brent Senior (UNC–Chapel Hill) found a cause larger than himself 14 years ago when he began traveling to Vietnam to provide ENT care to patients through medical centers in Ho Chi Minh City and Hanoi. Since then, Dr. Senior has raised money that has allowed him to take two chief residents with him, so that they, too, could work with other ENTs from the United States working side-by-side with Vietnamese colleagues. Dr. Senior made his 15th trip to Vietnam in the spring of 2012, which included plans to begin videoconferencing between UNC–Chapel Hill and the medical centers in Vietnam. In addition, his team visited Jakarta University in Indonesia. Dr. Karen Bednarski,[4] UNC–Chapel Hill graduate and ENT practitioner in Houston, Texas, described Dr. Senior's work in Vietnam,

Dr. Senior made a commitment to help these people, and he hasn't abandoned them to fly by the seat of their pants. He keeps going back and sticking with them. That dedication to helping another population advance their knowledge and skills is inspiring.

As business scholar Charles Handy points out, these kinds of leaders measure success "in terms of outcomes for others"[5] as well as for themselves.

Following 10 years in congregational ministry at Trinity Episcopal Church in Princeton, New Jersey, Rev. Jean Smith chose to leave parish work for a different kind of ministry. With this act, she enlarged her purpose by taking her ministry beyond the walls of her church and community to the Seamen's Church Institute (SCI) and mariners who travel the world and deliver goods to seaports worldwide, as well as to river mariners who ply the 2,200 miles of inland waterways from Pittsburgh to New Orleans.[6] The Reverend Smith described her decision to extend her ministry beyond suburbia,

When it was time for me to move on to another church, I thought it would be good to serve in a different environment, maybe the inner city. But as I began interviewing, I realized there was real hesitation about considering a small, 50-year-old woman to serve in an urban setting. It looked as if I would serve another church much like the one in Princeton.

When I received a call from Jim, the then-executive director of SCI, asking if I would be interested in the position of director of the International Seafarer Center, I hedged. I had only considered myself prepared to serve as clergy in a church setting. After a ship visit and first interview I was fascinated by the idea of serving with chaplains from different faith traditions, offering a ministry of presence to mariners, and becoming involved in advocating for workers in an ancient industry. When I was offered the position I grabbed it!

In addition, Rev. Smith found a new challenge, for herself, for her organization, and for those she served,

SCI depends upon its staff and board to be aware of changes underway in the maritime industry and especially those affecting the mariners. Our product is service to the worker, and for it to be of high quality, we need to know how their jobs impact their lives and what we could do in response to support them and their families. I liked the challenge to re-create SCI anew every day. This doesn't mean there are no policies, established programs, or that each day we tossed out of the window another version of the strategic plan. Rather, we focused on that plan, constantly reviewing our progress. Successful implementation depended on information gathered from seafarers and port workers as much as from staff and board members—especially in the rapidly changing maritime arena.

As the organization grew and changed, so did my responsibility. I was honored to become their COO and later SCI's first female executive director in its 175-year history.

When Aneil asked Rev. Smith what qualities are most critical for this type of position, she replied,

The job is a terrific one for someone who loves people and thrives in a multicultural setting . . . or would at least like to try it out. It requires self-confidence to forge ahead in uncharted territory and humility to be always learning from those we want to serve. If we don't trust ourselves and them—and ourselves with them—it's a no-go.

☐ Contribute Because You Care

Bob Lintz got involved serving the greater Cleveland community while still at GM. GM has always been supportive of community needs and Bob feels like giving back has been an important component to building his character. In fact, he feels strongly that young leaders should get involved in giving back to their communities. It is a way to learn from other outstanding leaders and to learn more about the community you live and work in. "Giving back can be as rewarding as your own job responsibilities."

Bob became more deeply involved with the Cleveland Clinic after they discovered his kidney cancer at a routine checkup. As he got to know the leaders there more, they invited him to join the board in 1991. Bob feels like his experience in employee engagement and quality improvement has been very helpful to the Cleveland Clinic. Bob serves on the Audit; Research & Education; and Safety, Quality & Patient Experience committees.[7] The Cleveland Clinic has been very focused on quality and patient experience, and Bob has been able to share his experience and expertise with both the trustees and the hospital employees. Employees of the Cleveland Clinic have also toured the Parma plant to learn more about General Motors' approaches to meeting and exceeding customers' expectations. Asked why he still spends so much time volunteering his efforts on behalf of the Cleveland Clinic trustees, Bob replied, "As long as they feel I'm contributing, I will continue to serve. I can't stop caring."[8]

☐ Remember Your Roots

For many years, Sheldon Yellen's firm, Belfor Holdings, has given its managers charitable allowances that "they can spend at Christmastime on local charities of their choice around the world."[9] In 2011, Sheldon expanded on this philanthropic tradition by establishing Belfor Cares, a "not-for-profit organization giving back to communities around the world."[10] He explained, "Our brand has become better known, but we've done everything philanthropic under the radar screen because our name didn't show up anywhere. So, I said, 'I think it's time for people to know that Belfor cares,' and so we created a registered charity called Belfor Cares."[11] At the end of 2011, Sheldon was talking with his wife, Iris, about the charities to which Belfor's managers were going to be donating that year,

> She says, "Do you ever lie back in bed and realize that you lived the American dream?"
> I said, "Iris, every minute of every day I think that—not just lying in bed. I think that every minute of every day."
> She says, "Isn't it sad that some kids don't have a bed?" And I said, "Yeah, okay," like, "what's your point?"
> She said, "Well, don't you think every child needs a place to dream?" And, I said, "Yes."
> She said, "Then why don't you give away beds to those that don't have beds? In fact, I got a great idea."
> I said, "What's that?"
> She says, "Kots for Kids," with the tagline, "Every child needs a place to dream." She just came up with this at a dinner out of nowhere, because she just thinks like that. She's just creative like that. She had a very successful sales career when we were first married and before we had children.[12]

Sheldon supported Iris's idea immediately, because he knew that Iris wanted to express her creativity while also helping others and because of his own childhood. As a child, Sheldon did not have a bed of his own, instead sleeping with two brothers in two beds put together. The three of them slept across the two beds so that they wouldn't fall between the two mattresses. As of early 2012, their new nonprofit, Kots for Kids, is in the process of securing thousands of beds and aims to distribute them to underprivileged children worldwide.

☐ Step Back and Then Walk Away

Sometimes a leader needs to step away from his or her leadership role and build trust that is sustainable over the long term, particularly with an eye toward the eventual time when he or she leaves the organization, either through retirement, moving to another organization, or some other transition. An effort to enlarge your purpose can also facilitate self-renewal, helping the leader find a new direction or a renewed spirit of enthusiasm for the job ahead. After watching a few episodes of the CBS series *Undercover Boss*, we noted that more than one Undercover Boss mentioned that he or she came back to work with a renewed sense of purpose about his or her job and mission and how he or she is accountable to the rest of the organization. Sometimes, a new view can help us gain a new perspective.

After leading Two Men and a Truck, International for more than a decade, Melanie Bergeron realized she needed to transition to a different role. The company needed to perform at a higher level, and her brother Brig was ready to succeed her as the company's top leader. After Brig returned from a sabbatical in the summer of 2007, Melanie had him assume full responsibilities as president and COO of the company. (He had taken on the title of president at the beginning of that year.)[13] A month or two later, at his request, Brig became responsible for all of the company's international operations as well. Since then, Melanie has relinquished the CEO title to Brig, and she has assumed the title of chair. She now represents the company to its external stakeholders among the franchise community and elsewhere. Despite giving up much of her formal leadership of the firm, or perhaps *because* she has done so, she has continued to thrive and grow. She explained, "It's an evolution. As I've been doing all this speaking, I'm mentoring so many people, and I learn so much."

The leadership changes at Two Men and a Truck also involved non–family members, and sometimes those changes have been quite painful, not only for those affected directly, but also for those who have had to initiate them. Again, Melanie,

> There's a time when you have to go from legacy management to professional management. It's one of the most difficult things the president or CEO has to do. To let go of people that had your back and have been so good to you and have lived the core values and worked hard. They haven't done anything wrong. But how humiliating for them to be let go because they don't have the skill set they need to take the company to the next level.
>
> A lot of company owners don't make that jump. I see it [among members] in the International Franchise Association. It is so difficult to make that jump. Because it looks like greed—people think you want to take it to a higher level just so you can make more money. That's where I had trouble with it. Jeff, our CFO, said, "Melanie, you're not going to be in business if you keep running things the way they are. TMT has to do this—think of your customers. TMT needs to make changes so that it is equipped to meet our customers' needs in the future. With better people you'll be able to better serve the customer."

I think of my mom and how she didn't have the energy to make our franchisees, some of which weren't paying royalties, do so, or be in compliance with their trucks' colors and logos. She didn't have the energy. I did that, though. But I was burned out after 14 years.

For example, with respect to our former head of IT, I knew things weren't right in that department. But I just didn't have the energy or the heart to make the changes that needed to be made. Brig did, thank God. It was just by the grace of God Brig jumped in. Brig's so strict. He does not care about being popular. He's not a people pleaser. So he has the perfect personality to handle this transition and was the leader that we needed at that time.

And as far as what keeps me going here, a couple years ago I asked myself, what am I going to do or what do I have to give back moving forward? Mary Ellen decided that she really wanted to retire, so I took over her public-speaking circuit. I gave 34 presentations in 2011, so I'm getting the hang of it! But it's funny—this is how God works. When one door closes, sure enough another one opens!

I think people enjoy it when I speak about the company, because I'm transparent. I also talk about the problems myself and the company have had, including health issues. Everyone is going through something. I think for many people it is comforting to know that they are not alone and that with perseverance they can get through it. The quote that sums it all up for me is by Frederick Douglas: "If there is no struggle, there is no progress."[14]

Beyond public speaking, Melanie is tangibly giving back, and enlarging her purpose, by mentoring other entrepreneurs, women, and young people. She described her current activities:

Now I'm mentoring several hardworking professionals. The people that I've talked to on the phone, they're just all trying to do the right thing and grow and create jobs. If I can help them not make the same mistakes I've made, or teach them through best practices, without expecting anything from them in return, it just feels so right. I feel like it gives me purpose. I mean, God gave me this incredible experience through everything I've done, every job I've ever had. It's just sharing the blessings that were given to me. What I'm hoping is that if I can share it to help others, they will also take all of their experience and continue to help others grow as well. You know—that is total trust.

Melanie does not charge for her speaking engagements, saying, "I enjoy it so much. Two Men and a Truck is making good money, and I still get a nice check, so I don't need to charge. I just like sharing. If I was charging, it would feel too much like a job." Melanie uses her speaking opportunities to talk about her involvement with not-for-profits, including Hidden Treasures, a Lansing, Michigan, thrift shop she started whose proceeds go to "providing an annual supplement to fund Lansing Christian School teachers' salaries with the goal of bringing them up to Christian Schools International (CSI) standards."[15] She discussed how Hidden Treasures fits into her enlarged picture,

> The people you speak to are coming from all different points in their career development, all different backgrounds, experiences, and angles. Some people will come up after a presentation and they want the courage to quit their jobs to start their own business. They ask, is it the right thing to do? I speak to many different groups of people. I speak to many women's groups. They have questions about being a woman in business. I tell them it just doesn't matter if you're a man or a woman. But they have questions about balancing home life if they have children and they're working and they've got so much going on. Then there are older people who want to retire. Their questions are about how do they step out, how do they do succession planning? What do they do to fulfill their lives now? That's where I talk about Hidden Treasures and how fulfilling it is to use your life skills to help a nonprofit get stronger.

Melanie's time and energy are not inexhaustible, however, and she applies the ROCC of Trust in determining with whom to share these resources,

> But there are people in life who make you feel like you're being used. I guess my lesson on that is you can't be a doormat; you need to set limits, listen to your gut. You have to be choosy about where you put your time and resources. I do love helping people, but not when they are undependable or unappreciative.
>
> For example, this one guy, he's got a great educational program for kids, a great concept. Three times he has set up an appointment to come meet with me and just did not show up. I thought, "I can't believe it." So then this happened a third time, I just threw his file in the garbage. Then, last night I get an email from him. He writes, "You know, I actually haven't heard from you in a long time. I've got a couple things I want to run by you. Can I stop by and see you this week?" I'm thinking, "Are you kidding?" I couldn't believe it. I guess I should have emailed back and said, "You know, 'no,' because . . ." I probably should have explained why, but I just deleted it.

☐ It's Really a Story About *Us*

Philosophers debate whether or not it is the individual or the corporation that has a responsibility to the community, can be held accountable, and must demonstrate itself to be trustworthy. Some management scholars ask whether a corporation can have a conscience and argue that it can.[16] In addition, Harvard Business School Professor Rosabeth Moss Kanter has argued that when a private company engages in public-sector partnership, the result can be solutions to real community problems and provide employees with renewed energy in their current jobs.[17] Ted Castle (Rhino Foods) exhibits this responsibility and partnership through his efforts to integrate Bosnian refugees into his company by teaching them English as a second language,

> I think some of the things that have changed are that we actually have gotten very big in hiring refugees. Burlington is an area where refugees are being resettled, and we've begun hiring Bosnian refugees since the late '90s. Now we actually have a lot of Africans, so 30% of our workforce is composed of refugees.
>
> So, we look at that as a good thing for our business. We look at that as bringing diversity to our business. We look at that as adding some real maturity to our work force; people appreciating their job, appreciating the company, wanting to work hard. We think it makes us a stronger company.
>
> So we look at this as something we embrace and want to get really good at, versus we just happen to have a bunch of refugees here. Vermont is not a diverse place, like other areas of the country, so we're looking at the diversity we have in our company and actually think that's really a great thing.
>
> So this isn't really a story about me anymore, but I think it's a story about us sort of falling into a situation where we never really wanted English as a second language at Rhino because we try to share so much information. We have company meetings; we have games that we play and try to turn people into, you know, stakeholders or owners. There's the thought of, "Oh, now they can't speak? English isn't their first language?" Then, it's like, "Oh my God, how are we going to do this?" and we were having trouble finding people. As we started doing it, there were some real challenges and difficulties to it, but now that we've worked ourselves through it, we look at this as actually a really powerful engine to our company now, that we have some pretty amazing people working here. So that's a story we tell and that's sort of a thing that's exciting about what's happening in our company now.

We're actually very interested in a program called "Bridges out of Poverty," which is looking at generational poverty. We think that we probably will be hiring people that have grown up in generational poverty more than first-class or wealthy environments. So, what is important to people in different segments of wealth, middle class, or poverty? How do we speak the right language and motivate people the right way? It means constantly looking at ourselves, our staff, and our people to understand what makes people tick. So I would just say that if you come and talk to me 10 years from now, it'll be different from what it is today.

We don't rely on old techniques; instead, we rely on creating an environment where people will speak up and they'll tell us what they think and an environment where people are good at listening and trying to make that work.

Indeed, at the end of 2012, more than five years after that interview with Ted, the Bridges out of Poverty program, now called Working Bridges, is stronger than ever.

☐ What Will You Do Next?

During our time serving as college professors, we have done our small part to enlarge our purpose to move beyond just teaching, by mentoring our students in their job and career goals. Our approach might be as a result of our human resources work at General Motors. We have found a niche in helping our students (and alumni) polish resumes and network with other professionals who might be able to help them in their job search, and by generally providing a listening ear and advice as they navigate the career paths ahead of them. While colleges and universities are focused on preparing students in their majors, they do not have a strong focus on how to prepare for a job search and what actions to take to actually land a job that is a good fit. This informal mentoring is how the Trust Network evolved, and it is something we find ourselves doing on a weekly basis. We agree with Melanie—if we charged for this service, we would never get any pleasure from it. We enjoy doing it because we are helping our students identify their strengths and match them to their place in the world. It helps connect us to each other and the greater community around us.

Now that you know how to build trust with employees, customers, and colleagues at a leader, what will you do to enlarge your purpose? How can you use your skills to help one person unselfishly today? How can you use your skills and passion to help a whole group of people tomorrow? Enlarging your purpose is about connecting our reliability, openness, and competence *with* our compassion to make the world around us a better place. We look forward to hearing from you as you move forward in your leadership journey.

Aneil K. Mishra and Karen E. Mishra, trustiseverything.com, 2012.

Trust Tips

1. Be **reliable** by continually showing others that you are there for them.
2. Be **open** and honest in how you share your successes and your struggles.
3. Be **competent** by following through and helping someone in a way that only you can.
4. Be **compassionate** by finding a purpose larger than yourself and committing to it.

APPENDIX A: LEADER AND SCHOLAR BIOGRAPHIES

☐ Leaders

George S. Barrett is chairman and chief executive officer of Cardinal Health, a company ranked number 19 on the Fortune 500 and dedicated to improving the cost-effectiveness of healthcare. Barrett has refocused the company on the "business behind healthcare," supporting hospitals, pharmacies, and alternative sites of care in their efforts to improve the quality and safety of patient care, while reducing costs and improving efficiency. Barrett joined Cardinal Health in 2008 as vice chairman and CEO of the company's Healthcare Supply Chain Services segment, where he was responsible for all of the company's supply chain businesses, including pharmaceutical distribution, medical/surgical distribution, nuclear pharmacy services, Presource® surgical kitting services, and the Medicine Shoppe International, Inc., retail pharmacy franchise operations. From 2005 to the end of 2007, Barrett served as president and CEO of North America for Teva Pharmaceutical Industries. During 2007, he also served as corporate executive vice president of the company's global pharmaceutical markets. He held the position of president of Teva USA from 1999 to the end of 2004. Prior to joining Teva, Barrett held various positions with Alpharma Inc., serving as president of US Pharmaceuticals from 1994 to 1997, and president of NMC Laboratories, prior to its acquisition by Alpharma in 1990. Barrett serves on the board of directors of Eaton Corporation, Nationwide Children's Hospital, and the President's Leadership Council of Brown University. He is a member of the board of trustees of the Healthcare Leadership Council and the Conference Board. He is also a member of the Business Roundtable, the Business Council, Ohio Business Roundtable and the Columbus Partnership. In addition, Barrett is a recipient of an Ellis Island Medal of Honor. Barrett received his BA from Brown University and an MBA from New York University. He also holds an honorary Doctor of Humane Letters degree from Long Island University's Arnold & Marie Schwartz College of Pharmacy and Health Sciences.

Melanie Bergeron, CFE, is the chair of Two Men and a Truck International, Inc., the largest moving franchise company in North America. Bergeron began as the company's first franchisee—the founder of the company is her mother, Mary Ellen Sheets. Bergeron became president in 1994 and together with her team grew the company from $6 million to $198 million.

The company has been featured on *The Today Show* and CNBC's *How I Made My Millions*. Bergeron has spoken at several universities and for many business groups to share best practices she has learned along the way. She also spends time mentoring other young entrepreneurs. In addition, Bergeron serves on the International Franchise Association board of directors. She is on the board of directors of the Lansing Regional Chamber of Commerce and is president of a nonprofit thrift store called Hidden Treasures. She is a graduate of Central Michigan University.

Lewis Broadnax is executive director of Lenovo.com sales and marketing. Lewis is responsible for driving the strategy and execution of Lenovo's e-commerce mission in the Americas. Lewis's team manages all aspects of the Lenovo.com business, including 4P strategy and management, site merchandising and enablement, affinity sales, demand generation, and inbound telesales and sales support. In addition to having P&L responsibility for U.S. and Canada e-commerce, he is responsible for leading Lenovo's e-commerce expansion into Latin America, including Mexico, Colombia, Brazil, and Argentina. Lewis has been with IBM and Lenovo for just over 11 years. Previous to Lenovo, Lewis held positions in marketing, web strategy, and product management for Research Triangle Park startup companies. Lewis was educated at Duke University and calls Durham, North Carolina, home.

Ted Castle is the owner and president of Rhino Foods, located in Burlington, VT. Rhino employs approximately 110 employees and manufactures a variety of frozen desserts and ice cream products that are distributed in North America and Europe. Rhino Foods manufactures cheesecake, ice cream cookie sandwiches, bakery products, and inclusions for ice cream manufacturers for some of the largest food companies in the world. Rhino Foods' purpose is to impact the manner in which business is done through its financial, customer and supplier, employee, and community principles. Rhino Foods has been recognized for its efforts with awards including the U.S. Chamber of Commerce Blue Chip Enterprise Award, Child Help USA for its efforts on behalf of Vermont children and families, the Optimas award for vision in the workplace (past winners include UPS, Coors, and 3M), *Inc. Magazine*'s best companies to work for, the United Way Cornerstone Award, the State of Vermont Climate Wise Award, the Excellence in Action Best Practice Award by the Vermont Council for Quality representing Human Resource Focus, the Special Recognition Award from the Vermont Refugee Resettlement Program, and the Vermont Governor's Council Rising Star Worksite Wellness Program Recognition Award. Castle was recognized with Vermont Small Business Person of the Year by the United States Small Business Administration, the Terry Ahrich Award for Socially Responsible Business by Vermont Businesses for Social

Responsibility, Chittenden County's United Way board member of the year, regional award winner in Ernst & Young's, and Inc. Magazine's Entrepreneur of the Year Award. Ted has served on the board of directors for Prevent Child Abuse Vermont, United Way of Chittenden County, and Shelburne Farms. Ted lives in Charlotte, Vermont, with his wife, Anne. Their two sons, Ned and Rooney, have graduated from college and are presently living in Vermont.

Alan Finkel, MD, is cofounder of the Carolina Headache Institute in Chapel Hill, North Carolina. Dr. Finkel earned his BA in English from Middlebury College in 1975 and his MD from School of Medicine at SUNY at Buffalo in 1985, where he did his honors thesis in neuroanatomy. He completed postgraduate medical education in internal medicine at the University of Alabama-Birmingham, and neurology at the University of North Carolina at Chapel Hill. He also completed a fellowship in pain management and headache medicine in the Department of Neurology at the University of North Carolina, at Chapel Hill, North Carolina. He has published over a dozen refereed journal articles and numerous book chapters on headache and facial pain. He serves or has served on the editorial boards of *Headache; Neurology; Cephalalgia; Lancet Neurology;* and *Neuropsychopharmacology.* Dr. Finkel is the recipient of several honors and awards including the John R Graham Senior Clinicians' Forum Award from American Headache Society (2006), the Teaching Excellence Award from the UNC School of Medicine (2005), and the Teacher Recognition Award from American Academy of Neurology (2006). He serves as chair of the Headache and Face Pain Section of the American Academy of Neurology (AAN), is a board member of the United Council of Neurologic Subspecialties (UCNS), and is a fellow of the American Headache Society (AHS).

Dr. Kevin Lobdell is the director of quality for the Sanger Heart & Vascular Institute, which is the Cardiovascular Service Line for the Carolinas HealthCare System (about 48,000 employees, 33 hospitals, and 600 points of care, with revenues of approximately $7 billion annually). Additionally, Dr. Lobdell is program director in Cardiothoracic Surgery and maintains board certification in general surgery, thoracic surgery, and critical care and has a Certificate in Medical Management. Dr. Lobdell's current professional efforts are focused on comprehensive performance management (through quality, analytics, and innovation) in cardiovascular care. These efforts have resulted in two programs receiving the highest ratings of three stars by the Society of Thoracic Surgeons (awarded to less than 15% of about 1045 programs in the USA). Dr. Lobdell has authored or co-authored more than 30 peer-reviewed publications and presented over 75 times in regional, national, and international forums.

Bob Lintz is a retired plant manager of General Motors Corporation. A native of Flint, Michigan, Bob Lintz received his bachelor's degree in industrial management from Michigan State University in East Lansing, Michigan, in 1963. He also attended the Management Excellence Program at Case Western University's Weatherhead School of Management. Bob began his General Motors career right after college as a College Graduate-in-Training at the Flint Metal Fabricating Plant. After serving in various positions there, he was named superintendent of inspection and quality control at the GM Bay City, Michigan, plant in 1972. In September 1974, he was transferred to the GM Parma Pressed Metal Plant as general superintendent manufacturing and on September 1, 1980, he was promoted to plant manager of the Pressed Metal operation. In February 1987, he became manager of the entire Parma complex. He retired from General Motors in 2000. Throughout his adult life, Bob has been very active in community affairs. Among his many current philanthropic and service activities, Bob is a member of the board of trustees of the Cleveland Clinic, where he serves on the Quality and Safety Committee, Research and Education Committee, and Audit Committee. He is also a member of the board of trustees for the Cleveland Clinic's Western Region hospitals, where he also serves as member of their Governance Committee. He has recently taken on limited consulting in an effort to share his expertise in employee engagement and developing trust. He also continues his passion for antique cars and coin-operated penny arcade machines from the early 1900s.

Dr. David Pawsat, DO, is founder and director of the Center for Optimal Health in East Lansing, Michigan. Physiology is the study of the mechanical, physical, and biochemical functions of living organisms. Dr. David Pawsat is a physiologist at heart. In 1985, he received a BS degree in physiology from Michigan State University. In order to understand more about the intricacies of physiology, Dr. Pawsat joined a research team at Henry Ford Hospital in Detroit, where he began research on neuropharmacologic and surgical treatments for Parkinson's. While attending Michigan State University's School of Osteopathic Medicine, he published award-winning research on the effects of estrogen in the brain. Upon graduation from medical school, he had a 12-year career in emergency medicine, serving as a site director and clinical professor of Michigan State University's Emergency Medicine. He became disheartened by a medical model that forces physicians to spend little time finding solutions to patients' needs and more time using drugs to suppress symptoms. Most importantly, he experienced the successes of those physicians who carefully listened and respected the power of each patient's individuality. It was these patients who tended to need fewer medications and who were more likely to survive an illness and/or be cured of a disease. What he did not realize at the time was that his energy, progressing fatigue, and 40-pound weight gain were due to an undiagnosed thyroid condition. After initiating conventional medical therapy with minimal improvement, Dr. Pawsat began to study the fields of Alternative, Integrative, and Anti-Aging Medicine. He found a prevalent part of the medical community in Europe, Asia, and even the West Coast of the United States used scientifically sound methods for creating physiologically sound healing. Upon leaving emergency medicine, Dr. Pawsat made three commitments. First and foremost, to heal himself. Second, to engage in formal training and intensive study in the fields of nutritional medicine and hormonal replacement therapies. Third, to make the first two commitments without distraction. In 2005, he took a year off medicine, developed a nutritional and thyroid hormone regimen for himself, and began using many diverse healing methods. The result of this regimen was a 40-pound weight loss, a huge improvement in energy, and an incredible passion to give back what he had received. During this time of healing, Dr. Pawsat received formal training through the Fellowship of Anti-Aging and Functional Medicine, where he studied cutting-edge bio-identical hormones and natural and integrative therapies. He is certified in Anti-Aging and Regenerative Medicine by the American Academy of Anti-Aging & Regenerative Medicine. Dr. Pawsat is an active member of the Institute for Functional Medicine. The Center for Optimal Health has been open since February 2006. Dr. Pawsat has had thousands of patient interactions and has developed an incredible patient community of very proactive, committed patients from very diverse backgrounds. The premise that medicine should begin by treating the cause, not the symptoms, is the centerpiece of the practice. The skillful integration of conventional medicine combined with nutritional and hormonal therapies is the cornerstone of his care. Dr. Pawsat feels blessed to have found a way to help himself, but feels even more blessed to be able to share the skills, experience, and knowledge in helping so many others regain their health.

Dennis Quaintance began his hospitality and entrepreneurial career at age 15 as a housekeeper's assistant at a hotel in Missoula, Montana. In 1988, Dennis teamed up with Mike Weaver to form Quaintance-Weaver and opened Lucky 32 restaurant in Greensboro in 1989. Today, the Quaintance-Weaver family includes a second Lucky 32 Kitchen and Wine Bar in Cary. The four-diamond, 131-room O. Henry Hotel and the adjacent Green Valley Grill opened in Greensboro in 1998. The four-diamond 147-room Proximity Hotel and neighboring Print Works Bistro opened in 2007 and are the first hotel and restaurant to gain Platinum certification with the U.S. Green Building Council's Leadership in Energy and Environmental Design program. He is a recipient of the Junior Achievement of the Triad Spirit of Entrepreneurship Award in 2006, and winner of the 2011 Brotherhood/Sisterhood Citation Award from the National Conference for Community and Justice of the Piedmont Triad. Dennis serves a board member for the Johnnetta B. Cole Global Institute for Diversity and Inclusion. He and his wife, Nancy King Quaintance, have twin children, Kathleen Troy and Dennis Carlisle.

Bruce Kalman Rubin, MD, received his BS, Master of Engineering, and MD degrees from Tulane University in New Orleans. After completing medical studies, he went to Oxford University as a Rhodes Scholar to do postdoctoral research in biomedical engineering. He completed an MBA at the Babcock School of Management, Wake Forest University, in 2004. In 1983 Rubin joined the faculty of Queen's University in Kingston, Ontario, as Chief of Paediatric Respirology and Critical Care. From 1991–1997, he was Professor of Pediatrics and Chief of Pediatric Pulmonary at St. Louis University, and from 1997–2009, he was at Wake Forest University as professor and Vice Chair for Research in Pediatrics. In July 2009, he joined the faculty of Virginia Commonwealth University as the Jessie Ball duPont Distinguished Professor and Chairman of the Department of Pediatrics and physician in chief of the Children's Hospital of Richmond. He is also a professor of biomedical engineering, physiology, and biophysics at VCU. Dr. Rubin is on the editorial board of 12 pulmonary journals and is associate editor of six. He has published more than 200 research papers and chapters and holds six patents. Dr. Rubin received the ACCP Young Investigator award in 1989, the Critical Care Research Award in 1990, and the Alfred Soffer Award for Editorial Excellence in 2004. He received the Prix Extraordinaire by the International Congress of Pediatric Pulmonology in 2008, the Forrest Bird Lifetime Scientific Achievement award by the AARC in 2008, and gave the Donald Egan Memorial Lecture at the 2009 AARC meeting, and the Phil Kittredge Memorial lecture in 2011. In 2011, he also received the Robert A. Bageant Award from the Virginia Society for Respiratory Care. He is listed in *Who's Who in the United States*, *The Best Doctors in America*, and Castle Connolly's *America's Top Doctors*. He is a fellow of the Royal College of Physicians of Canada, the American College of Chest Physicians, the American Pediatric Association, and the AARC, and is a trustee of the American Respiratory Care Foundation. In 2012, Dr. Rubin received the Jimmy A. Young Medal from the Respiratory Care International Organization (AARC), with over 50,000 members. This medal is the highest award presented by the AARC and honors an individual who has "exceeded all expectations for meritorious service to the AARC and advancement of the respiratory care professions." It is given to professionals who have given a lifetime of service which has benefited both mankind and the health profession of respiratory care. Dr. Rubin's research is on regulation of mucus clearance in health and disease, airway immune modulation, and aerosol delivery of medications. He directs the only mucus clearance clinic in North America for the assessment and treatment of adults and children with difficult-manage mucus problems, as well as a dedicated Pediatric Chronic Cough clinic. The goal of his research group is to develop new therapies for asthma, cystic fibrosis, chronic bronchitis, and plastic bronchitis. Dr. Rubin is also a magician, elected to membership in the International Brotherhood of Magicians and the Society of American Magicians. In the past 20 years, he has performed and taught "medical magic" in 20 countries on five continents.

Brent A. Senior, MD, FACS, FARS, is Nathaniel and Sheila Harris Distinguished Professor and professor of otolaryngology and neurosurgery at the University of North Carolina at Chapel Hill, where he also serves as vice chair of Academic Affairs and director of Rhinology, Allergy, and Endoscopic Skull Base Surgery. He is immediate past president of the American Rhinologic Society and president of the Christian Society of Otolaryngologists. He has authored over 80 scientific papers, texts, and textbooks and serves as an associate editor of the *International Forum of Allergy and Rhinology*. Among his honors are inclusion in Castle Connelly's *America's Top Doctors* and *Best Doctors* in both the United States and North Carolina; the Distinguished Service Award; the Medal for People's Health from the Minister of Health of Vietnam, Hanoi, Vietnam; and the People's Medal from People's Committee HCMC, Vietnam, for service to people of Ho Chi Minh City, Vietnam.

Mary Ellen Sheets is the founder of Two Men and a Truck International. In less than 20 years, Mary Ellen Sheets has taken her sons' small moving business and driven it to an international corporation with more than 1,300 trucks and more than 200 locations worldwide. After her sons, Brig and Jon Sorber, left for college, the business continued to receive numerous requests, so Sheets decided to take it over. She purchased an old moving truck for $350—the only money she ever invested in the company—and hired two movers. The business grew steadily and Sheets's entrepreneurial spirit became well known in the Lansing area. Eventually, she quit her state government job (forgoing her retirement) to put 100% into her thriving moving business. She awarded the first franchise to her daughter, Melanie Bergeron, a year later. It was located in Atlanta, Georgia. By 1989, Sheets had developed the business into the first and only local moving franchise in the country. Last year, Two Men and a Truck International's annual revenue was $193.3 million. Sheets considers herself fortunate to have all three children actively involved in running the company. Brig Sorber is presently president and CEO. Melanie Bergeron acts as chair of the board of directors. Jon Sorber is executive vice president. "When I look back, I can't believe this all happened," she says. "I am in shock and so grateful. I definitely think this is the American dream. We live in a wonderful country."

The Rev. Jean R. Smith, DD, assists in her local parish and works part-time for the Episcopal Bishop of Vermont, consulting with churches in transition and in conflict transformation. Working initially as a speech therapist, she retired in December 2007 after 10 years of parish ministry followed by 17 years with the Seamen's Church Institute of NY, NJ. A 1964 graduate of Northwestern University in speech, she graduated from Church Divinity School of the Pacific and was ordained in 1980. Jean is married to her husband, Peter, whose loving support makes the challenges of a dual-career family not only possible, but also fun.

Peter T. Smith is a part-time marketing consultant and writer living in Vermont. He retired from full-time employment in 2007 after 43 years in senior marketing positions with organizations around the world, including Procter & Gamble, McCann Erickson, Johnson & Johnson, Inter-Continental Hotels, and Recording for the Blind & Dyslexic (now Learning Ally). A 1964 graduate of Northwestern University's Medill School of Journalism, he and his wife, the Rev. Jean R. Smith, DD, will celebrate 48 years of marriage this year. They are parents of a daughter, Lindsay, and a son, Davis, and have four granddaughters.

Ross Smith is director of test for Office Communicator and Design Group at Microsoft Corporation, and has been in the software industry for over 20 years, developing and testing software on everything from mainframe systems to handheld devices and PCs. He began his Microsoft career in product support in 1991 and has been a test lead, test manager, and test architect. He has been a longtime member of the Test Architect's Group, and has worked on almost every version of Windows and Office since 1995. He is one of the authors of *The Practical Guide to Defect Prevention* and holds five software patents. Over the last couple years, he has nurtured a management innovation initiative called 42projects, aspiring to inject cultural change and "bring back the buzz to the hallways" at Microsoft. He has been a guest poster on Google's Testing Blog. The London School of Business and the Management Innovation Lab published a case study of 42projects titled, "Game On: Theory Y meets Generation Y." His team's work on productivity games was mentioned in *The Economist*, and in the recent book *Changing the Game: How Video Games are Transforming the Future of Business*. He is experimenting with how gaming can improve productivity among next-generation workers, and the impact of games and social networking tools on management education and requisite skills for new managers. He has been interviewed in Dr. Dobb's, MSDN, and others, and has spoken recently at Google's Test Automation Conference in Zurich, Corbis, MIT's Innovation Lab, AACSB Dean's Conference, and a Web 2.0 conference in London.

Brig Sorber is CEO of the award-winning Two Men and a Truck International, based in Lansing, Michigan. He is also is one of the original "two men," along with younger brother Jon Sorber. He has also spoken about Two Men and a Truck and franchising at Wake Forest University's undergraduate and graduate business schools, the University of Texas El Paso, and the University of Michigan Ross School of Business. He is a frequent speaker for Connecting Business Men to Christ, a ministry to the marketplace. Brig has also been a guest instructor for the Institute for Biblical Business and Entrepreneurship. Brig is the past president of the Okemos Baseball/Softball Club and is a current member of the Knights of Columbus. He is an active member of the Detroit chapter of the Young Presidents' Organization and a local group of Lansing, Michigan, CEOs. He is also on the board of directors for the Business Leaders for Michigan, a nonprofit, executive organization geared toward making Michigan a "top 10" state for job and economic growth. He was awarded the 2008 Alumni Award by the Okemos Education Foundation. Brig is a graduate of Northern Michigan University, where he earned the 2010 Distinguished Alumni Award. He also earned the title of Certified Franchise Executive, which is recognized as a standard of excellence in the franchise industry.

Jon Sorber is one of the original two men, along with older brother Brig Sorber. The two started the business in the early 1980s in Okemos, Michigan, to earn spending money. Using a 1967 pickup truck, the brothers placed an ad in a local shopping guide that read "Men At Work Movers . . . Two Men and A Truck." The ad also included a stick-figure logo designed by their mother, Mary Ellen Sheets. This logo remains the corporate symbol for what is now Two Men and a Truck International. After Jon left home to attend Northern Michigan University, Sheets decided to keep the business rolling. Upon graduation from NMU in 1988, Sorber accepted a loss-prevention job with General Motors in Lansing, Michigan. A year later, he accepted a job at UPS in Grand Rapids, Michigan, where he would move with his newlywed wife, Gabrielle, to start his Two Men and a Truck franchise. When he first opened his franchise, he worked at his childhood desk, behind the couch, in their one-bedroom apartment that also served as his office. At that time, Sorber was only earning about $50 a week from his franchise and continued working at UPS from 4 a.m. to 8 a.m., then focusing on his Two Men and a Truck franchise from 8 a.m. to 5 p.m. Sorber then did additional paperwork at night. In 1991, he quit his UPS job to focus solely on the family business. In the early '90s, at the request of his mother, Sorber took over the original Two Men and a Truck moving company in Lansing, Michigan, in addition to the franchise he was building in Grand Rapids. In 2008, Sorber sold his franchises in Grand Rapids to focus more time at

Two Men and a Truck and work alongside his brother, Brig, sister, Melanie, and mother, Mary Ellen Sheets. At its peak, Two Men and a Truck of Grand Rapids had 21 trucks and about 75 employees. Sorber owned and operated that franchise for 18 years. In 2007, Sorber assumed the title executive vice president of Two Men and a Truck. Sorber believes his 10 years of experience as a mover and driver and 18 years of experience as a successful franchisee help him work with Home Office staff and franchisees to help make Two Men and a Truck a powerhouse in the moving Industry. Sorber enjoys spending his time on the operational and strategic growth areas of the business.

Jim Wenger is an ordained Lutheran pastor of the Evangelical Lutheran Church in America. He received his bachelor's degree from Wartburg College in Waverly, Iowa, and his master's of divinity from Wartburg Seminary in Dubuque, Iowa. He is the son and grandson of Lutheran pastors, but most importantly, he is a servant of the most high God, who is most clearly known in the person of Jesus of Nazareth, by the power of the Holy Spirit.

Sheldon Yellen is CEO of Belfor Holdings, Inc. into the 21st century. Belfor Holdings, Inc. is a $1.5-billion diversified building services company which owns Belfor Property Restoration. Prior to the management-led buyout of Belfor International in 2006, Sheldon was the CEO of Belfor USA. Sheldon's journey as the eldest of four boys from a poor family on welfare to an owner of a worldwide company is an unbelievable one. Working since the age of 11 and bringing his paycheck home to his mother to help support the family taught him many important life lessons that he implements every day. A 53-year-old businessman who is driven by perfection, Sheldon continues to be up early and work late, which sets the example for everyone to follow. Sheldon has found success in his unique business style, which goes against the grain of "traditional" business management. He hates meetings, he dislikes committees, and he believes layers of a corporate hierarchy bring nothing more than road blocks and additional overhead costs—he is anything but conventional! Failure is not in his vocabulary, and when asked about the recession, his comments were simple and to the point: "Belfor will not participate." Driven by his relentless business sense and work ethic, Sheldon has created an unconventional company culture based on one premise: "doing the right thing." "It's easy to do the right thing when everybody is watching, but Belfor people do the right thing when nobody is watching," Sheldon proclaims. His management style has many conflicts; while watching every penny that is spent, he won't waste a second to get on his private plane to visit a sick employee or customer.

Celebrating with families at weddings and births is also part of Sheldon's "job description" as CEO. Although some would consider the private plane a luxury, to Sheldon it is just another tool to get the job done. One can't make 85 acquisitions and grow a company from one office into a worldwide company sitting in the airport wasting time, and he is known for being in four or five cities in a day. "Time is the enemy," one can often hear him say.

When asked about his family he enthusiastically says it's grown to over 6,000 people. He truly believes that Belfor people throughout the world are part of his family, and he rarely separates his business and personal lives. Although he is *always* available for his personal family, and Sunday-night dinners are mandatory for all involved, he barely differentiates. His love for people cannot be underestimated. Sheldon continues to pave the way for the people who work "with him" to run more than 250 offices in 29 countries throughout the world. He still keeps everything in balance in his quest to continue to grow the company. To this day, with over 6,000 employees, he continues to handwrite personalized birthday cards—a task he started many years ago when there were just 19 employees in the company. Refusing to give in to the impersonal technology era of email and phone texts, Sheldon still believes in the old-fashioned personal touch of handwritten notes and phone calls. The true passion and compassion Sheldon has for his Belfor employees awarded him an Emmy-nomination of the Belfor episode on CBS's hit series *Undercover Boss*. A popular speaker and motivator, Sheldon has also appeared at several events and conferences where he shares his unconventional yet effective business sense with groups of all ages, backgrounds, and interests. Sheldon and his wife, Iris, have two sons and are very involved in the community. In 2011, Sheldon launched Belfor Cares, a nonprofit organization giving back to communities around the world. Kots for Kids, a Belfor Cares charity created by his wife, Iris, continues the message that Belfor cares about communities, large and small. Being able to provide children with the ability to dream the dream that he has lived in real life is the basis of these charities. Today, under Sheldon's leadership, Belfor has grown to be the global leader in integrated disaster recovery and restoration services. Belfor Holdings, Inc. is the parent company of the Belfor Franchise Group, consisting of Ductz and Hoodz, the world's largest air-duct cleaning and kitchen-exhaust cleaning organizations, respectively; Greenblendz; the Professional Group; and more. A true entrepreneur at heart, Sheldon is always looking ahead for the next opportunity. Sheldon has an ingratiating personality, a keen business sense, and a terrific sense of humor. If you are given the opportunity to meet him, if only for a few minutes, he will make a significant impact on you.

☐ Scholars

Johnston (Jack) Beach is a senior leadership development consultant at IBM. He currently manages the Leadership Strategy & Research Group and has oversight of the Executive Leadership Development Programs. In that role he has had a great impact on IBM's recognition over the last several years as the number one corporation in leadership development. Prior to coming to IBM, Jack was a colonel in the United States Army and professor of psychology, who helped to build the Department of Behavioral Sciences and Leadership at the United States Military Academy, West Point, New York. He has consulted extensively on leadership development and leadership education throughout the world. Jack is the author of *Leadership in My Rearview Mirror: Reflections from Vietnam, West Point, and IBM*, published by MC Press.

Brenda Bernstein, founder and senior editor of The Essay Expert LLC, has been coaching professionals and students on their writing projects for more than 12 years. Her team works closely with clients to create effective written expressions of who they are and what they have to offer. The Essay Expert's customers reliably produce compelling business documents, attain sought-after job interviews, and receive offers of admission to top schools.

Jeff DeGraff is clinical professor of management and organizations at the University of Michigan Ross School of Business. He is coauthor of the books *Creativity at Work*, *Leading Innovation*, *Competing*, and *Innovation You*. He also has a PBS program titled *Innovation You*. He is founder of the Innovatrium Institute for Innovation, with labs in Ann Arbor, Michigan, and Atlanta, Georgia. Jeff writes a column for *Psychology Today* and the *Huffington Post*. He can be followed at www.JeffDeGraff.com.

Will Ford is a business-intelligence architect and blogger at www.willfuldevelopment.com, where he offers book reviews and ideas on the implications of intentional living and design on personal and professional success. Beyond business intelligence and its strategic implications, his passions include educational marketing, the impacts of technology, and personal development.

Dr. John David Gordon has consistently been listed as one of Washington's Top Doctors in the *Washingtonian Magazine*. Dr. Gordon is the editor of *Obstetrics, Gynecology, and Infertility* and is the author of many scientific publications, and he blogs at www.100infertilityquestions.com, a project that he launched in conjunction with the publication of his book,

100 Questions and Answers About Infertility. Dr. Gordon is a *Clinical Professor of Obstetrics and Gynecology* at George Washington University in Washington, DC. He has been honored on numerous occasions for his educational activities and is a three-time recipient of the Council on Resident Education in Obstetrics and Gynecology National Resident Teaching Award.

Doug Hoogervorst owns a high-service boutique business-intelligence software called Business Impact, which helps the "un-teched" use their business data without being held back by IT. The company is virtual with employees and contractors around the U.S., and he appreciates Aneil and Karen's work on trust to have helped in establishing trust with employees, contractors, customers, and vendors.

Eric Kutner is a homeland security specialist and founder of Emergency Response Design Group (ERDG), a consultancy focused on the homeland security realm. ERDG is involved with emergency preparedness, emergency management, planning, and business continuity, with high-level strategic partners in other areas that include physical security and continuity of government. He draws from his broad experience as a management/business development consultant with a background in leadership and management, and is an expert on social networks and relationship-building across many industries. Active in innovation, entrepreneurship, and science and technology education circles, he serves on the management or planning committees of several entrepreneurial and social enterprise endeavors.

David Lassman is vice president of operations for Leed's, a leader in the corporate promotional products industry. At Leed's, David is responsible for an operation that employees more than 700 people in manufacturing, warehousing, order processing, and customer service. In addition to his position at Leed's, David is an adjunct professor at Carnegie Mellon University's Heinz College of Public Policy and Management, where he teaches organizational management. He also teaches managing change as a guest lecturer in various executive education programs at Carnegie Mellon's Heinz College of Public Policy and Carnegie Mellon's Tepper School of Business.

Julie Mitchell, MA, offers integrated coaching and consulting services to organizations ranging from Fortune 500 corporations to universities, healthcare providers, and startups. Areas of expertise include communication skills development, strategic thinking, and advising leaders through challenges, opportunities, and change. An award-winning speaker and experienced educator, Julie delivers keynotes, brown-bag workshops, and in-depth seminars.

Gretchen Spreitzer is Professor of Management and Organizations at the University of Michigan Ross School of Business. She is also the codirector of the Ross Leadership Initiative. She joined the Michigan faculty in 2001 after spending nine years on the faculty at the University of Southern California Marshall School of Business. Her research focuses on employee empowerment and leadership development, particularly within a context of organizational change and decline. Her most recent research is examining how organizations can enable thriving. This is part of a new movement in the field of organizational behavior, known as positive organizational scholarship (www.bus.umich.edu/positive). Gretchen currently teaches electives on leading organizational change for MBAs and BBAs, and the Multidisciplinary Action Project (MAP) Program. She also is a core faculty member in the Leading the Positive Organization, Management of Managers, and Emerging Leaders executive education programs at Michigan.

APPENDIX B: VALIDATED TRUST SCALE

1.	Management is straightforward with me (open)	1	2	3	4	5
2.	Management is competent and knowledgeable (competent)	1	2	3	4	5
3.	Management does not try to get out of its commitments (reliable)	1	2	3	4	5
4.	Management does not take advantage of me (compassion)	1	2	3	4	5
5.	Management communicates honestly with me (open)	1	2	3	4	5
6.	Management can contribute to this organization' success (competent)	1	2	3	4	5
7.	Management behaves consistently (reliable)	1	2	3	4	5
8.	Management does not exploit me (compassion)	1	2	3	4	5
9.	Management does not mislead me in their communications (open)	1	2	3	4	5
10.	Management can help this organization survive during the next decade (competent)	1	2	3	4	5
11.	Management is reliable (reliable)	1	2	3	4	5
12.	Management cares about my best interests (compassion)	1	2	3	4	5
13.	Management does not withhold important information from me (open)	1	2	3	4	5
14.	Management is concerned for my welfare (compassion)	1	2	3	4	5
15.	Management can be counted on (reliable)	1	2	3	4	5
16.	Management can help solve important problems faced by this organization (competent)	1	2	3	4	5
17.	Management can be trusted (trust)	1	2	3	4	5

This instrument (in its current form or in previous versions) was originally published in:

Brockner, Joel, Spreitzer, Gretchen M., Mishra, Aneil, K., Hochwarter, Wayne, Pepper, Lewis, & Weinberg, Janice. (2004). Perceived control as an antidote to the negative effects of layoffs on survivors' organizational commitment and job performance. *Administrative Science Quarterly, 49*(1/March): 76–100.

Mishra, Aneil K., & Mishra, Karen E. (1994) The role of mutual trust in effective downsizing strategies. *Human Resource Management, 33*(2), 261–279.

It has been subsequently published by us in:

Mishra, Karen E., Spreitzer, Gretchen M., & Mishra, Aneil K. (1998). Preserving employee morale during downsizing. *Sloan Management Review, 39*(2), 83–95.

Other researchers have used this instrument in their published articles, as well:

Spreitzer, Gretchen. M., and Mishra, Aneil K. (1999). Giving up control without losing control: Trust and its substitutes' effects on managers' involving employees in decision making. *Group and Organization Management, 14*(2), 155–187.

Spreitzer, Gretchen M., & Mishra, Aneil K. (2002). To stay or to go: Voluntary survivor turnover following a downsizing. *Journal of Organizational Behavior, 23*(September), 707–729.Appendix B: Validated Trust Scale

APPENDIX C: TRUST CONTRACT EXAMPLE

1. We promise to be reliable in our work together. We promise to tell each other if there are problems that will keep us from meeting our agreed-upon deadlines.
2. We promise to be open and honest with each other. We agree to tell the truth about our work together.
3. We promise to do our best work for each other. We plan to exceed each other's expectations.
4. We promise to care about each other's interests and to promote each other's well-being.

Me _____   You _____

NOTES

☐ 1 Trust Is Needed Now More Than Ever

1. http://trade.gov/static/2011Parts.pdf
2. http://www.edelman.com/trust/2011/
3. http://trust.edelman.com/trust-download/executive-summary/, 2012, p. 3.
4. http://www.edelman.com/trust/2011/
5. http://trust.edelman.com/trust-download/executive-summary/, 2012, p. 6.
6. http://www.gallup.com/poll/5392/Trust-Government.aspx
7. http://www.gallup.com/poll/152528/Congress-Job-Approval-New-Low.aspx?utm_source=alert&utm_medium=email&utm_campaign=syndication&utm_content=morelink&utm_term=All%20Gallup%20Headlines
8. http://politicalticker.blogs.cnn.com/2011/09/28/cnn-poll-trust-in-government-at-all-time-low/
9. http://www.gallup.com/poll/149888/Local-State-Governments-Retain-Positive-Ratings.aspx
10. http://www.gallup.com/poll/149678/Americans-Express-Historic-Negativity-Toward-Government.aspx
11. http://trust.edelman.com/trust-download/executive-summary/, 2012, p. 2.
12. http://trust.edelman.com/trust-download/executive-summary/, 2012, p. 2.
13. "Hating what you do: Disenchantment with work is growing. What can be done it? *The Economist*, October 8, 2009. http://www.economist.com/node/14586131
14. Rosenthal, S. A. (2011). National leadership index 2011: A national study of confidence in leadership. Cambridge, MA: Center for Public Leadership, Harvard Kennedy School, Harvard University.
15. http://trust.edelman.com/trust-download/executive-summary/, 2012, p. 7.
16. http://www.edelman.com/trust/2011/
17. Interview with Sheldon Yellen, January 4, 2012.
18. http://www.politico.com/blogs/politico-live/2011/12/huntsman-addresses-the-trust-deficit-in-washington-106819.html
19. Putnam, R. D. (2000). *Bowling alone: The collapse and revival of American community*. New York, NY: Simon & Schuster.
20. http://faithpopcorn.com
21. Mishra, Aneil K., Mishra, Karen E., & Spreitzer, Gretchen M. (2009, Spring). How to downsize your company without downsizing morale. *MIT Sloan Management Review*, 39–44.
22. http://en.wikipedia.org/wiki/Hewlett-Packard_spying_scandal
23. http://www.economist.com/blogs/banyan/2012/01/japans-nuclear-crisis
24. http://www.economist.com/node/21549095
25. http://www.forbes.com/2011/09/26/ubs-ceo-resigns-board-affirms-commitment-to-investigation-changes-marketnewsvideo.html

26. Stroh, Linda K. (2007). *Trust rules: How to tell the good guys from the bad guys in work and life* (p. 4). Westport, CT: Praeger.
27. http://www.dw-world.de/dw/article/0,,5493641,00.html
28. http://en.wikipedia.org/wiki/George_Alan_Rekers
29. Malhotra, D., & Lumineau, F. (2011). Trust and collaboration in the aftermath of conflict: The effects of contract structure. *Academy of Management Journal, 54*(5), 981–998.
30. Luhmann, N. (1979). *Trust and power*. Hoboken, NJ: Wiley.
31. Luhmann, N. (1988). Familiarity, confidence, trust: Problems and alternatives. In D. Gambetta (Ed.), *Trust: Making and breaking cooperative relations* (pp. 94–107). Cambridge, MA: Basil Blackwell.
32. Fukuyama, F. (1995). *Trust: The social virtues and the creation of prosperity*. New York, NY: Free Press.
33. Mishra, A. K. (1996). Organizational responses to crisis: The centrality of trust. In R. Kramer & T. Tyler (Eds), *Trust in organizations* (pp. 261–287). Newbury Park, CA: Sage.
34. Mishra, Aneil K., & Spreitzer, Gretchen M. (1998). Explaining how survivors respond to downsizing: The roles of trust, empowerment, justice and work redesign. *Academy of Management Review, 23*(3), 567–588.
35. Deutsch, M. (1962). Cooperation and trust: Some theoretical notes. In Marshall R. Jones (Ed.), *Nebraska symposium on motivation* (pp. 275–319). Lincoln, NE: University of Nebraska Press.
36. Zand, D. (1972). Trust and managerial problem solving. *Administrative Science Quarterly, 17*, 229–239.
37. Granovetter, M. (1985). Economic action and social structure: The problem of embeddedness. *American Journal of Sociology, 91*(3) (November), 481–510.
38. Deutsch, M. (1973). *The resolution of conflict: Constructive and destructive processes*. New Haven, CT: Yale University Press.
39. Lewis, J. D., & Weigert, A. (1985). Trust as a social reality. *Social Forces, 63*, 967–985.
40. Kramer, R. (1999). Trust and distrust in organizations: Emerging perspectives, enduring questions. *Annual Review of Psychology, 50*, 569–598.
41. Mayer, R. C., Davis, J. H., & Schoorman, F. D. (1995). An integrative model of organizational trust. *Academy of Management Review, 20*, 709–734.
42. Rousseau, D. M., Sitkin, S. B., Burt, R. S., & Camerer, C. (1998). Not so different after all: A cross-discipline view of trust. *Academy of Management Review, 23*, 393–404.
43. Mishra, Aneil K. (1996). Organizational responses to crisis: The centrality of trust. In Roderick Kramer & Thomas Tyler (Eds), *Trust in organizations: Frontiers of theory and research* (pp. 261–287). Thousand Oaks, CA: Sage.
44. Mishra, Aneil K., & Mishra, Karen E. (2008). *Trust is everything: Become the leader others will follow*. Chapel Hill, NC: Lulu.
45. Mishra, Aneil K. (1996). Organizational responses to crisis: The centrality of trust. In Roderick Kramer & Thomas Tyler (Eds), *Trust in organizations: Frontiers of theory and research* (pp. 261–287). Thousand Oaks, CA: Sage.
46. Mishra, Aneil K., and Spreitzer, Gretchen M. (1998). Explaining how survivors respond to downsizing: The roles of trust, empowerment, justice and work redesign. *Academy of Management Review, 23*(3), 567–588.

47. Mishra, Aneil K., & Mishra, Karen E. (2008). *Trust is everything: Become the leader others will follow*. Chapel Hill, NC: Lulu.
48. Ibid.
49. Ibid.
50. Mishra, A. K., & Mishra, K. E. (2012). Positive organizational scholarship and trust in leaders. In K. S. Cameron & G. M. Spreitzer (Eds), *The Oxford handbook of positive organizational scholarship* (pp. 449–461). New York, NY: Oxford University Press.
51. http://insight.kellogg.northwestern.edu/index.php/Kellogg/article/cultures_of_trust/#When:06:55:24Z
52. Ibid.
53. Dirks, K. T., & Ferrin, D. L. (2002). Trust in leadership: Meta-analytic findings and implications for research and practice. *Journal of Applied Psychology, 87*(4), 611–628.
54. Colquitt, J. A., Scott, B. A., & LePine, J. A. 2007). Trust, trustworthiness, and trust propensity: A meta-analytic test of their unique relationships with risk taking and job performance. *Journal of Applied Psychology, 92*(4), 909.
55. Gabarro, J. (1987). *The dynamics of taking charge*. Boston, MA: Harvard Business School Press.
56. Collins, Jim. (2001). *Good to great: Why some companies make the leap . . . and others don't*. New York, NY: Harper Business.
57. Buckingham, Marcus, & Coffman, Curt. (1999). *First, break all the rules: What the world's greatest managers do differently*. New York, NY: Simon & Schuster.
58. Quinn, Robert E. (2004). *Building the bridge as you walk on it: A guide for leading change*. San Francisco, CA: Jossey-Bass.
59. Rath, Tom, & Conchie, Barry. (2009). *Strengths-based leadership*. New York, NY: Gallup.
60. Johnson, Andrew M., Vernon, Philip A., McCarthy, Julie M., Molson, Mindy, Harris, Julie A., & Lang, Kerry L. (1998). Nature vs. nurture: Are leaders born or made? A behavior genetic investigation of leadership style. *Twin Research, 1*, 216–223.
61. Yukl, Gary. (2009). *Leadership in organizations* (7th ed.). Englewood Cliffs, NJ: Prentice-Hall.
62. Ibid.
63. Luthans, Fred, & Avolio, Bruce. (2003). Authentic leadership: A positive development approach. In Kim S. Cameron, Jane E. Dutton, & Robert E. Quinn (Eds), *Positive organizational scholarship: Foundations of a new discipline*, (pp. 241–261). San Francisco, CA: Berrett-Koehler.
64. Golembiewski, R., & McConkie, M. (1975). The centrality of trust in group processes. In Cary L. Cooper (Ed.), *Theories of group processes* (pp. 131–185) New York, NY: Wiley.
65. http://www.twomenandatruck.ca/the-grandma-rule-
66. Likert, R. (1961). *New patterns of management*. McGraw-Hill, New York.
67. Gabarro, John J. (1978). The development of trust, influence and expectations. In Anthony Athos & John J. Gabarro (Eds), *Interpersonal Behavior* (pp. 295–298). Englewood Cliffs, NJ: Prentice Hall.
68. Kramer, R. (1999). Trust and distrust in organizations: Emerging perspectives, enduring questions. *Annual Review of Psychology, 50*, 569–598.

69. Interview with Dr. Bruce Rubin, December 30, 2011.
70. Mishra, Aneil K., & Mishra, Karen E. (2008). Trust is everything: Become the leader others will follow. Chapel Hill, NC: Lulu.
71. Handy, C. (2002, December). What's a business for? *Harvard Business Review*.
72. http://www.edelman.com/trust/2009/

☐ 2 What Trust Is and Why It Matters

1. Granovetter, M. (1985). Economic action and social structure: The problem of embeddedness. *American Journal of Sociology, 91* (3) (November), 481–510.
2. Lewis, J. D., & Weigert, A. (1985). Trust as a social reality. *Social Forces, 63*, 967–985.
3. Mishra, A. K. (1996). Organizational responses to crisis: The centrality of trust. In R. Kramer and T. Tyler (Eds), *Trust in organizations* (pp. 261–287). Newbury Park, CA: Sage.
4. Mayer, R. C., Davis, J. H., & Schoorman, F. D. (1995). An integrative model of organizational trust. *Academy of Management Review, 20*, 709–734.
5. Sitkin, S. B., & Roth, N. L. (1993). Explaining the limited effectiveness of legalistic "remedies" for trust/distrust. *Organization Science, 4*, 367–92.
6. Rousseau, D. M., Sitkin, S. B., Burt, R. S., & Camerer, C. (1998). Not so different after all: A cross-discipline view of trust. *Academy of Management Review, 23*, 393–404.
7. Mayer, R. C., Davis, J. H., & Schoorman, F. D. (1995). An integrative model of organizational trust. *Academy of Management Review, 20*, 709–734.
8. Simons, Tony. (2008). The integrity dividend: Leading by the power of your word. San Francisco, CA: Jossey-Bass.
9. Hart, Paul, & Saunders, Carol. (1997). Power and trust: Critical factors in the adoption and use of electric data interchange. *Organization Science, 8*, 23–42.
10. Luhmann, N. (1979). *Trust and power*. New York, NY: J. Wiley.
11. Deutsch, M. (1962). Cooperation and trust: Some theoretical notes. In M. R. Jones (Ed.), *Nebraska symposium on motivation* (pp. 275–319). Lincoln, NE: University of Nebraska Press.
12. Deutsch, M. (1973). *The resolution of conflict: Constructive and destructive processes*. New Haven, CT: Yale University Press.
13. Luhmann, N. (1988). Familiarity, confidence, trust: Problems and alternatives. In D. Gambetta (Ed.), *Trust: Making and breaking cooperative relations* (pp. 94–107). Cambridge, MA: Basil Blackwell.
14. Deutsch, M. (1973). *The resolution of conflict: Constructive and destructive processes*. New Haven, CT: Yale University Press.
15. Gabarro, J. (1987). *The dynamics of taking charge* (p. 104). Boston, MA: Harvard Business School Press.
16. McGregor, D. (1967). *The professional manager*. New York: McGraw-Hill.
17. Gabarro, J. (1987). *The dynamics of taking charge* (p. 104). Boston, MA: Harvard Business School Press.
18. Ouchi, William G. (1981). *Theory Z: How American business can meet the Japanese challenge*. Reading, MA: Addison-Wesley.

19. Kirkpatrick, S., & Locke, E. (1991). Leadership: Do traits matter? *Academy of Management Executive, 5*(2), 48–60.
20. Nanus, B. (1989). *The leader's edge: The seven keys to leadership in a turbulent world* (p. 102). Chicago, IL: Contemporary Books.
21. Ouchi, William G. (1981) *Theory Z: How American business can meet the Japanese challenge*. Reading, MA: Addison-Wesley.
22. Gabarro, J. (1987). *The dynamics of taking charge*. Boston, MA: Harvard Business School Press.
23. Nanus, B. (1992). *Visionary leadership: Creating a compelling sense of direction for organizations*. San Francisco, CA: Jossey-Bass.
24. Kilpatrick, S. A. & Locke, E. A. (1991). Leadership: Do traits matter? *Academy of Management Executive, 5*(2), 50–60.
25. Davis, S., & Lawrence, P. (1977). *Matrix*. Reading, MA: Addison-Wesley.
26. Nooteboom, B. (2002). *Trust: Forms, foundations, functions, failures and figures*. Cheltenham, U.K.: Edward Elgar.
27. Mayer, R. C., Davis, J. H., & Schoorman, F. D. (1995). An integrative model of organizational trust. *Academy of Management Review, 20,* 709–734.
28. Szulanski, G., Cappetta, R., & Jensen, R. J. (2004) When and how trustworthiness matters: Knowledge transfer and the moderating effect of causal ambiguity. *Organization Science, 15,* 600–613.
29. Shapiro, D., Sheppard, B.B., & Cheraskin, L. (1992). Business on a handshake. *Negotiation Journal, 8,* 365–377.
30. Liu, Steven S. (2009).The roles of competence trust, formal contract, and time horizon in interorganizational learning. *Organization Studies, 30,* 333–353.
31. McClelland, David C., and Burham, David H. (1976). Power is the great motivator. *Harvard Business Review, 54*(2), 100–110.
32. Dunleavy, K. N., Chory, R. M., & Goodboy, A. K. (2010). Responses to deception in the workplace: perceptions of credibility, power, and trustworthiness. *Communication Studies, 61,* 239–255.
33. Dunleavy, K. N., Chory, R. M., & Goodboy, A. K. (2010). Responses to deception in the workplace: perceptions of credibility, power, and trustworthiness. *Communication Studies, 61,* 243.
34. Gabarro, J. (1987). *The dynamics of taking charge*. Boston, MA: Harvard Business School Press.
35. Kilpatrick, S. A. & Locke, E. A. (1991). Leadership: Do traits matter? *Academy of Management Executive, 5*(2), 50–60.
36. Janowicz-Panjaitan, M., & Krishnan, R. (2009). Measures for dealing with competence and integrity violations of interorganizational trust at the corporate and operating levels of organizational hierarchy. *Journal of Management Studies, 46*(2), 245–268.
37. Mishra, A. K. (1996). Organizational responses to crisis: The centrality of trust. In R. Kramer and T. Tyler (Eds), *Trust in organizations* (266). Newbury Park, CA: Sage.
38. McGregor, D. (1967). *The professional manager*. New York: McGraw-Hill.
39. Cummings, L., & Bromiley, P. (1996). The organizational trust inventory (OTI): Development and validation. *Trust in organizations: Frontiers of theory and research* (pp. 302–330).

40. Kanter, R. (1983). *The change masters: Innovation and entrepreneurship in the American corporation*. New York, NY: Simon & Schuster.
41. Kanter, R. (1989). *When giants learn to dance*. New York: Simon & Schuster.
42. Kotter, J., & Schlesinger, L. (1979). Choosing strategies for change. *Harvard Business Review, 57* (2), 106–114.
43. Pascale, R. (1990). *Managing on the edge: How the smartest companies use conflict to stay ahead*. New York, NY: Simon & Schuster.
44. http://www.industryweek.com/articles/cutting_costs_without_cutting_people_24095.aspx?ShowAll=1&SectionID=3
45. http://www.rhinofoods.com/stuff/contentmgr/files/1/f06979adb30 aad81d139a595b01ad0b0/download/guide___working_bridges_version_3_15_11.pdf
46. Interview with Sheldon Yellen, January 4, 2012.
47. Dirks, K. T., & Ferrin, D. L. (2002). Trust in leadership: Meta-analytic findings and implications for research and practice. *Journal of Applied Psychology, 87*, 618.
48. Mayer, R. C., & Gavin, M. B. (2005). "Trust in management and performance: Who minds the shop while the employees watch the boss?" *The Academy of Management Journal, 48*(5), 874–888.
49. http://www.khpi.com/Current-R-D/WorkTrends/Trust-Matters
50. Salamon, S. D., and Robinson, S. L. (2008). Trust that binds: The impact of collective felt trust on organizational performance. *Journal of Applied Psychology, 93*, 593.
51. Personal communication from Ranjay Gulati, January 7, 2012.
52. http://www.rhinofoods.com/stuff/contentmgr/files/1/f06979adb30aad 81d139a595b01ad0b0/download/guide___working_bridges_version_3_15_11.pdf
53. http://www.rhinofoods.com/stuff/contentmgr/files/1/e71ff89d5551 f4467c8058ec2e329013/download/guide___eep_version_2_14_11.pdf
54. Lobdell, K., Camp, S., Stamou, S., Swanson, R., Reames, M., Madjarov, J., . . . Robicsek, F. (2009). Quality improvement in cardiac critical care. *HSR Proceedings in Intensive Care and Cardiovascular Anesthesia, 1*(1): 22–26.

☐ 3 Leaders Are Born *and* Made

1. Johnson, Andrew M., Vernon, Philip A., McCarthy, Julie M., Molson, Mindy, Harris, Julie A., & Lang, Kerry L. (1998). Nature vs. nurture: Are leaders born or made? A behavior genetic investigation of leadership style. *Twin Research, 1*, 216–223.
2. Locke, E., & Kirkpatrick, S. (1999). *The essence of leadership: The four keys to leading successfully*. New York, NY: Lexington Books.
3. Gardner, J. W. (1993). *On leadership*. New York, NY: Free Press.
4. McCauley, C. D. (2001). Leader training and development. In S. J. Zaccaro & R. J. Klimoski (Eds), *The nature of organizational leadership* (pp. 347–383). San Francisco, CA: Jossey-Bass.

5. Kouzes, J., & Posner, B. (2002). *The leadership challenge*. San Francisco, CA: Jossey-Bass.
6. McCauley, C.D. (2001). Leader training and development. In S. J. Zaccaro & R. J. Klimoski (Eds), *The nature of organizational leadership* (347–383). San Francisco, CA: Jossey-Bass.
7. Interview with Pastor James Wenger, December 14, 2010.
8. Arvey, Richard D., Rotundo, Maria, Johnson, Wendy, Zhang, Zhen, & McGue, Matt. (2006). The determinants of leadership role occupancy: Genetic and personality factors. *The Leadership Quarterly, 17*, 1–20.
9. Zhang, Zhen, Ilies, Remus, & Arvey, Richard. (2009). Beyond genetic explanations for leadership: The moderating role of the social environment. *Organizational behavior and human decision processes, 110*, 118–128.
10. Ibid.
11. Interview with Dr. Kevin Lobdell, November 28, 2011.
12. Interview with Dr. Bruce Rubin, December 30, 2011.
13. Ibid.
14. http://www.bersinassociates.com/fr3/annualreport.pdf
15. McCallum, S., & O'Connell, D. (2008). Social capital and leadership development: Building stronger leadership skills through enhanced relationship skills. *Leadership & Organization Development Journal, 30*(2), 152–166.
16. Dirks, K. T., & Ferrin, D. L. (2002). Trust in leadership: Meta-analytic findings and implications for research and practice. *Journal of Applied Psychology, 87*(4), 611–628.
17. Gabarro, J. J. (1987). *The dynamics of taking charge*. Boston, MA: Harvard Business School Press.
18. Dirks, K. T., & Ferrin, D. L. (2002). Trust in leadership: Meta-analytic findings and implications for research and practice. *Journal of Applied Psychology, 87*(4), 611–628.
19. Bai, Y. T., Li, P. P., & Xi, Y. M. (2012). The distinctive effects of dual-level leadership behaviors on employees' trust in leadership: An empirical study. *Asia Pacific Journal of Management, 29*(2), 213–237.
20. Our thinking about these three levels of change has been influenced by Aneil's colleagues in the Stephen M. Ross School of Business executive education programs at the University of Michigan: Kim Cameron, Bob Quinn, Jeff DeGraff, and Gretchen Spreitzer. See also Cameron, Kim S., Freeman, Sarah J., & Mishra, Aneil K. (1991). Best practices in white-collar downsizing: Managing contradictions. *Academy of Management Executive, 5*(3), 57–73; Cameron, Kim S., Freeman, Sarah J., & Mishra, Aneil K. (1993). Organizational downsizing. In George Huber & William Glick (Eds), *Organizational change and redesign: ideas and insights for improving performance* (pp. 19–65). New York, NY: Oxford University Press.
21. Mishra, A., & Mishra, K. (2008). *Trust is everything: Become the leader others will follow*. Chapel Hill, NC: Lulu.
22. Saparito, P. A., C. C. Chen, & Sapienza, H.J. (2004). The role of relational trust in bank–small firm relationships. *The Academy of Management Journal, 47*(3), 400–410.
23. Mishra, A., & Mishra, K. (2012). Trust in leaders and lasting positive change. In Kim Cameron & Gretchen Spreitzer (Eds), *Handbook of Positive*

Organizational Scholarship (pp. 449–461). New York, NY: Oxford University Press.

24. Hofstede, Geert. (1980). Motivation, leadership, and organization: Do American theories apply abroad? *Organizational Dynamics, 9*(1), 42–63.

25. Fichman, M. (2003). Straining towards trust: Some constraints essay on studying trust in organizations. *Journal of Organizational Behavior, 24*(2), 133–157.

26. Li, P. P., Bai, Y., & Xi, Y. (2012). The contextual antecedents of organizational trust: A cross-level analysis. *Management and Organizational Review, 8,* 371–396.

27. Mishra, A., & Mishra, K. (2008). *Trust is everything: Become the leader others will follow.* Chapel Hill, NC: Lulu.

28. Norman, Steven M., Avolio, Bruce J., & Luthans, Fred. (2010). The impact of positivity and transparency on trust in leaders and their perceived effectiveness. *The Leadership Quarterly, 21*(3), 350–364.

29. Worline, M. C., & Quinn, R. (2003). Positive organizational scholarship: foundations of a new discipline. In K. Cameron, J. Dutton, & R. Quinn (Eds), *Positive organizational scholarship: Foundations of a new discipline* (pp. 138–161). San Francisco, CA: Berrett-Koehler.

30. Luthans, F., & Avolio, B. (2003). Authentic leadership development. In K. Cameron, J. Dutton, & R. Quinn (Eds) *Positive organizational scholarship: Foundations of a new discipline* (pp. 240–258). San Francisco, CA: Berrett-Koehler.

31. Mishra, A., & Mishra, K. (2008). *Trust is everything: Become the leader others will follow.* Chapel Hill, NC: Lulu.

32. Rotter, J. B. (1967). A new scale for the measurement of interpersonal trust. *Journal of Personality, 35,* 651–65.

33. Nielsen, R., Marrone, J. A., & Slay, H. S. (2010). A new look at humility: Exploring the humility concept and its role in socialized charismatic leadership (SCL). *Journal of Leadership & Organizational Studies, 17*(1), 33–43.

34. Luthans, F., & Avolio, B. (2003). Authentic leadership development. In Cameron, Dutton, & Quinn (Eds), *Positive organizational scholarship: Foundations of a new discipline* (pp. 240–258). San Francisco, CA: Berrett-Koehler.

35. Nielsen, R., Marrone, J. A., & Slay, H. S. (2010). A new look at humility: Exploring the humility concept and its role in socialized charismatic leadership (SCL). *Journal of Leadership & Organizational Studies, 17*(1), 33–43.

36. Owens, B. P., Rowatt, W. C., & Wilkins, A. L. (2012). Exploring the relevance and implications of humility in organizations. In K. S. Cameron & G. M. Spreitzer (Eds), *Handbook of positive organizational scholarship* (pp. 260–272). New York, NY: Oxford University Press.

37. Walumbwa, F. O., Avolio, B. J., Gardner, W. L., Wernsing, T. S., & Peterson, S. J. (2008). Authentic leadership: Development and validation of a theory-based measure. *Journal of Management, 34,* 89–126.

38. Luthans, F., & Avolio, B. (2003). Authentic leadership development. In Cameron, Dutton, & Quinn (Eds), *Positive organizational scholarship: Foundations of a new discipline* (pp. 240–258). San Francisco, CA: Berrett-Koehler.

39. Ibid.

40. Helland, M. R., & Winston, B. E. (2005). Towards a deeper understanding of hope and leadership. *Journal of Leadership and Organizational Studies, 12*(2), 42–54.

41. Mishra, A., & Mishra, K. (2008). *Trust is everything: Become the leader others will follow.* Chapel Hill, NC: Lulu.
42. Mishra, A. & Mishra, K. (2012). Trust in leaders and lasting positive change. In K.S. Cameron and G.M. Spreitzer (Eds), *Handbook of positive organizational scholarship* (pp. 449–461). New York, NY: Oxford University Press.
43. Owens, B. P., Rowatt, W. C., & Wilkins, A. L. (2012). Exploring the relevance and implications of humility in organizations. In K.S. Cameron & G.M. Spreitzer (Eds), *Handbook of positive organizational scholarship* (260–272) New York, NY: Oxford University Press.
44. Luthans, F., & Avolio, B. (2003). Authentic leadership development. In Cameron, Dutton, & Quinn (Eds), *Positive organizational scholarship: Foundations of a new discipline* (pp. 240–258). San Francisco, CA: Berrett-Koehler.
45. Ibid.
46. Ibid.
47. Walumbwa, F. O., Luthans, F., Avey, J. B., & Adegoke, O. (2011). Authentically leading groups: The mediating role of collective psychological capital and trust. *Journal of Organizational Behavior, 32*(1), 4–24.
48. Interview with Sheldon Yellen, January 4, 2012.
49. Ibid.
50. Spreitzer, G. M. (2006). Leading to grow and growing to lead: Leadership development lessons from positive organizational studies. *Organizational Dynamics, 35*(4), 305–315.
51. http://www.bus.umich.edu/Positive/POS-Teaching-and-Learning/ReflectedBestSelfExercise.htm
52. http://strengths.gallup.com/110440/About-StrengthsFinder-2.aspx

☐ 4 Developing Your Own Trust Network

1. Gerbasi, Alexandra & Cook, Karen S. (2008).The effect of perceived trustworthiness on affect in negotiated and reciprocal exchange. In Jody Clay-Warner and Dawn T. Robinson (Eds), *Social structure and emotion* (pp. 141–165). New York, NY: Elsevier.
2. Quinn, R. *Leading Change* executive education program, the University of Michigan Ross School of Business, October 1998, Ann Arbor, MI.
3. Quinn, Robert. (1998). Remarks given during *Leading Change* program, University of Michigan Executive Education.
4. Gerbasi, Alexandra & Cook, Karen S. (2008).The effect of perceived trustworthiness on affect in negotiated and reciprocal exchange. In Jody Clay-Warner and Dawn T. Robinson (Eds), *Social structure and emotion* (pp. 141–165). New York, NY: Elsevier.
5. Granovetter, Mark S. (1973). The strength of weak ties. *The American Journal of Sociology, 78*(6), 1360–1380.
6. Granovetter, Mark S. (1985). Economic action and social structure: The problem of embeddedness. *American Journal of Sociology, 91*(3), 481.
7. http://www.princeton.edu/main/news/archive/S31/80/01M66/
8. http://www.princeton.edu/pub/oc/schedule/

9. Although we reviewed the Freshman Orientation calendar of events, we couldn't determine whether students today still actually receive the lecture about alumni generosity during the fire safety presentation, as Aneil and his 1984 classmates did, or at some other point during Freshman Week.

10. Dr. Albertson not only agreed to discuss Aneil's case with Aneil's brother, but also intervened when four pathologists initially could not agree as to the type of thyroid cancer in question, sending some of Aneil's lab tissue to one of the country's leading experts, Dr. Ronald DeLellis of Brown University. Dr. Albertson also coordinated Aneil's treatment with Dr. Kathryn Morton, now at the University of Utah, the nuclear medicine specialist who treated Aneil with radioactive iodine. Dr. Morton responded quickly when the side effects of withdrawing Aneil's thyroid hormone prior to receiving radiation resulted in a physical crisis of exhaustion and insomnia.

11. http://www.bumc.bu.edu/endo/faculty/braverman/

12. Lawler, Edward J. (2001). An affect theory of social exchange. *The American Journal of Sociology, 107*(2), 321–352.

13. Granovetter, Mark S. (1985.) Economic action and social structure: The problem of embeddedness. *American Journal of Sociology, 91*(3), 481–493.

14. Gerbasi, Alexandra & Cook, Karen S. (2008). The effect of perceived trustworthiness on affect in negotiated and reciprocal exchange. In Jody Clay-Warner and Dawn T. Robinson (Eds), *Social structure and emotion* (pp. 141–165). New York, NY: Elsevier.

☐ 5 Building Trust Within Teams

1. Katzenbach, Jon R., & Smith, Douglas K. (1992). *The wisdom of teams: Creating the high-performance organization.* Cambridge, MA: Harvard Business School Press.

2. Sundstrom, E., DeMeuse, K. P., & Futrell, D. (1990). Work teams: Applications and effectiveness. *American, 45*(2), 120–133.

3. Mathieu, J., Maynard, M. T., Rapp, T., & Gilson, L. (2008). Team effectiveness 1997–2007: A review of recent advancements and a glimpse into the future. *Journal of Management, 34*(3), 410–476.

4. Argote, L., & McGrath, J. E. (1993). Group process in organization: Continuity and change. In C. I. Cooper & I. T. Robertson (Eds), *International Review of Industrial and Organizational Psychology* (Vol. 8, pp. 333–389. New York: John Wiley.

5. Goodman, P. S. (1986). The impact of task and technology on group performance. In P. Goodman & Associates (Eds), *Designing effective work groups* (pp. 120–167). San Francisco, CA: Jossey-Bass.

6. Barrick, M. B., Bradley, B. H., Kristof-Brown, A. L., & Colbert, A. E. (2007). The moderating role of top management team interdependence: Implications of real teams and working groups. *Academy of Management Journal, 50*, 544–557.

7. Lencioni, Patrick M. (2002). *The Five Dysfunctions of a Team.* San Francisco, CA: Jossey-Bass.

8. Colquitt, J. A., LePine, J. A., Zapata, C. P., & Wild, R. E. (2011). Trust in typical and high-reliability contexts: Building and reacting to trust among firefighters. *The Academy of Management Journal, 54*(5), 999–1015.

9. De Jong, B. A., & Elfring, T. (2010). How does trust affect the performance of ongoing teams? The mediating role of reflexivity, monitoring, and effort. *The Academy of Management Journal, 53*(3), 535–549.

10. Langfred, C. W. (2004). Too much of a good thing? Negative effects of high trust and individual autonomy in self-managing teams. *The Academy of Management Journal, 47*(3), 385–399.

11. Langfred, C. W. (2007). The downside of self-management: A longitudinal study of the effects of conflict on trust, autonomy, and task interdependence in self-managing teams. *The Academy of Management Journal, 50*(4), 885–900.

12. Ross, Judith A. (2006, June). Trust makes the team go 'round. *Harvard Management Update*, pp. 3–6.

13. Schaubroeck, J., Lam, S. S. K., & Peng, A. C. (2011). Cognition-based and affect-based trust as mediators of leader behavior influences on team performance. *Journal of Applied Psychology, 96*(4), 863.

14. Lau, Dora, & Liden, Robert C. (2008). Antecedents of coworker trust: Leaders' blessings. *Journal of Applied Psychology, 93*(50), 1130–1138.

15. Mathieu, J., Maynard, M. T., Rapp, T., & Gilson, L. (2008). Team effectiveness 1997–2007: A review of recent advancements and a glimpse into the future. *Journal of Management, 34*(3), 410–476.

16. Likert, Rensis (1967). *The human organization: Its management and value.* New York, NY: McGraw-Hill.

17. Lawler, E. E. (1993). Managing employee involvement. In W. F. Christopher and C. G. Thor (Eds), *Handbook for productivity measurement and improvement* (pp. 10.1.3–10.1.13). Cambridge, MA: Productivity Press.

18. Lencioni, Patrick. (2002). *The five dysfunctions of a team: A leadership fable.* San Francisco, CA: Jossey-Bass.

19. Steil, Lyman K., Barker, Larry L., & Watson, Kittie W. (1983). *Effective listening: Key to your success* (p. 5). New York, NY: Random House.

20. Hackman J. R. & Wageman, R. (2005). A theory of team coaching. *Academy of Management Review, 30*(2), 269–287.

21. Mathieu, J., Maynard, M. T., Rapp, T., & Gilson, L. (2008). Team effectiveness 1997–2007: A review of recent advancements and a glimpse into the future. *Journal of Management, 34*(3), 410–476.

22. Ibid.

23. Costa, A. C., Roe, R. A., & Tallieu, T. (2001). Trust within teams: The relation with performance effectiveness. *European Journal of Work and Organizational Psychology, 10*(3), 225–244.

24. Peters, L., & Karren, R. (2009). An examination of the roles of trust and functional diversity on virtual team performance ratings. *Group & Organization Management, 34*(4), 479–504.

25. Kiffin-Petersen, S. (2004). Trust: A neglected variable in team effectiveness research. *Journal of Management & Organization, 10*(1), 38–53.

26. Robert, L. P., Jr., Dennis, A. R., & Hung, Y. C. (2009). Individual swift trust and knowledge-based trust in face-to-face and virtual team members. *Journal of Management Information Systems, 26*(2), 241–279.

27. Garfield, J., & Stanton, K. (2005, November). Building effective teams in real time. *Harvard Management Update*, 3–5.
28. Ross, Judith A. (2006, June). Trust makes the team go 'round. *Harvard Management Update*, 3–6.
29. Spreitzer, G. M., Noble, D. S., Mishra, A. K., & Cooke, W. N. (1999). Predicting process improvement team performance in an automotive firm: Explicating the roles of trust and empowerment. In R. Wageman (Ed.), *Research on managing groups and team: Groups in context* (Vol. 2, pp. 71–92). Stamford, CT: JAI.
30. De Jong, B. A., & Elfring, T. (2010). How does trust affect the performance of ongoing teams? The mediating role of reflexivity, monitoring, and effort. *Academy of Management Journal*, *53*(3), 535–549.
31. Penteli, N., & Tucker, R. (2009). Power and trust in global virtual teams. *Communications of the Association for Computing Machinery*, *52*(12), 113–115.
32. Katzenbach, Jon R., & Smith, Douglas K. (1992). *The wisdom of teams: Creating the high-performance organization*. Cambridge, MA: Harvard Business School Press.
33. Field, A. (2006, August). Are you rewarding solo performance at the team's expense? *Harvard Management Update*, 3–5.
34. Robert L. P., Jr., Dennis, A. R., & Hung, Y. C. (2009). Individual swift trust and knowledge-based trust in face-to-face and virtual team members. *Journal of Management Information Systems*, *26*(2), 241–279.
35. Ross, Judith A. (2005, November). Team camaraderie: Can you have too much? *Harvard Management Update*, 3–4.
36. Long, C. P., & Sitkin, S. B. (2006). Trust in the balance: How managers integrate trust-building and task control. In R. Bachmann & A. Zaheer (Eds), *Handbook of trust research* (pp. 87–106). Cheltenham, England: Edward Elgar.
37. Ross, Judith A. (2005, November). Team camaraderie: Can you have too much? *Harvard Management Update*, 3–4.
38. Atwater, Eastwood. (1992). *I Hear You*. New York, NY: Walker & Company.
39. Ibid.
40. Gibson, C. B., & Cohen, S. G. (2003). *Virtual teams that work: Creating conditions for virtual team effectiveness* (p. 73). San Francisco, CA: Jossey-Bass.
41. Ramsey, R. P., & Sohi, R. S. (1997). Listening to your customers: The impact of perceived salesperson listening behavior on relationship outcomes. *Journal of the Academy of Marketing Science*, *25*(2), 127–137.
42. Aggarwal, P., Castleberry, S. B., Ridenour, R., & Shepherd, C. D. (2005). Salesperson empathy and listening: Impact on relationship outcomes. *Journal of Marketing Theory and Practice*, 16–31.
43. Mechanic, David, & Meyer, Sharon. (2000). Concepts of trust among patients with serious illness. *Social Science & Medicine*, *51*(5), 657–668.
44. Holton, J. A. (2001). Building trust and collaboration in a virtual team. *Team Performance Management*, *7*(3/4), 36–47.
45. Steil, Lyman K., Barker, Larry L., & Watson, Kittie W. (1983). *Effective listening: Key to your success* (p. 5). New York, NY: Random House.
46. Wacker, K. G., & Hawkins, K. (1995). Curricula comparison for classes in listening. *International Journal of Listening*, *9*, 14–28.

47. Cannon-Bowers, J.A., Tannenbaum, S. I., Salas, E., & Volpe, C. E. (1995). Defining team competencies and establishing team training requirements. In E. Salas (Ed.), *Team effectiveness and decision making in organizations* (pp. 333–380). San Francisco, CA: Jossey-Bass.

48. Moreland, R. L., Argote, L., & Krishnan, R. (1998). *Training people to work in groups.* In G. M. Wittenbaum, S. I. Vaughan, G. Stasser, & R. S. Tindale (Eds), *Theory and research on small groups* (pp. 37–61). New York, NY: Plenum.

49. Ross, Judith A. (2005, November). Team camaraderie: Can you have too much? *Harvard Management Update,* 3–4.

50. Hackman, J. R. (1987). The design of work teams. In J. W. Lorsch (Ed.), *Handbook of organizational behavior* (pp. 315–342). Englewood Cliffs, NJ: Prentice Hall; Ross, Judith A. (2005, November). Team camaraderie: Can you have too much? *Harvard Management Update,* 3–4.

51. Mickaitis, A. I., Rose, E. L., & Zettinig, P. (2009). The determinants of trust in multicultural global virtual teams. *Academy of Management Proceedings,* 1–6, New York, NY: Pace University.

52. Blatt, R. (2009). Tough love: How communal schema and contracting practices build relational capital in entrepreneurial teams. *Academy of Management Review, 34*(3), 533–551.

53. Panteli, N., & Tucker, R. (2009). Power and trust in global virtual teams. *Communications of the ACM, 52*(12), 113–115.

54. Field, A. (2006, August). Are you rewarding solo performance at the team's expense? *Harvard Management Update,* 3–5.

55. Ross, Judith A. (2005, November). Team camaraderie: Can you have too much? *Harvard Management Update,* 3–4.

56. Ross, Judith, A. (2008, December). Make your good team great. *Harvard Management Update,* 3–5.

☐ 6 Making Change Last by Creating a Culture of Trust

1. Kramer, Roderick M. (2010). Collective trust within organizations: Conceptual foundations and empirical insights. *Corporate Reputation Review, 13*(2), 82–97.

2. Barber, Benard. (1983). *The logic and limits of trust.* New Brunswick, NJ: Rutgers University Press.

3. Gambetta, Diego. (1988). Can we trust trust? In Diego Gambetta (Ed.), *Trust: Making and breaking cooperative relationships* (pp. 213–237). Cambridge, MA: Basil Blackwell.

4. Kramer, Roderick M., & Cook, Karen S. (2006). *Trust and distrust within organizations.* New York, NY: Russell Sage Foundations.

5. Kouzes, J. M, & Posner, B. Z. (1996). Envisioning your future: Imagining ideal scenarios. *The Futurist, 30*(3), 14–19.

6. Gould-Williams, J., & Davies, F. (2005). Using social exchange theory to predict the effects of HRM practice on employee outcomes: An analysis of public sector workers. *Public Management Review, 7*(1), 25–47.

7. For a recent discussion, please see Mishra, Karen E., Schwarz, Gavin M., & Mishra, Aneil K. (2011). The evolution of trust and control as evidenced through an organization's human resources practices. In Rosalind Searle & Denise Skinner (Eds), *Trust and human resource management* (pp. 42–64). London, England: Edward Elgar.

8. Sheppard, B. H., & Tuchinsky, M. (1996). Micro-OB and the network organization. In Roderick Kramer & Thomas Tyler (Eds), *Trust in organizations: Frontiers of theory and research* (pp. 140–165). Thousand Oaks, CA: Sage.

9. Shapiro, D., Sheppard, B. H., & Cheraskin, L. (1992, October). Business on a handshake. *The Negotiation Journal, 8*, 365–378.

10. Denison, Daniel R. (1990). *Corporate culture and organizational effectiveness* (p. 2). New York: Wiley.

11. Mishra, A. K., & Mishra, K. E. (2012). Trustworthy leadership for lasting positive change. In G. M. Spreitzer & K. S. Cameron (Eds), *Handbook of positive organizational scholarship* (pp. 449–461). New York, NY: Oxford University Press.

12. Cameron, K. S. (2007). Positive organizational scholarship. In S. Clegg & J. Bailey (Eds), *International encyclopedia of organizational studies*. Beverly Hills, CA: Sage.

13. Spreitzer, G. M. (2006). Leading to grow and growing to lead: Leadership development lessons from positive organizational studies. *Organizational Dynamics, 35*(4), 305–315.

14. Spreitzer, G. M., Stephens, J. P., & Sweetman, D. (2009). The reflected best self field experiment with adolescent leaders: Exploring the psychological resources associated with feedback source and valence. *Journal of Positive Psychology, 4*(5), 331–348.

15. Cameron, K. S. (2008). *Positive leadership: Strategies for extraordinary performance* (p. 23). San Francisco, CA: Berrett-Koehler.

16. Ibid.

17. Rath, T., & Conchie, B. (2009). *Strengths-based leadership: Great leaders, teams, and why people follow*. New York, NY: Gallup.

18. Cameron, K. S. (2008). *Positive leadership: Strategies for extraordinary performance* (p. 23). San Francisco, CA: Berrett-Koehler.

19. Ibid.

20. Interview with George Barrett, November 23, 2011.

21. Likert, R. (1967). *The Human Organization: Its management and value*. New York, NY: McGraw-Hill.

22. Ibid.

23. Dolphin, R. R. (2005). Internal communications: Today's strategic imperative. *Journal of Marketing Communications, 11*(3), 171–190.

24. Kalla, H. K. (2005). Integrated internal communications: A multidisciplinary perspective. *Corporate Communications, 10*(4), 302–314.

25. Therkelsen, D. J., & Fiebich, C. L. (2003). The supervisor: The linchpin of employee relations. *Journal of Communication Management, 8*(2), 120–129.

26. Huang, X., Iun, J., Aili, L. (2010). Does participative leadership enhance work performance by inducing empowerment or trust? The differential effects on managerial and non-managerial subordinates. *Journal of Organizational Behavior, 31*(1), 122–143.

27. Argenti, P. (1998). Strategic employee communications. *Human Resource Management, 37*(3–4), 199–206.

28. Wright, D. K. (1995). The role of corporate public relations executives in the future of employee communications. *Public Relations Review, 21*(3), 181–198.
29. Dolphin, R. R. (2005). Internal communications: Today's strategic imperative. *Journal of Marketing Communications, 11*(3), 171–190.
30. Mishra, A. K., & Mishra, K. E. (1994). The role of mutual trust in effective downsizing strategies. *Human Resource Management, 33*(2), 261–279.
31. Graen, G. B., & Uhl-Bien, M. (1995). Relationship-based approach to leadership: Development of leader-member exchange (LMX) theory of leadership over 25 years: Applying a multi-level multi-domain perspective. *Leadership Quarterly, 6*, 219–247.
32. Ibid.
33. Brower, H. H., Schoorman, F. D., & Tan, H. H. (2000). A model of relational leadership: The integration of trust and leader- member exchange. *Leadership Quarterly, 11*, 229.
34. *The Harbour Report* North America (2008). Retrieved from http://www.oliverwyman.com/content_images/OW_EN_Automotive_Press_2008_HarbourMedia08.pdf, slide 14.
35. http://media.gm.com/media/us/en/gm/company_info/facilities/stamping/parma.html
36. http://www.cleveland.com/business/index.ssf/2011/05/general_motors_parma_metal_cen.html
37. http://media.gm.com/media/us/en/gm/company_info/facilities/stamping/parma.html

☐ 7 Trust and Innovation

1. Bronson, P., & Merryman, A. (2010). The creativity crisis. *Newsweek,* July 19. Retrieved from http://www.thedailybeast.com/newsweek/2010/07/10/the-creativity-crisis.html
2. http://finance.yahoo.com/career-work/article/109596/what-chief-executives-really-want?mod=career-leadership
3. Bidault, Francis, & Castello, Alessio. (2010). Why too much trust is death to innovation. *MIT Sloan Management Review, 51*(4/Summer), 1–5. Retrieved from http://sloanreview.mit.edu/the-magazine/articles/2010/summer/51411/why-too-much-trust-is-death-to-innovation/
4. Bronson, P., & Merryman, A. (2010). The creativity crisis. *Newsweek.*
5. Ibid.
6. http://www.aacsb.edu/resources/innovation/business-schools-on-an-innovation-mission.pdf
7. Wilson, H. J. (2010). What *Mad Men* gets right about innovation. Retrieved from http://blogs.hbr.org/research/2010/07/where-mad-men-gets-innovation.html
8. Mishra, Aneil K., Mishra, Karen E., & Spreitzer, Gretchen M. (2009). How to downsize your company without downsizing morale. *MIT Sloan Management Review, 50*(3), 39–44.
9. Kanter, R.J. (2006). Innovation: The classic traps. *Harvard Business Review, 84*(11), 72–83.

10. Hamel, Gary. (2009). Moon shots for management. *Harvard Business Review, 87*(2), 91–98.
11. Ibid.
12. Ibid.
13. Bidault, Francis, & Castello, Alessio. (2010). Why too much trust is death to innovation. *MIT Sloan Management Review, 51*(4/Summer), 1–5. Retrieved from http://sloanreview.mit.edu/the-magazine/articles/2010/summer/51411/why-too-much-trust-is-death-to-innovation/
14. Interview with Sheldon Yellen, January 4, 2012.
15. Muethel, J., Siebdrat, F., & Hoegl, J. (2009). Perceived trustworthiness in innovation teams and the moderating effect of virtuality. *Academy of Management Proceedings*. New York: Pace University.
16. Hamel, Gary. (2009). Moon shots for management. *Harvard Business Review, 87* (2), 91–98.
17. http://en.wikipedia.org/wiki/Creative_destruction
18. Betta, M., Jones, R., & Latham, J. (2010) Entrepreneurship and the Innovative self: a Schumpeterian reflection, *International Journal of Entrepreneurial Behaviour and Research*, 16 (3), 229–244.
19. Ibid.
20. http://www.twomenandatruck.com/community-service
21. Ibid.
22. Interview with Melanie Bergeron, December 12, 2011.
23. http://www.bus.umich.edu/MAP/Dev/WhatisMAP.htm
24. Drucker, Peter F. (1985). *Innovation and entrepreneurship*. New York, NY: Collins Business.
25. Ibid.
26. Ibid.
27. http://www.productivityhacks.com/small-business-topics/google-8020-ito-can-the-innovation-time-off-method-benefit-your-workplace/
28. http://www.fastcodesign.com/1663137/how-3m-gave-everyone-days-off-and-created-an-innovation-dynamo
29. Ted Castle's visit to Aneil's MBA class, October 29, 2002.
30. Ibid.
31. Dobbs, L. (Producer). (1995, March 18). *Managing with Lou Dobbs* [Television broadcast]. CNN.
32. Interview with Ted Castle, January 7, 2012.
33. Ibid.

☐ 8 Trust Across Borders

1. Davidow, William H., & Malone, Michael S. (1993). *The virtual corporation: Structuring and revitalizing the corporation for the 21st century*. New York, NY: Harper.
2. Ashkenas, Ron, Ulrich, Dave, Jick, Todd, & Kerr, Steve. (1993). *The boundaryless organization: Breaking the chains of organization structure*. San Francisco, CA: Jossey-Bass.

3. Personal communication from Dr. Ranjay Gulati, January 7, 2012.
4. http://www.fastcompany.com/magazine/12/freeagent.html
5. http://www.crainsdetroit.com/article/20090128/FREE/901289979/25-of-u-s-workers-self-employed-kelly-services-reports#
6. http://articles.economictimes.indiatimes.com/2011-06-25/news/29747818_1_rural-areas-casual-labourers-urban-areas
7. http://www.nytimes.com/2011/07/31/business/siemens-ceo-on-building-trust-and-teamwork.html?pagewanted=1&emc=eta1
8. Joshi, A., Lazarova, M. B., & Liao, H. (2009). Getting everyone on board: The role of inspirational leadership in geographically dispersed teams. *Organization Science, 20*(1), 240–252.
9. Panteli, Niki, &Tucker, Robert. (2009). Power and trust in global virtual teams. *Communications of the ACM, 51*(12), 113–115.
10. Ross, Judith A. (2006, June). Trust makes the team go 'round. *Harvard Management Update,* 3–6.
11. Walther, Joseph B., & Bunz, Ulla. (2005, December). The rules of virtual groups: Trust, liking, and performance in computer-mediated communication (CMC). *Journal of Communication, 55*(4), 828–846.
12. Ibid.
13. Ibid.
14. Ibid.
15. http://www.bain.com/Images/BAIN_BRIEF_Management_Tools.pdf
16. Sako, M. (1992). *Prices, quality, and trust: Inter-firm relations in Britain & Japan.* New York, NY: Cambridge University Press.
17. Barber, B. (1983). *The logic and limits of trust.* New Brunswick, NJ: Rutgers University Press.
18. Sako, M. (1992). *Prices, quality, and trust: Inter-firm relations in Britain & Japan.* New York, NY: Cambridge University Press.
19. Bradach, J., & Eccles, R. (1989). Rice, authority, and trust: From ideal types to plural forms. *Annual Review of Sociology, 15,* 97–118.
20. Beamish, Paul W., & Lupton, Nathaniel C. (2009). Managing joint ventures. *Academy of Management Perspectives, 23*(2), 75–94.
21. Sako, Mari. (2006). Does trust improve business performance? In Roderick M. Kramer (Ed.), *Organizational trust: A reader* (pp. 267–292). Oxford, England: Oxford University Press.
22. Ibid.
23. Bidault, Francis, & Castello, Alessio. (2009). Trust and creativity: Understanding the role of trust in creativity oriented joint developments. *R&D Management, 39*(3), 259–270.
24. Fang, Eric, Palmatier, Robert W., Scheer, Lisa K., & Li, Ning. (2008). Trust at different organizational levels. *Journal of Marketing, 72*(2), 80–98.
25. Beamish, Paul W., & Lupton, Nathaniel C. (2009). Managing joint ventures. *Academy of Management Perspectives, 23*(2), 83.
26. Jeffries, F. L., & Reed, R. (2000). Trust and adaptation in relational contracting. *Academy of Management Review,* 873–882.
27. Krishnan, R., Martin, X., & Noorderhaven, N. (2006). When does trust matter to alliance performance? *The Academy of Management Journal, 49*(5), 894–917.

28. Perrone, V., Zaheer, A., & McEvily, B. (2003). Free to be trusted? Organizational constraints on trust in boundary spanners. *Organization Science*, 422–439.

29. Gulati, Ranjay, & Nickerson, Jack A. (2008). Interorganizational trust, governance choice, and exchange performance. *Organization Science, 19*(5), 703.

30. Gulati, Ranjay, & Nickerson, Jack A. (2008). Interorganizational trust, governance choice, and exchange performance. *Organization Science, 19*(5), 688–708.

31. Huff, L., & Kelley, L. (2003). Levels of organizational trust in individualist versus collectivist societies: A seven-nation study. *Organization Science*, 81–90.

32. http://hbswk.hbs.edu/item/6761.html

33. http://www.livemint.com/2012/01/08202107/Developing-tomorrow 8217s-le.html?h=C

☐ 9 Trust and Healthcare

1. http://nchc.org/node/1171

2. https://www.cms.gov/NationalHealthExpendData/25_NHE_Fact_Sheet.asp

3. Abelson, J., Miller, F., & Giacomini, M. (2009). What does it mean to trust a health system? A qualitative study of Canadian health care values. *Health Policy, 91*(1), 63–70.

4. http://online.wsj.com/article/SB10001424052702304506904575180331528424238.html

5. Interview with George S. Barrett, November 23, 2010.

6. http://net.acpe.org/MembersOnly/pejournal/2011/MarchApril/Fibuch.pdf

7. http://www.gallup.com/poll/120890/Healthcare-Americans-Trust-Physicians-Politicians.aspx

8. http://www.ama-assn.org/amednews/2011/03/14/bisd0315.htm

9. http://www.commonwealthfund.org/Publications/In-the-Literature/2009/Feb/High-Medical-Cost-Burdens--Patient-Trust--and-Perceived-Quality-of-Care.aspx

10. http://healthaffairs.org/blog/2012/02/08/new-health-affairs-some-physicians-not-always-honest-with-patients/

11. Interview with Dr. Kevin Lobdell, November 28, 2011.

12. Interview with Dr. Brent Senior, November 2, 2011.

13. Interview with Dr. Bruce Rubin, December 30, 2011.

14. Shore, D. A. (2007). The (sorry) state of trust in the American healthcare enterprise. In David A. Shore (Ed.), *The trust crisis in healthcare: Causes, consequences, and cures*, pp. 3–20. Oxford: Oxford University Press.

15. Lee, Thomas H. (2010, April). Turning doctors into leaders. *Harvard Business Review, 88*(4), 54.

16. Safran, D. G. (2007). Patients' trust in their doctors: are we losing ground? In David A. Shore (Ed.), *The trust crisis in healthcare: Causes, consequences, and cures*. Oxford University Press.

17. Rose, R., & Calnan, M. (2006). Trust relations in healthcare: The new agenda. *European Journal of Public Health, 16*, 4–6.

18. Shore, D. A. (2007). The (sorry) state of trust in the American healthcare enterprise. In David A. Shore (Ed.), *The trust crisis in healthcare: Causes, consequences, and cures* (p. 3–20). Oxford: Oxford University Press.
19. Interview with Dr. Brent Senior, November 2, 2011.
20. Interview with Dr. Bruce Rubin, December 30, 2011.
21. Interview with Dr. Brent Senior, November 2, 2011.
22. Interview with Dr. Bruce Rubin, December 30, 2011.
23. Interview with Dr. Brent Senior, November 2, 2011.
24. Interview with Dr. Bruce Rubin, December 30, 2011.
25. Interview with Dr. John Gordon, January 25, 2012.
26. Rose, R., & Calnan, M. (2006). Trust relations in healthcare: The new agenda. *European Journal of Public Health, 16*, 4–6.
27. Hall, Mark A., Zheng, Beiyao, Dugan, Elizabeth, Camacho, Fabian, Kidd, Kristin E., Mishra, Aneil K., & Balkrishnan, Rajesh. (2002). Measuring patients' trust in their primary care providers. *Medical Care Research and Review, 59*(3/September), 293–318.
28. Rose, R., & Calnan, M. (2006). Trust relations in healthcare: The new agenda. *European Journal of Public Health, 16*, 4–6.
29. Shore, D. A. (2007). The (sorry) state of trust in the American healthcare enterprise. In David A. Shore (Ed.), *The trust crisis in healthcare: Causes, consequences, and cures* (pp. 3–20). Oxford: Oxford University Press.
30. H all, Mark A., Zheng, Beiyao, Dugan, Elizabeth, Camacho, Fabian, Kidd, Kristin E., Mishra, Aneil K., & Balkrishnan, Rajesh. (2002). Measuring patients' trust in their primary care providers. *Medical Care Research and Review, 59*(3/September), 293–318.
31. Safran, D. G. (2007). Patients' trust in their doctors: are we losing ground? In David A. Shore (Ed.), *The trust crisis in healthcare: Causes, consequences, and cures*. Oxford University Press.
32. Hall, Mark A., Zheng, Beiyao, Dugan, Elizabeth, Camacho, Fabian, Kidd, Kristin E., Mishra, Aneil K., & Balkrishnan, Rajesh. (2002). Measuring patients' trust in their primary care providers. *Medical Care Research and Review, 59* (3/September), 293–318.
33. Rose, R., & Calnan, M. (2006). Trust relations in healthcare: The new agenda. *European Journal of Public Health, 16*, 4–6.
34. Interview with Dr. Brent Senior, November 2, 2011.
35. Firth-Cozens, J. (2004). Organisational trust: The keystone to patient safety. *Qual Saf Health Care, 13*, 56–61.
36. Hernandez, James S. (2010). The spectrum of medical leadership roles. *Physician Executive, 36*(5), 56–59.
37. http://net.acpe.org/MembersOnly/pejournal/2011/MarchApril/Tiffan.pdf
38. Lee, Thomas H. (2010, April). Turning doctors into leaders. *Harvard Business Review, 88*(4), 50–58.
39. Interview with Dr. Kevin Lobdell, November 28, 2011.
40. http://www.sts.org/quality-research-patient-safety/sts-public-reporting-online/explanation-quality-rating-composite-sco
41. http://www.nytimes.com/2011/07/11/health/policy/11docs.html
42. Lee, Thomas H. (2010, April). Turning doctors into leaders. *Harvard Business Review, 88*(4), 50–58.

43. Rose, R., & Calnan, M. (2006). Trust relations in healthcare: The new agenda. *European Journal of Public Health, 16*, 4–6.
44. Shore, D. A. (2007). The (sorry) state of trust in the American healthcare enterprise. In David A. Shore (Ed.), *The trust crisis in healthcare: Causes, consequences, and cures* (pp. 3–20). Oxford: Oxford University Press.
45. Blendon, R. J. (2007). Why Americans don't trust the government and don't trust healthcare. In David A. Shore (Ed.), *The trust crisis in healthcare: Causes, consequences, and cures* (pp. 21–31). Oxford: Oxford University Press.
46. Alderman, Leslie. (2011, August 11). The doctor will see you . . . eventually. *The New York Times*, p. D6.
47. Hernandez, James S. (2010). The spectrum of medical leadership roles. *Physician Executive, 36*(5), 56–59.
48. Shore, D. A. (2007). The (sorry) state of trust in the American healthcare enterprise. In David A. Shore (Ed.), *The trust crisis in healthcare: Causes, consequences, and cures* (pp. 3–20). Oxford: Oxford University Press.
49. Rose, R., & Calnan, M. (2006). Trust relations in healthcare: The new agenda. *European Journal of Public Health, 16*, 4–6.
50. Ibid.
51. Hall Mark A., Zheng, Beiyao, Dugan, Elizabeth, Camacho, Fabian, Kidd, Kristin E., Mishra, Aneil K., & Balkrishnan, Rajesh. (2002). Measuring patients' trust in their primary care providers. *Medical Care Research and Review, 59*(3/September), 293–318.
52. Firth-Cozens, J. (2004). Organisational trust: The keystone to patient safety. *Qual Saf Health Care, 13*, 56–61.
53. Cook, K. S., Kramer, R. M., Thom, D. H., Stepanikova, I., Mollborn, S. B., & Cooper, R. M. (2004). Trust and distrust in patient–physician relationships: Perceived determinants of high- and low-trust relationships in managed-care settings. In R. M. Kramer & K. S. Cook (Eds), *Trust and distrust in organizations: dilemmas and approaches* (pp. 65–98). New York, NY: Sage.
54. Hall, Mark A., Zheng, Beiyao, Dugan, Elizabeth, Camacho, Fabian, Kidd, Kristin E., Mishra, Aneil K., & Balkrishnan, Rajesh. (2002). Measuring patients' trust in their primary care providers. *Medical Care Research and Review, 59*(3/September), 293–318.
55. Rose, R., Calnan, M. (2006). Trust relations in healthcare: The new agenda. *European Journal of Public Health, 16*, 4–6.
56. Ibid.
57. Shore, D. A. (2007). The (sorry) state of trust in the American healthcare enterprise. In David A. Shore (Ed.), *The trust crisis in healthcare: Causes, consequences, and cures*. Oxford University Press.
58. Cook, K. S., Kramer, R. M., Thom, D. H., Stepanikova, I., Mollborn, S. B., & Cooper, R. M. (2004). Trust and distrust in patient–physician relationships: Perceived determinants of high- and low-trust relationships in managed-care settings. In R. M. Kramer & K. S. Cook (Eds), *Trust and distrust in organizations: Dilemmas and approaches* (p. 70). New York, NY: Sage.
59. Mishra, Aneil K., & Mishra, Karen E. (2008). *Trust is everything: Become the leader others will follow*. Chapel Hill, NC: Lulu.
60. Hall, Mark A., Zheng, Beiyao, Dugan, Elizabeth, Camacho, Fabian, Kidd, Kristin E., Mishra, Aneil K., & Balkrishnan, Rajesh. (2002). Measuring

patients' trust in their primary care providers. *Medical Care Research and Review, 59*(3/September), 293–318.

61. Cook, K. S., Kramer, R. M., Thom, D. H., Stepanikova, I., Mollborn, S. B., & Cooper, R. M. (2004). Trust and distrust in patient–physician relationships: Perceived determinants of high- and low-trust relationships in managed-care settings. In R. M. Kramer & K. S. Cook (Eds), *Trust and distrust in organizations: Dilemmas and approaches* (pp. 65–98). New York, NY: Sage.

62. Dr. Rubin is also a practicing magician and a member of the International Brotherhood of Magicians; see http://www.news.vcu.edu/news/VCU_Pediatrics_Spring_Conference_Features_Workshops_on_Magic

63. http://www.cfohealth.com/dr-david-e-pawsat-do.php

64. Firth-Cozens, J. (2004). Organisational trust: The keystone to patient safety. *Qual Saf Health Care, 13*, 56–61.

65. Interview with George Barrett, November 23, 2010.

66. Ibid.

67. Ibid.

68. http://net.acpe.org/MembersOnly/pejournal/2011/MarchApril/Tiffan.pdf

69. Interview with Dr. Bruce Rubin, December 30, 2011.

70. Lobdell, K., Camp, S., Stamou, S., Swanson, R., Reames, M., Madjarov, J., Robicsek, F. (2009). Quality improvement in cardiac critical care. *HSR Proceedings in Intensive Care and Cardiovascular Anaesthesia, 1*(1), 22–26.

71. Thom, D. H., Wong, S. T., Guzman, D., Wu, A., Penko, J., Miaskowski, C., & Kushel, M. (2011). Physician trust in the patient: Development and validation of a new measure. *Annals of Family Medicine, 9*(2), 148–154.

72. Dowling, M. J. (2007). Building trust in a healthcare system. In David A. Shore (Ed.), *The trust crisis in healthcare: Causes, consequences, and cures* (pp. 172–179). Oxford: Oxford University.

☐ 10 Rebuilding Trust

1. Tomlinson, E. C., & Mayer, R. C. (2009). The role of causal attribution dimension in trust repair. *Academy of Management, 34*(1), 85–104.

2. Lewicki, R. J., Tomlinson, E. C., & Gillespie, N. (2006). Models of interpersonal trust development: Theoretical approaches, empirical evidence, and future directions. *Journal of Management, 32*(6), 991–1022.

3. Janowicz-Panjaitan, J., & Krishan, R. (2009). Measures for dealing with competence and integrity violations of interorganizational trust at the corporate and operating levels of organizational hierarchy. *Journal of Management Studies, 46*(2), 245–268.

4. Lewicki, R. J., & Wiethoff, C. (2000). Trust, trust development, and trust repair. In Morton Deutsch & Peter T. Coleman (Eds), *The Handbook of conflict resolution: Theory and practice* (pp. 86–107). San Francisco, CA: Jossey-Bass.

5. Govier, T. (1994). An epistemology of trust. *International Journal of Moral and Social Studies, 8,* 155–74.
6. Sitkin, S. B., & Roth, N. L. (1993). Explaining the limited effectiveness of legalistic "remedies" for trust/distrust. *Organization Science, 4*(3), 367–392.
7. Luhmann, N. (1979). *Trust and power.* New York, NY: John Wiley & Sons.
8. Lewicki, R. J., Tomlinson, E. C., & Gillespie, N. (2006). Models of interpersonal trust development: Theoretical approaches, empirical evidence, and future directions. *Journal of Management, 32*(6), 991–1022.
9. Deustch, M. (1958). Trust and suspicion. *Journal of Conflict Resolution, 2,* 265–279.
10. Kramer, R. M. (1999). Trust and distrust in organizations. *Annual Review of Psychology, 50,* 569–598.
11. Tomlinson, E. C., & Mayer, R. C. (2009). The role of causal attribution dimension in trust repair. *Academy of Management, 34*(1), 87.
12. Kramer, R. M., & Lewicki, R. J. (2010). Repairing and enhancing trust: Approaches to reducing organizational trust deficits. *The Academy of Management Annals, 4*(1), 245–277.
13. Ferrin, D. L., Bligh, M. C., & Kohles, J. C. (2007). Can I trust you to trust me: A theory of trust, monitoring and cooperation in interpersonal and intergroup relations. *Group & Organization Management, 32*(4), 465–499.
14. Tomlinson, E., Dineen, B., & Lewicki, R. (2004). The road to reconciliation: Antecedents of victim willingness to reconcile following a broken promise. *Journal of Management, 31,* 165–187.
15. Simons, Tony. (2008). *The integrity dividend: Leading by the power of your word.* San Francisco, CA: Jossey-Bass.
16. Stroh, Linda K. (2007). *Trust rules: How to tell the good guys from the bad guys in work and life.* Westport, CT: Praeger.
17. Tomlinson, E., Dineen, B., & Lewicki, R. (2004). The road to reconciliation: Antecedents of victim willingness to reconcile following a broken promise. *Journal of Management, 31,* 165–187.
18. Frost, Peter. (2003). *Toxic emotions at work: How compassionate managers handle pain and conflict.* Boston, MA: HBS.
19. Interview with Dr. Kevin Lobdell, November 28, 2011.
20. Ferrin, D. L., Kim, P. H., Cooper, C. D., & Dirks, K. T. (2007). Silence speaks volumes: The effectiveness of reticence in comparison to apology and denial for responding to integrity- and competence-based trust violations. *Journal of Applied Psychology, 92*(4), 893.
21. Hui, C. H., Lau, F. L. Y., Tsang, L., & Pak, S. (2011). The impact of post-apology behavioral consistency on victim's forgiveness intention: A study of trust violation among coworkers. *Journal of Applied Social Psychology, 41*(5), 1214–1236.
22. Schoorman, F. D., Mayer, R. C., et al. (2007). An integrative model of organizational trust: Past, present, and future. *The Academy of Management Review, 32*(2), 344–354.
23. Kramer, R. M., & Lewicki, R. J. (2010). Repairing and enhancing trust: Approaches to reducing organizational trust deficits. *The Academy of Management Annals, 4*(1), 245–277.
24. Stroh, Linda K. (2007). *Trust rules: How to tell the good guys from the bad guys in work and life* (p. 111). Westport, CT: Praeger.

25. Kim, P. H., Dirks, K. T., & Cooper, C. D. (2009). The repair of trust: A dynamic bilateral perspective and multilevel conceptualization. *Academy of Management Review, 34*(3), 401–422.
26. Ibid.
27. Ibid.
28. Williams, 2001: 379.
29. Tomlinson, E. C., & Mayer, R. C. (2009). The role of causal attribution dimensions in trust repair. *Academy of Management Review, 34*(1), 85–104.
30. Lewicki, R. J., & Tomlinson, E. C. (2003, December) Trust and trust building. In Guy Burgess and Heidi Burgess (Eds), *Beyond intractability*. Conflict Research Consortium, University of Colorado Boulder. Retrieved from http://www.beyondintractability.org/essay/trust_building/
31. Kramer, R. M. (1999). Trust and distrust in organizations. *Annual Review of Psychology, 50,* 569–598.
32. Krosgaard, M. A., Brodt, S. E., et al. (2002). Trust in the face of conflict: The role of managerial trustworthy behavior and organizational context. *Journal of Applied Psychology, 87*(2), 312.
33. Kramer, R. M. (1999). Trust and distrust in organizations. *Annual Review of Psychology, 50,* 569–598.
34. Frost, Peter. (2003). *Toxic emotions at work: How compassionate managers handle pain and conflict.* Boston, MA: HBS.
35. http://defectprevention.cloudapp.net/PairsLB.aspx?group=31a3675c-bbb3-4b91-9f76-08ee3a12f5b5
36. Fraser, W. (2010). *Trust and repair: An exploration of how work groups repair a violation of trust.* (Unpublished doctoral dissertation). Fielding Graduate University, Santa Barbara, CA.
37. Gillespie, N., & G. Dietz (2009). Trust repair after an organization-level failure. *The Academy of Management Review, 34*(1), 127–145.
38. Mishra, Aneil K. (1996). Organizational responses to crisis: The centrality of trust. In Roderick Kramer & Thomas Tyler (Eds), *Trust in organizations: Frontiers of theory and research* (pp. 261–287). Thousand Oaks, CA: Sage.
39. Mishra, Karen E., Mishra, Aneil K., & Spreitzer, Gretchen M. (1998, Winter). Maintaining trust and empowerment during downsizing. *MIT Sloan Management Review, 39*(2), 38–95.
40. Mishra, Aneil K., Mishra, Karen E., & Spreitzer, Gretchen M. (2009, Spring). How to downsize your company without downsizing morale. *MIT Sloan Management Review,* 39–44.
41. Ibid.
42. Ibid.
43. Hermann, C. (1963). Some consequences of crisis which limit the viability of organizations. *Administrative Science Quarterly, 8,* 61–82.
44. Turner, B. 1976. The organizational and interorganizational development of disasters. *Administrative Science Quarterly, 21,* 378–397.
45. Starbuck, W., & Hedberg, B. (1977). Saving an organization from a stagnating environment. In H. Thorelli (Ed.), *Strategy + structure = performance* (pp. 249–258). Bloomington, IN: Indiana University Press.
46. Webb, E. (1994). Trust and crisis. In R. Kramer & T. Tyler (Eds), *Trust in organizations* (288–301). Newbury Park, CA: Sage.

47. James, E. H., & Wooten, L. P. (2005). Leadership as (un)usual: How to display competence in times of crisis. *Organizational Dynamics, 34*(2), 141–152.
48. Pearson, C.M., & Mitroff, I.I. (1993). From crisis prone to crisis prepared: A framework for crisis management. *Academy of Management Executive,* 7(1), 48–59.
49. Coombs, W.T. (1999). Information and compassion in crisis responses: A test of their effects. *Journal of Public Relations Research, 11*(2), 125–143.
50. Interview with Eric Kutner, February 18, 2012.
51. http://www.road2resilience.org/gulf-coast-resilience-an-american-tale-video/, 8:20 time mark.
52. http://www.road2resilience.org/gulf-coast-resilience-an-american-tale-video/, 9:10 time mark.
53. http://www.road2resilience.org/gulf-coast-resilience-an-american-tale-video/, 11:00 time mark.
54. http://www.nytimes.com/2010/01/18/business/18drug.html
55. Stephens, K. K., Malone, P. C., & Bailey, C. M. (2005). Communicating with stakeholders during a crisis. *Journal of Business Communication, 42*(4), 390–419.
56. Ibid.
57. Ibid.

☐ 11 Making Trust Last by Enlarging Your Purpose

1. http://en.wikipedia.org/wiki/Charles_Handy
2. Handy, Charles (2002, December). What's a business for? *Harvard Business Review.*
3. Handy, Charles (2002, December). What's a business for? *Harvard Business Review,* 8.
4. http://www.texallergy.com/providers-otolaryngologists.php
5. Handy, Charles (2002, December). What's a business for? *Harvard Business Review,* 8.
6. http://www.seamenschurch.org/about-us
7. http://my.clevelandclinic.org/about-cleveland-clinic/overview/leadership/board-of-trustees.aspx
8. Interview with Bob Lintz, January 6, 2012.
9. Interview with Sheldon Yellen, January 4, 2012.
10. Sheldon Yellen's official biographical statement, repeated in this book's appendix.
11. Interview with Sheldon Yellen, January 4, 2012.
12. Ibid.
13. Mishra, Aneil K., & Mishra, Karen E. (2008). *Trust is everything: Become the leader others will follow.* Chapel Hill, NC: Lulu.
14. http://www.blackpast.org/?q=1857-frederick-douglass-if-there-no-struggle-there-no-progress

15. http://www.shophiddentreasures.com/about.htm
16. Goodpaster, Kenneth, & Mathews, John B., Jr. (1982, Jan–Feb). Can a corporation have a conscience? *Harvard Business Review*.
17. Kanter, Rosabeth Moss. (1999). From spare change to real change: The social sector as beta site for business innovation. *Harvard Business Review, 77*(3), 122–132.

AUTHOR INDEX

SUBJECT INDEX

A

accountability: in care organizations 115, 119–20; modeling of 138; philosophical debates about 154; Rhino Foods example 92–3; of team leaders 32; of team members 57, 61–2, 130, 151; Two Men and a Truck example 98–9

active listening 12, 63–4, 124

active watching 12

"all the time" relationships 42–3

Alumni Schools Committee (Princeton University) 49–51

Annual Giving Campaign (Princeton University) 49–51

Argentina, trust building in 107–9

Asia: distrust of government in 3; healthcare methods 123, 161

Association to Advance Collegiate Schools of Business (AACSB) 85–6

Australia, low trust ratings in 2

authentic leadership: Castle/Rhino foods example 39–40; defined 38–9; Yellen/Belfor Holdings example 40–3

automobile industry see General Motors (Parma, Ohio plant)

B

Babson College innovation study 86

Bain & Company survey 106

Belfor Cares charity 150, 167

Belfor Holdings: compassion for employees at 71; courage, humility, authenticity example 40–4; employee empowerment example 87–8; philanthropic tradition at 150; and ROCC of Trust 23, 40

The Boundaryless Organization (Ashkenas, Ulrich, Jick, Kerr) 103

Brazil, low trust ratings in 2–3

Bridges Out of Poverty program 22, 155

C

Canada: building ROCC of Trust in 12; low trust ratings 2; Two Men and a Truck in 36

Cardinal Health: governmental healthcare issues 111–12; healthcare industry

systemic trust 125–6; hospital arena efficiency improvements 127; open communication at 73; pharmaceutical sector efficiency improvements 126–7

Carolinas HealthCare System 112–13, 128

Center for Work-Life Policy survey (2007–2008) 3

Centers for Medicare and Medicaid Services (U.S.) 111

Chapel Hill Pediatrics and Adolescents 125

Children's Hospital of Richmond (Virginia) 113–14

China, low trust rating in 2–3

Circle of Trust: creation of, by leaders 11; development of 12, 53; ROCC of Trust combined with 13

Cleveland Clinic 120–1, 149

CNN/ORC International poll (2011) 2

coaches (coaching): one-on-one, group settings 61; resistance encountered by 47; and ROCC of Trust 8, 17; of team leaders 31; team leaders as 60–1; *see also* team leaders

collaboration: at General Motors Parma 11–12, 81; in humble, trustworthy organizations 9, 11; and innovation 89; at the interpersonal level 33, 91; modern society's loss of 5; and organizational customer centricity 25; and organizational trust 69; requirement of trust for 88; at Rhino Foods 101; at Two Men and a Truck 101; at Working Bridges Program 22

collective trust 69–70, 75–6

Columbia University Business School 135

Communication Studies (2010 article) 21

communication training 63–4

compassion: at Belfor Holdings 71; at CBS/*Undercover Boss* 42, 71; described 7, 21–2, 27; at General Motors 10; in healthcare 117, 119, 122, 124–5, 129, 130; and leadership 13–14, 65, 66, 70–1; of physicians 14, 23; in rebuilding trust 138–9, 144; at Rhino Foods 22, 40; ROCC of Trust explanation 18; and trust networks 48, 54, 60; trust tips for 83

restrictions 116–17; and ROCC of Trust 111–12, 121–2, 129–30; trust at the interpersonal level 121–5; trust at the personal level 119–21; trust at the systemic level 125–30; trust-building challenges 115–18
humility, leadership through 36–8
Hurricane Katrina 141–2

I

IBM CEO poll of creativity 85
Income Advance Loan program 22
India: low trust ratings 2; self-employment data 104
Indonesia, low trust ratings 2
innovation: Babson College study 86; collective effort and 57; contributions of trust to 6; IBM CEO creativity poll 85; at the interpersonal level 91–2; as a leadership imperative 19, 85–6; and mutual trust between leaders and followers 86–9; and organizational reinvigoration 97–101; ROCC of Trust and cultures of 89; at the systemic level 92
International Franchise Association 77
International Seafarer Center 148
international trust 107–9
interpersonal change 33–4
interpersonal trust 6, 33, 89, 110
Ireland: building ROCC of Trust in 12; Two Men and a Truck in 36
Italy: distrust of government in 3; low trust ratings 2

J

Japan: Fukushima nuclear reactor meltdown 4–5; openness in 106
Johnson Controls 106–7
Johnson & Johnson 142–3, 142–4

K

Kelly Services survey (2011) 104

L

Latin America, distrust of government in 3
leader member exchange (LMX) theory 76
leaders (leadership): through authenticity 38–43; birth of/making of leaders 10–11, 29–45; challenges in rebuilding trust

137; characteristics of 8–10; through courage 35–6; emphasis on ROCC of Trust factors 32, 69–70; empowerment role 8, 9, 24, 34–5, 86–7; environmental factors 29–30; genetic factors 10, 29–30; Hoogervorst on 31–2; through humility 36–8; innovation, mutual trust with followers 86–9; knowing when to step down 150–3; as linking pins 74–6; mastery of three levels of change 33–4; organizational building role 32–3; in positive organizations 70–2; relationships to others 30–1; role of middle managers 75; Rubin, Senior, and Lobdell on 31; see also coaches (coaching); team leaders
The Leader's Edge: The Seven Keys to Leadership in a Turbulent World (Nanus) 18–19
Leadership Development Program (Duke University) 105
Lenovo: e-commerce trust building at 107; team building at 24; trust building at 13, 33–4
listening skills, in teams 63–6; see also active listening
LMX theory of leadership see leader member exchange theory
Lockheed bribery scandals 4

M

Malaysia, low trust ratings 2
management manifesto (of Hamel) 86
MAP see Multidisciplinary Action Project
McNeil Consumer Products 142, 143–4
Medical College of Virginia/Virginia Commonwealth University School of Medicine 117–18
Mexico, low trust ratings 2
Michigan State University (MSU) 41, 62, 131–2
Minnesota Twin Registry 29
MIT Sloan Management Review (2009) 54
Multidisciplinary Action Project (MAP) 92
Myers-Briggs Type Indicator 29

N

National Leadership Index survey (2011) 3
networking 49
Newsweek article 85